AF887272

maranGraphics'™

Simplified Computer Guide

Word for Windows™ 2

Ruth Maran

maranGraphics Inc.

Mississauga, Ontario, Canada

Distributed in United States
by Regents/Prentice Hall
Telephone: 1-800-223-1360
Fax: 1-800-445-6991

Distributed in Canada
by Prentice Hall Canada
Telephone: 1-800-567-3800
Fax: 416-299-2529

Distributed Internationally
by Simon & Schuster
Telephone: 201-767-4990
Fax: 201-767-5625

Published 1992.

Canadian Cataloguing in Publication Data

Maran, Ruth, 1970–
MaranGraphics' simplified computer guide
Word for Windows 2

Includes index.
ISBN 0-13-001067-7

1. Microsoft Word (Computer file). 2. Microsoft Word for Windows (Computer file). 3. Word processing – Computer programs. 4. WINDOWS (Computer file). I. Title.

Z52.5.M523M37 1992 652.5'536 C92-095483-9

Acknowledgements

Special thanks to Jeffrey Smith of Microsoft Canada Inc., and to Saverio C. Tropiano, B.Sc., B.A. for their support and consultation.

To the dedicated staff at maranGraphics Inc. and HyperImage Inc., including Monica DeVries, Matthew Korchinski, Béla Korcsog, Jim C. Leung, Robert Maran, and Dave Ross for their contributions.

To Eric Feistmantl who was always there to solve my technical and operational problems.

To Maxine Maran for providing the organizational skill to keep the project under control.

And finally, a special appreciation to Richard Maran who originated the easy-to-use graphic format of this guide. Thank you for your inspiration and guidance.

Trademark Acknowledgements

Cover Design & Graphics Consultant:
Jim C. Leung

Art Director:
Jim C. Leung

Production:
Béla Korcsog
Jim C. Leung
Dave Ross

Film generated on maranGraphics' Linotronic L-330 imagesetter at 2540 dpi resolution.

Table of Contents

TYPICAL TWO-PAGE FORMAT

This guide uses a unique two-page format, with text and graphics tightly integrated on each two-page spread. This means each spread can present a great deal of condensed information in an accessible way.

A typical spread is shown at the right. Notice how the topic is presented as a screen-by-screen flow that shows exactly what you see at each step. Red lines and callouts emphasize the key points of each step.

Another unique element is the visual key system, at the right and top edges of each spread.

The key at the right edge shows all the chapters in the guide. The current chapter is highlighted in red type.

The key at the top shows all the topics in the current chapter. The current topic is highlighted in red type.

With this visual key for guidance, you can see in a flash where you are in the guide.

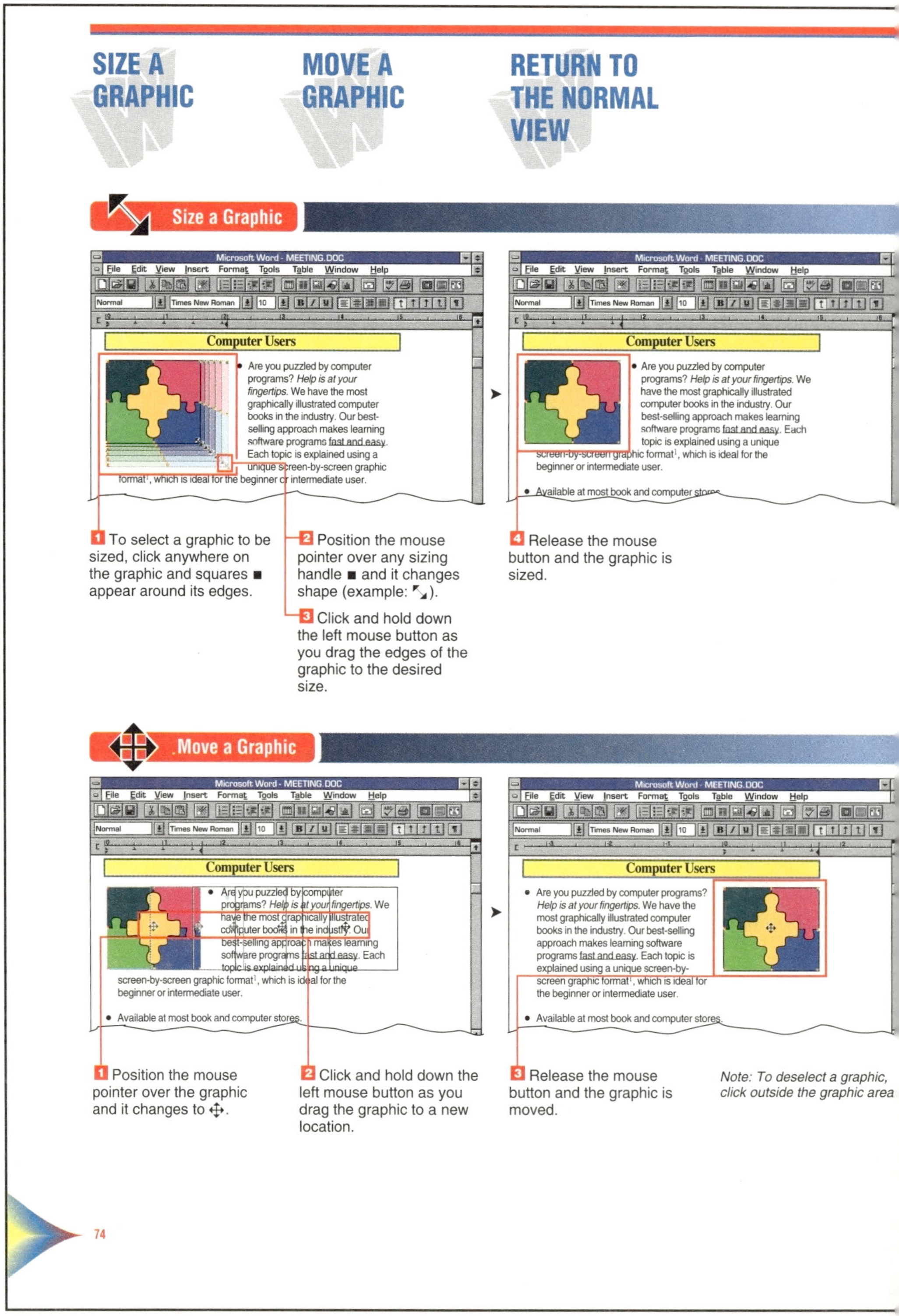

■ All topics in the current chapter are displayed. The current topic is highlighted in red type.

■ All chapters in the guide are displayed. The current chapter is highlighted in red type.

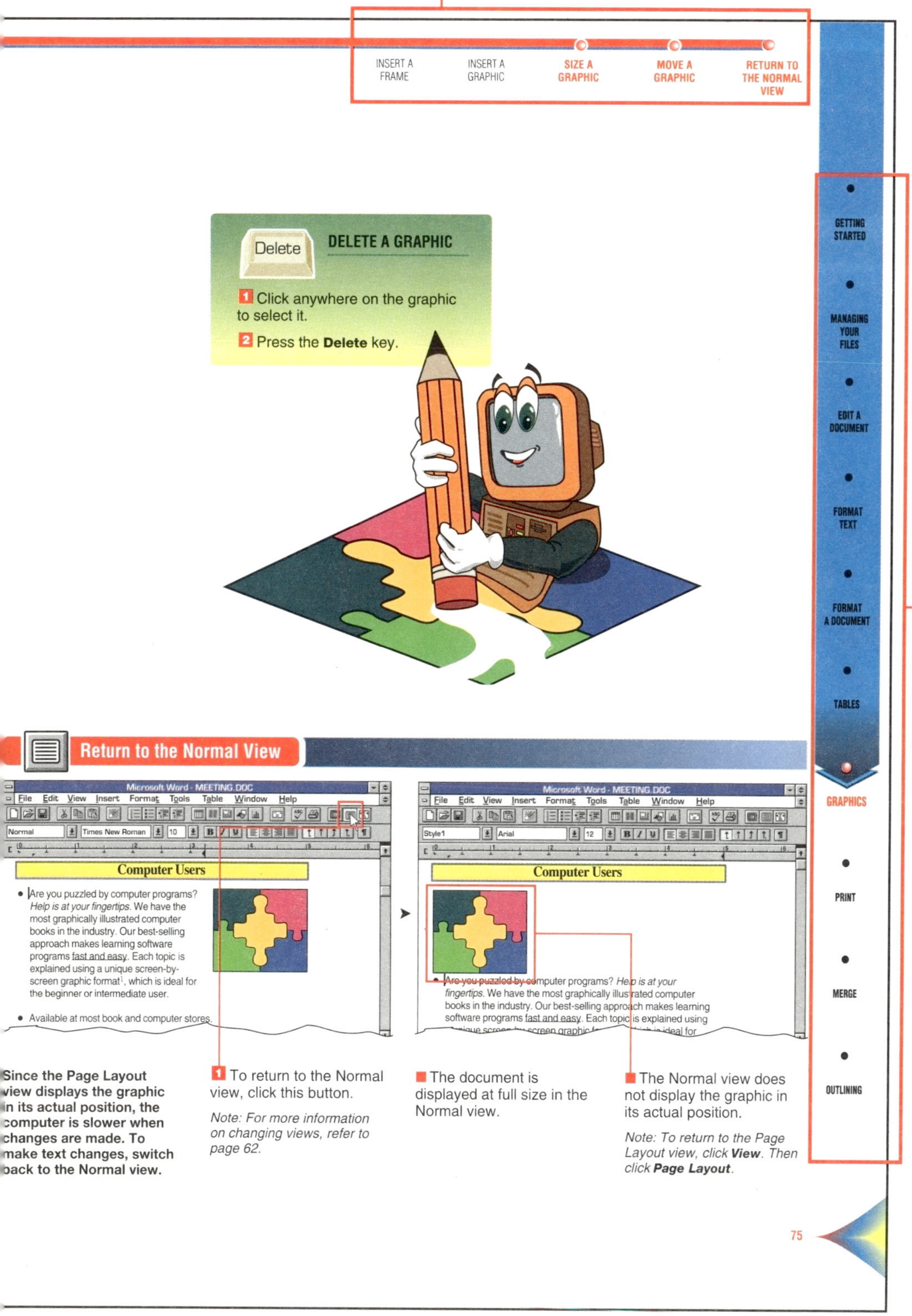

INSERT A FRAME | INSERT A GRAPHIC | SIZE A GRAPHIC | MOVE A GRAPHIC | RETURN TO THE NORMAL VIEW

GETTING STARTED | MANAGING YOUR FILES | EDIT A DOCUMENT | FORMAT TEXT | FORMAT A DOCUMENT | TABLES | GRAPHICS | PRINT | MERGE | OUTLINING

DELETE A GRAPHIC

1 Click anywhere on the graphic to select it.

2 Press the **Delete** key.

Return to the Normal View

Since the Page Layout view displays the graphic in its actual position, the computer is slower when changes are made. To return to make text changes, switch back to the Normal view.

1 To return to the Normal view, click this button.

Note: For more information on changing views, refer to page 62.

■ The document is displayed at full size in the Normal view.

■ The Normal view does not display the graphic in its actual position.

*Note: To return to the Page Layout view, click **View**. Then click **Page Layout**.*

75

START WORD

USING THE MOUSE

Start Word for Windows

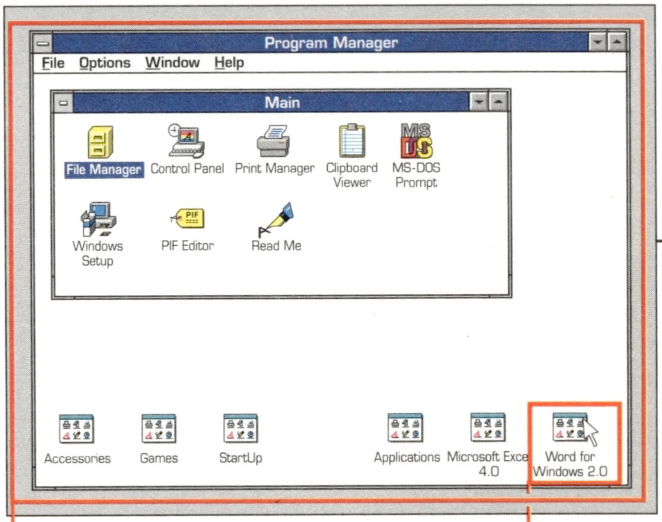

1 To start Microsoft® Word for Windows™ 2.0 from MS-DOS, type **win** and then press **Enter**.

■ The **Program Manager** window is displayed.

All your programs (example: **Microsoft Word for Windows**, **Microsoft Excel for Windows**) are started from the Program Manager.

2 To open the **Word for Windows 2.0** group icon, move the mouse pointer over its icon and double click the left mouse button.

- Windows is installed on your hard disk in a directory named windows.
- Microsoft Word for Windows is installed on your hard disk using the "Complete Installation" option. Default settings are used.
- A mouse is used with Microsoft Word for Windows.

Using the Mouse

MOUSE POINTER SHAPES

As you move the mouse on your desk, the mouse pointer on the computer screen also moves. The mouse pointer's shape changes, depending on the current task, or the position of the pointer on the screen. Here are some examples:

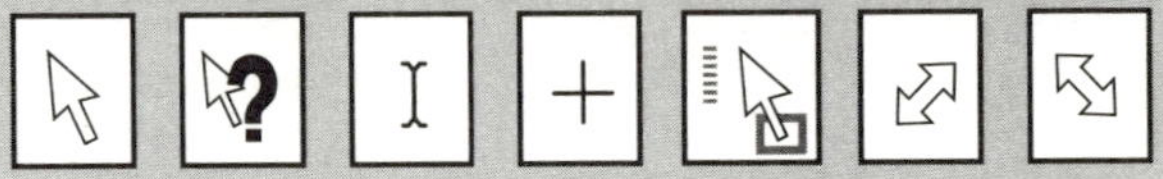

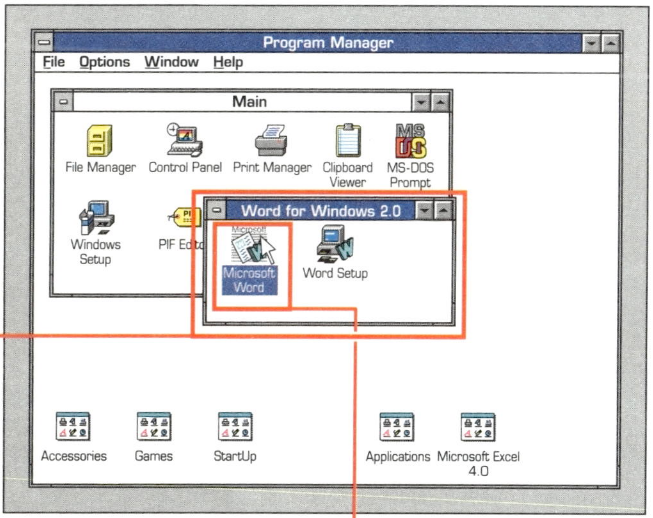

The **Word for Windows 2.0** group window appears.

3 To start the Microsoft Word application, move the mouse pointer over its icon and double click the left mouse button.

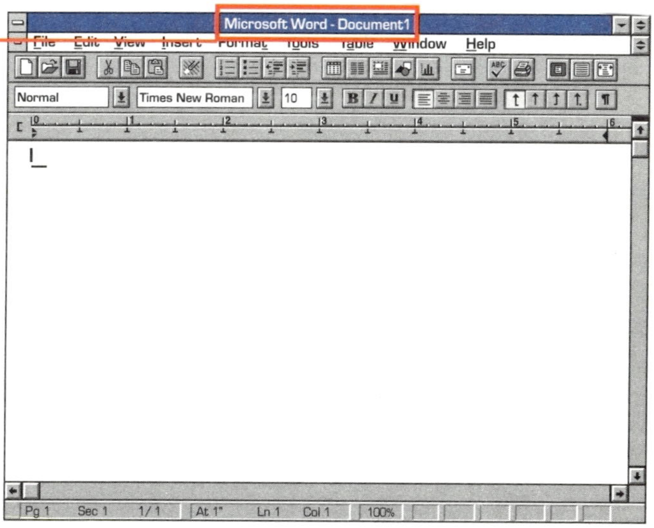

Word opens a new document called **Document1**.

MOUSE POINTER ACTIONS

There are two actions you can perform with the mouse pointer.

Click

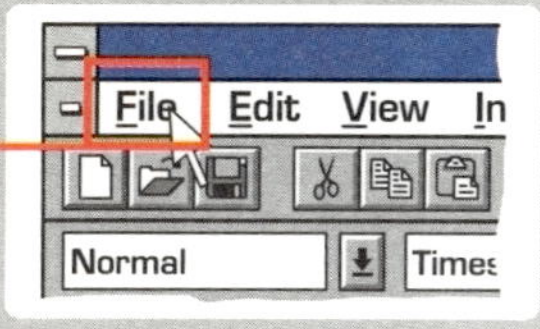

Move the mouse pointer over the item (example: **File**) and click the **left** mouse button.

Double click

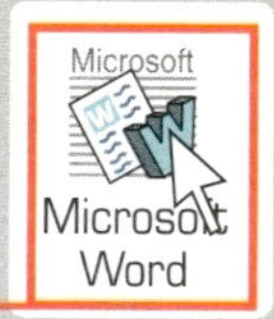

Move the mouse pointer over the item (example: **Microsoft Word**) and click the **left** mouse button twice in quick succession.

USING THE KEYBOARD

If key names are separated by a plus sign (+), press and hold down the first key before pressing the second key (example: **Shift+F1**).

If key names are separated by a comma (,), press and release the first key before pressing the second key (example: **Alt**,**F**).

RESTORE AND MAXIMIZE A DOCUMENT

ENTER TEXT

 Restore and  Maximize a Document

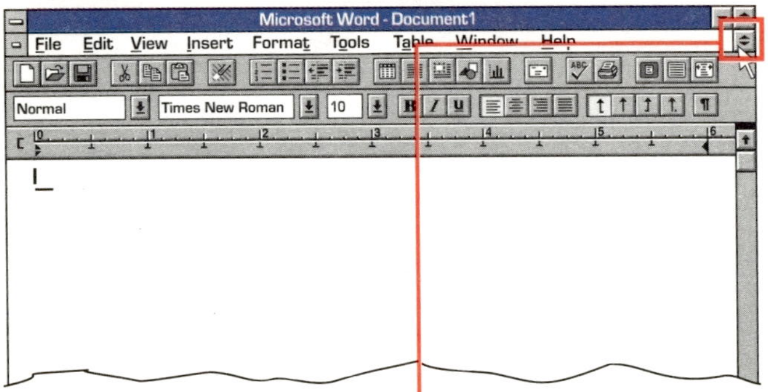

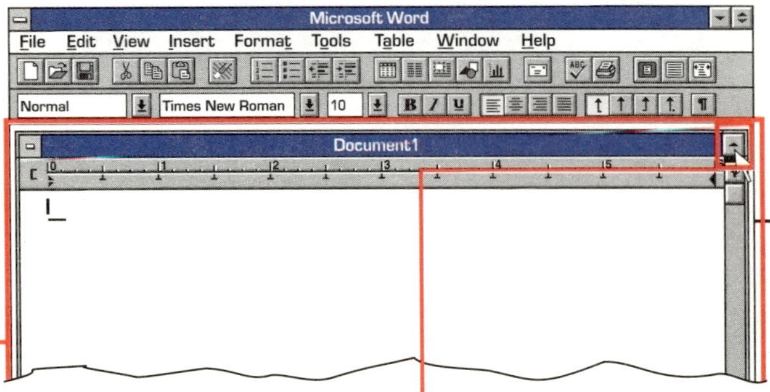

The size of the document window can be made smaller or larger.

1 To make the size of the document window smaller, click the document's **Restore** button.

■ The document window is reduced (restored) to a smaller size.

2 To make the size of the document window larger, click the document's **Maximize** button.

Enter Text

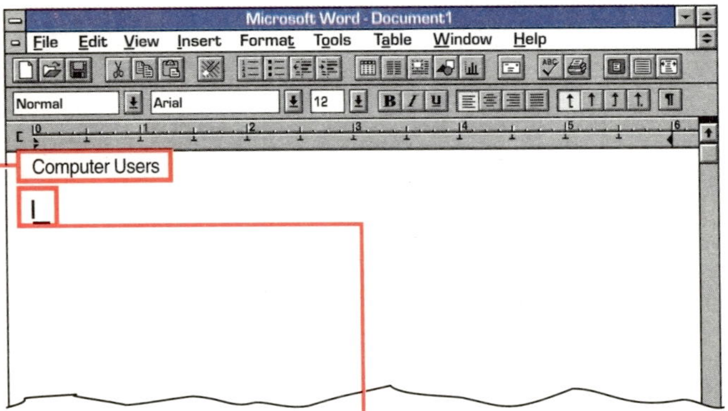

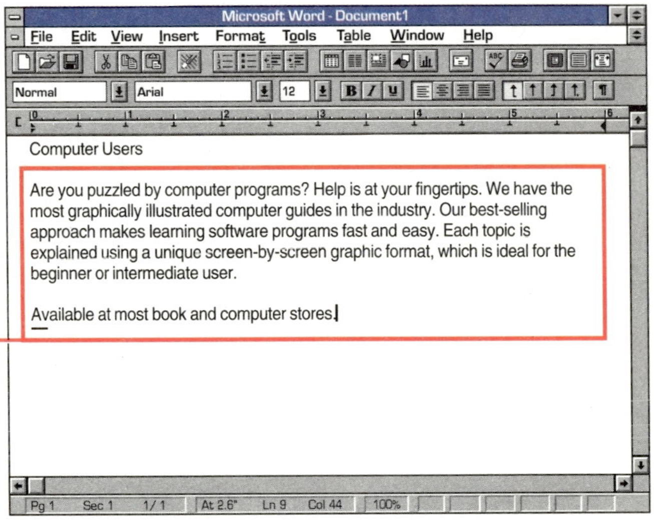

The insertion point (the flashing vertical line I) indicates where the text you type will appear in the document.

1 Type the first line of text.

Note: To display the examples in this guide more clearly, the font was changed to Arial, 12 point. For more information on changing fonts and point sizes, refer to page 40.

2 Press **Enter** to return to the left margin.

3 Press **Enter** again to leave one blank line before typing the next line of text.

4 Type the remaining text.

■ Press **Enter** only when you want to start a new line or paragraph.

Note: Word automatically moves the insertion point to the next line as you type.

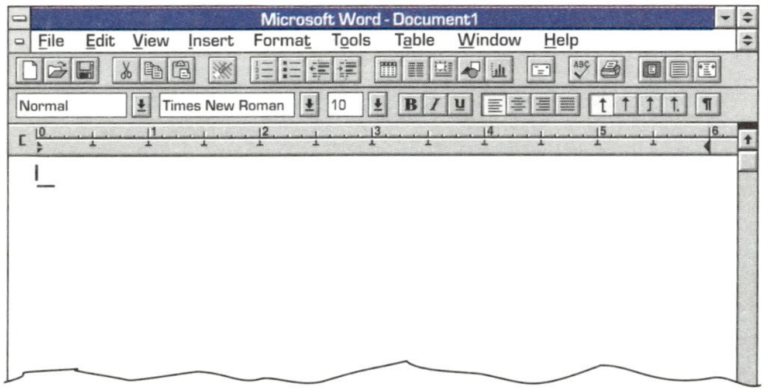

■ The document window is enlarged to occupy the complete screen area.

RESTORE AND MAXIMIZE THE WORD WINDOW

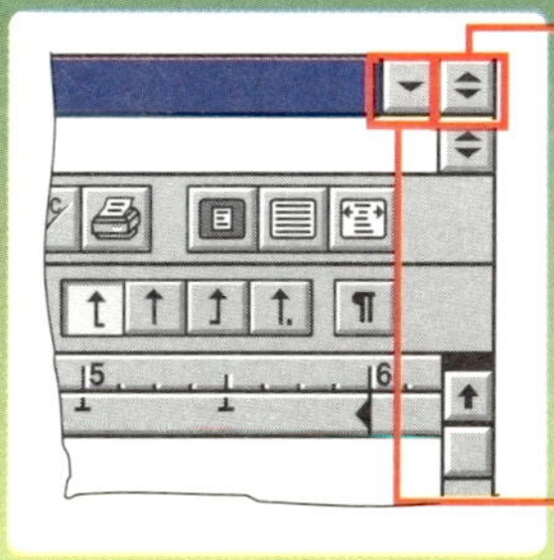

1 To make the size of the Word window smaller, click its **Restore** button.

*Note: To enlarge the Word window to fill the entire screen, click its **Maximize** button* ▲.

2 To shrink the Word window to an icon, click its **Minimize** button.

Note: To restore the Word window, double click its icon.

The position of the insertion point is indicated at the bottom of your screen.

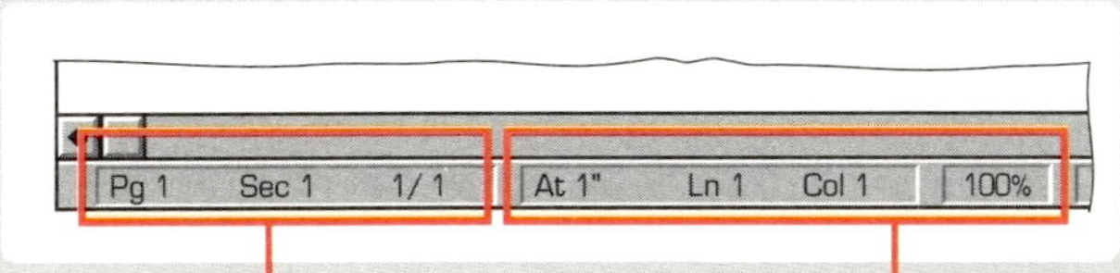

Pg 1	Page the insertion point is currently in.
Sec 1	Section the insertion point is currently in.
1/1	Number of pages from the beginning of the document to the insertion point/ the total number of pages in the document.

At 1"	Distance between the top of the page to the insertion point.
Ln 1	Number of lines from the top of the page to the insertion point.
Col 1	Number of characters from the left margin to the insertion point.
100%	Percent magnification or reduction of text in the document.

MOVE AROUND A DOCUMENT

Using the Mouse

MOVE TO ANY POSITION ON THE SCREEN

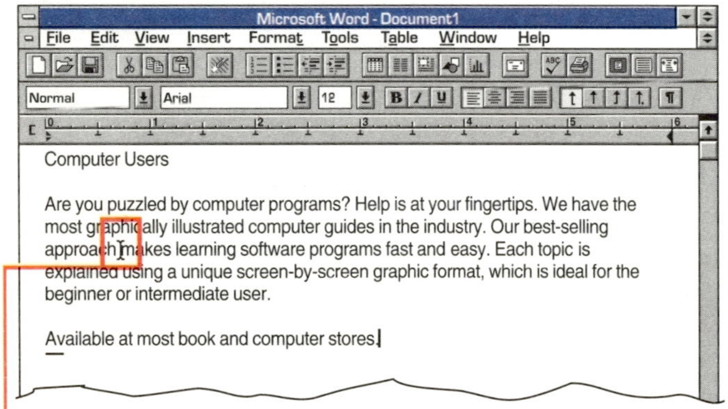

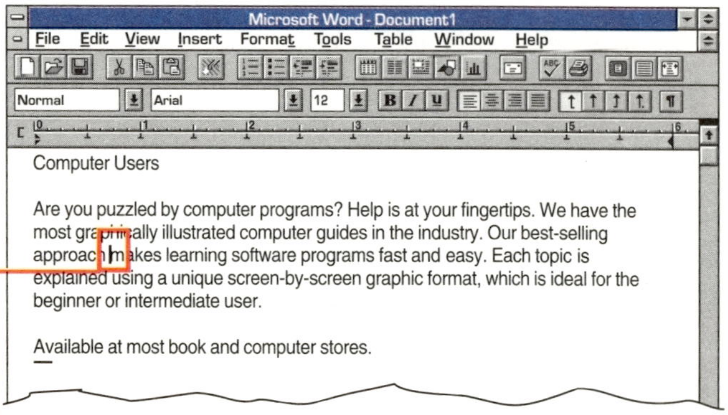

1 Position the mouse pointer I over the location you want to move to.

2 Click the left mouse button and the insertion point is moved.

Note: The insertion point (flashing vertical line |) indicates where the text you type will appear in the document.

MOVE TO ANY POSITION IN THE DOCUMENT (if the document extends beyond the current window)

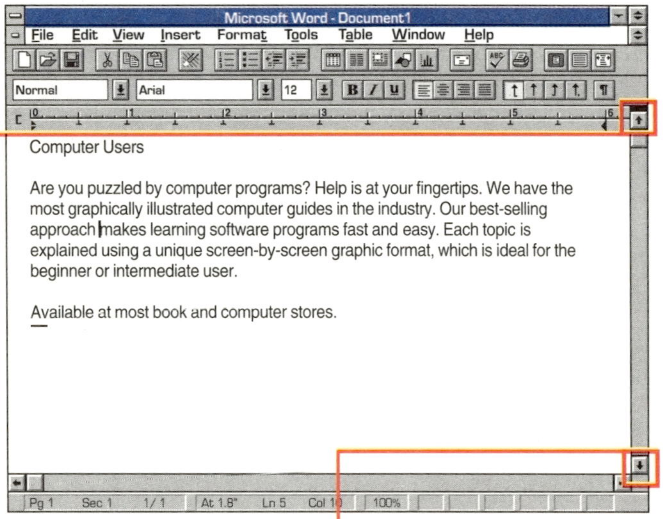

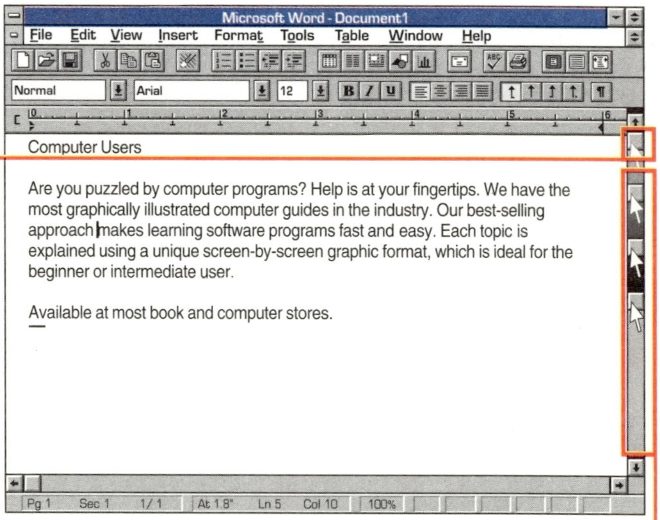

Scroll up

1 Click the **up arrow**.

Scroll down

1 Click the **down arrow**.

Scroll vertically to any position in the document

1 Position the mouse pointer over the **Scroll box**. Click the left mouse button and hold it down.

2 To move proportionally down the document, drag the **Scroll box** proportionally (example: **halfway**) down the Scroll bar. Then release the button.

Note: This only works if the text extends beyond the middle of the screen.

Using the Keyboard

TO MOVE THE INSERTION POINT...

ONE LINE UP OR DOWN	Press ↑ to move up one line. Press ↓ to move down one line.
ONE CHARACTER LEFT OR RIGHT	Press ← to move left one character. Press → to move right one character.
ONE WORD LEFT OR RIGHT	Press Ctrl + ← to move left one word. Press Ctrl + → to move right one word.
TO THE START OR END OF A LINE	Press Home to move to the start of a line. Press End to move to the end of a line.
ONE PARAGRAPH UP OR DOWN	Press Ctrl + ↑ to move up one paragraph. Press Ctrl + ↓ to move down one paragraph.
ONE SCREEN UP OR DOWN	Press Page Up to move up one screen. Press Page Down to move down one screen.
TO THE START OR END OF THE DOCUMENT	Press Ctrl + Home to move to the start of the document. Press Ctrl + End to move to the end of the document.

*Note: You cannot move the insertion point past the horizontal line — displayed on the screen. If you want to move past this line, press **Enter** several times after the last character in the document.*

NUM LOCK

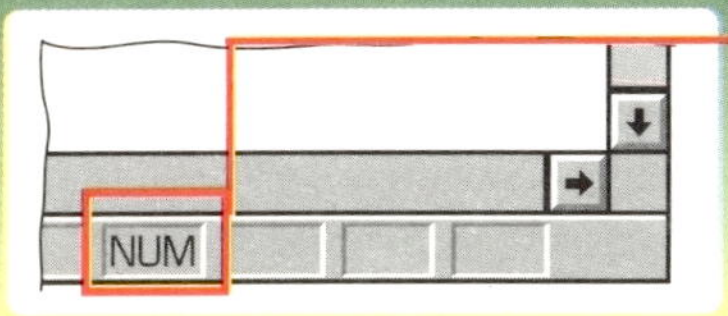

- To use the numeric keypad's arrows, PgUp, PgDn, Home and End keys, the **NUM** on the Status bar must be **off**.
- If **NUM** on the Status bar is **on** (is displayed on the Status bar), press Num Lock to turn it **off**.

SELECT TEXT

You must select the text you want to work with before starting most tasks in Word.

Select a Word

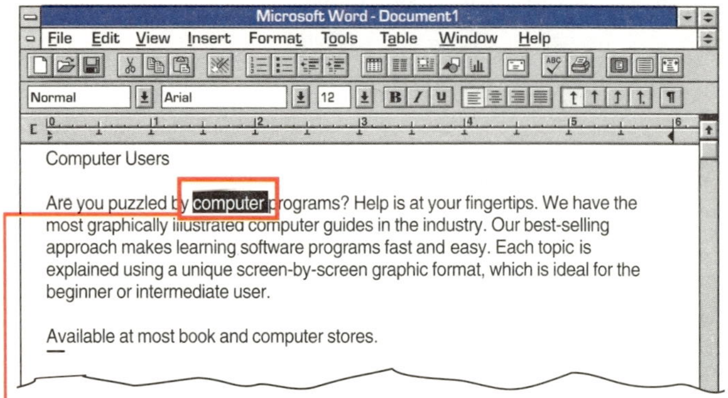

1 Position the mouse pointer I over the word you want to select (example: **computer**).

2 Double click the left mouse button.

Note: To deselect a word, click anywhere on the screen.

Select a Line

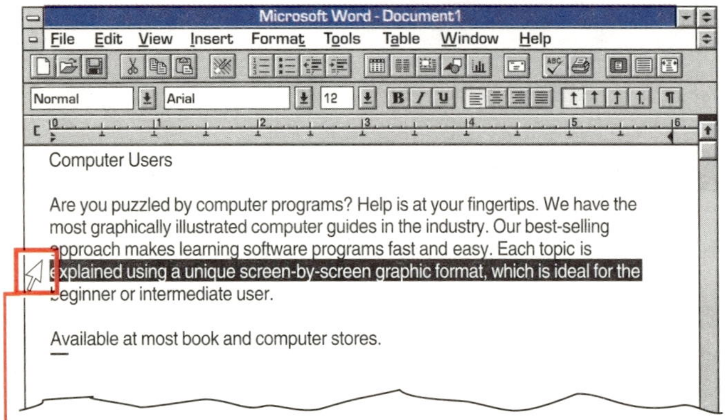

1 Position the mouse pointer I to the left of the line you want to select and it turns into ↖.

2 Click the left mouse button.

Note: To deselect a line, click anywhere on the screen.

Select Multiple Lines

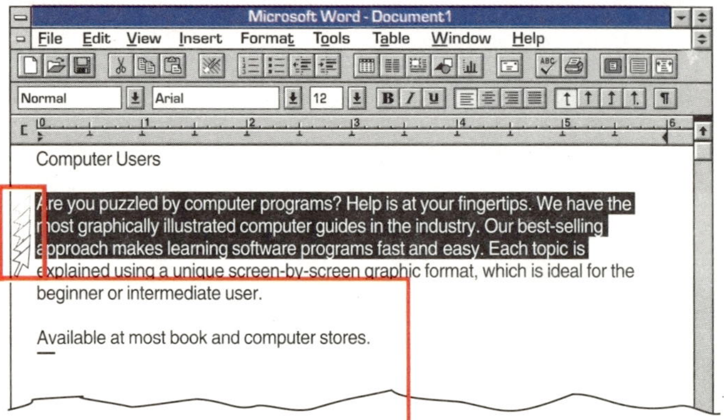

1 Position the mouse pointer I to the left of the first line you want to select and it turns into ↖.

2 Click and hold down the left mouse button as you drag to select the lines. Then release the mouse button.

Note: To deselect the lines, click anywhere on the screen.

Select a Sentence

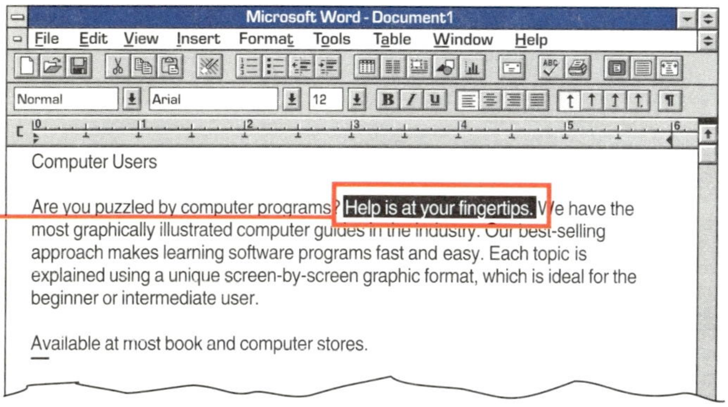

1 Press and hold down the **Ctrl** key.

2 Position the mouse pointer I anywhere over the sentence you want to select.

3 Click the left mouse button. Then release the **Ctrl** key.

Note: To deselect a sentence, click anywhere on the screen.

Select any Amount of Text

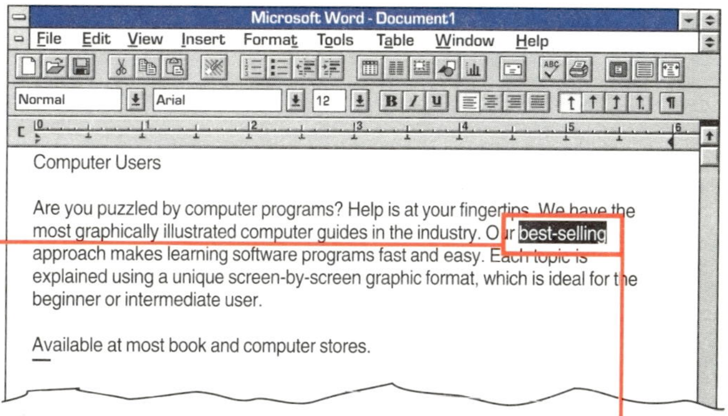

1 Position the mouse pointer I over the first character of the text you want to select.

2 Click and hold down the left mouse button as you drag the mouse pointer over the text you want to select. Then release the mouse button.

Note: To deselect text, click anywhere on the screen.

Select a Paragraph

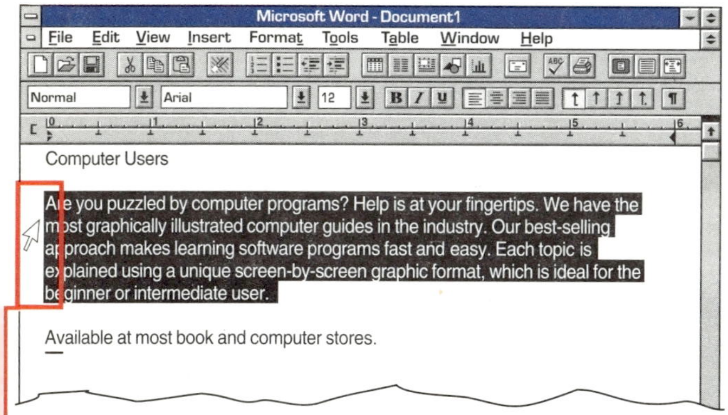

1 Position the mouse pointer I to the left of the paragraph you want to select and it turns into ↖.

2 Double click the left mouse button.

Note: To deselect a paragraph, click anywhere on the screen.

Select the Entire Document

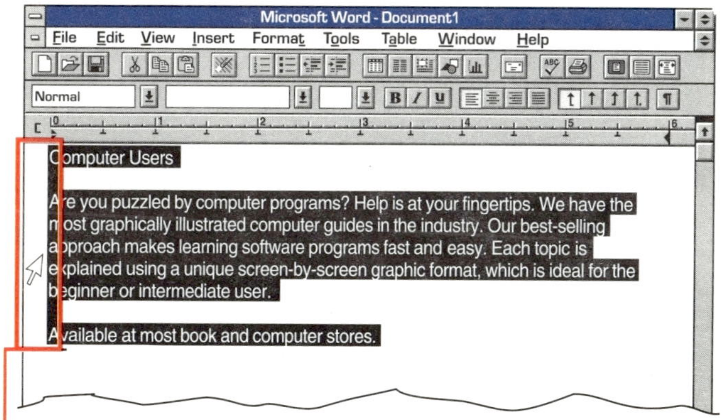

1 Press and hold down the **Ctrl** key.

2 Position the mouse pointer I anywhere to the left of the document and it turns into ↖.

3 Click the left mouse button. Then release the **Ctrl** key.

Note: To deselect the entire document, click anywhere on the screen.

HELP

Help Index

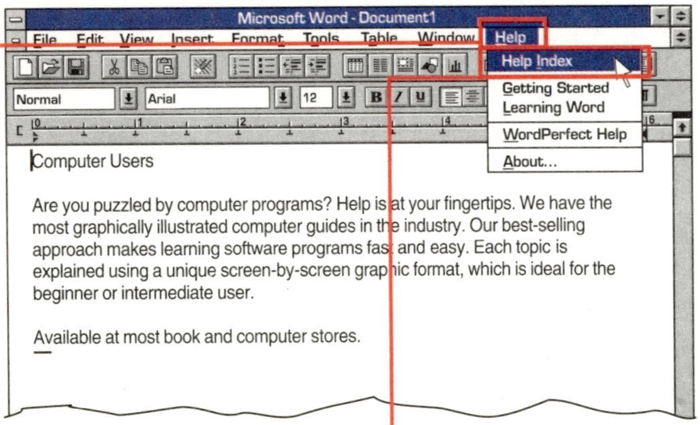

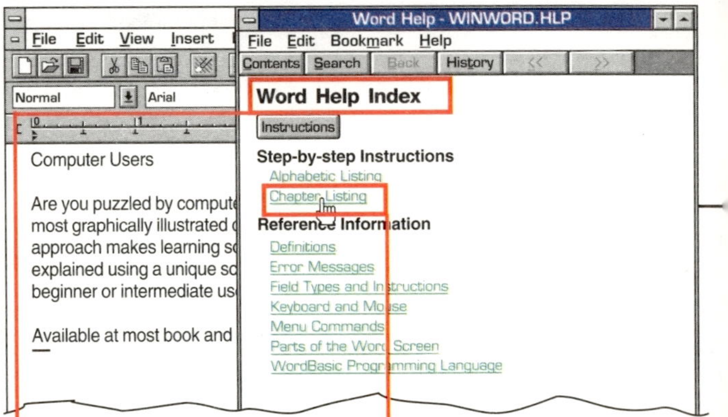

The Word Help Index offers step-by-step instructions and reference information.

1 Click **Help** to open its menu.

2 Click **Help Index** to see a list of the help topics.

■ The **Word Help Index** appears.

3 Move the mouse pointer over the topic of interest (example: Chapter Listing) and it turns into a hand pointer. Then click the left mouse button.

Note: This only applies to green/dimmed, underlined text.

Context Sensitive Help

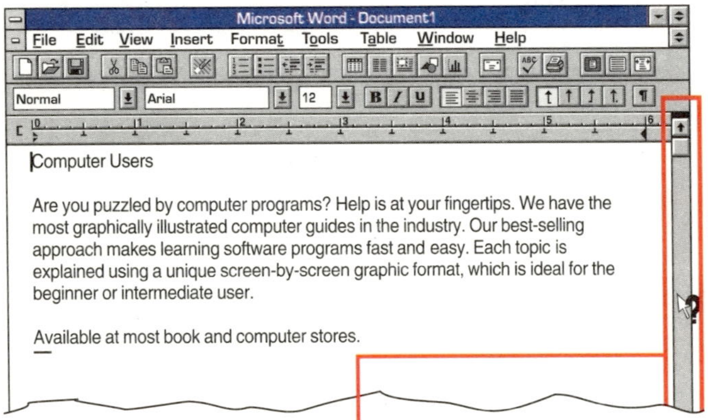

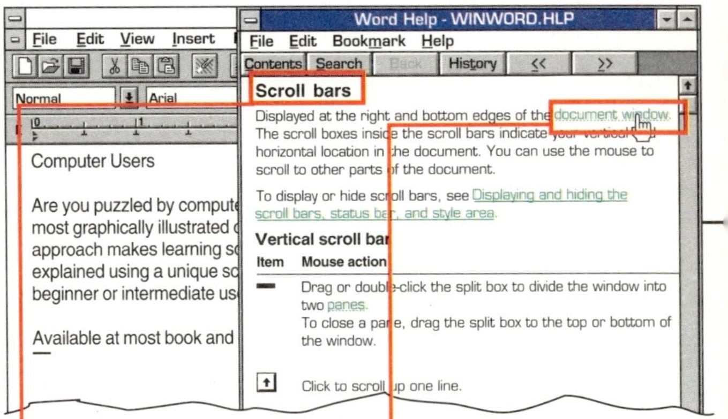

This feature allows you to receive help information for any item on the screen by clicking that item.

1 Press **Shift+F1** and the mouse pointer changes to a question-mark pointer.

2 To receive help for an item on the screen, click that item.

*Note: If you need help while performing a task in Word, press **F1** and context-sensitive help will appear for that task.*

3 Help information appears on the item you selected (example: **Scroll bars**).

4 To view a definition on any dotted, underlined term (example: document window), move the mouse pointer over the term and it turns into a hand pointer. Then click the left mouse button.

Note: This only applies to green/dimmed, dotted underlined text.

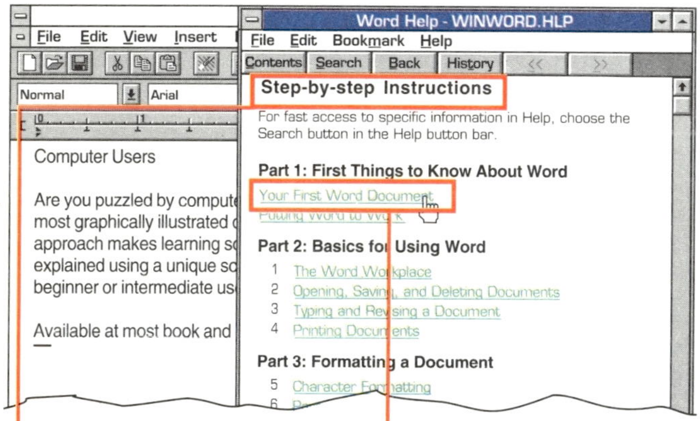

■ **Step-by-step Instructions** are offered for many different topics.

4 Press the ⬇ key to view more topics.

5 Move the mouse pointer ↖ over the topic of interest (example: Your First Word Document) and it turns into ☝. Then click the left mouse button.

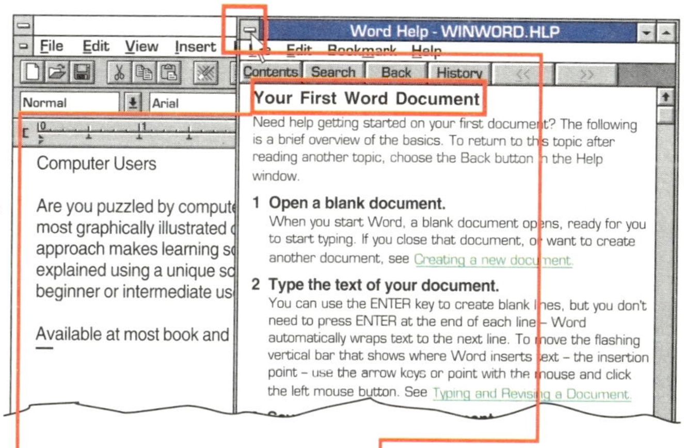

■ A detailed explanation of that topic appears.

6 To receive help on another underlined term move the mouse pointer ↖ over the topic and it turns into ☝. Then click the left mouse button.

7 To exit **Word Help**, double click its Control-menu box ▭ .

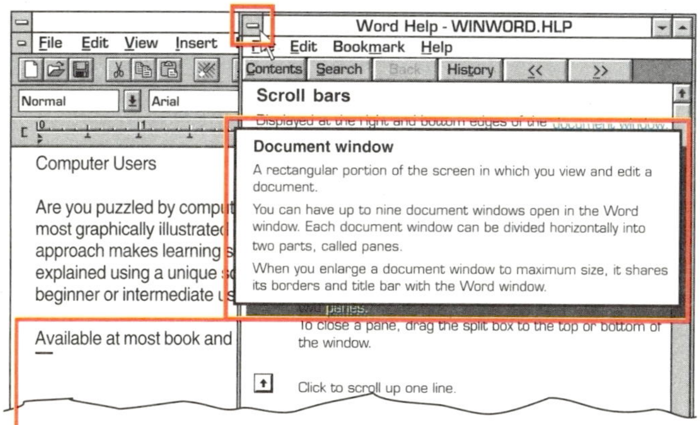

■ A detailed explanation of that term appears.

5 To remove the explanation, click anywhere on the screen.

6 To receive help on another underlined term move the mouse pointer ↖ over the topic and it turns into ☝. Then click the left mouse button.

7 To exit **Word Help**, double click its Control-menu box ▭.

HELP BUTTONS

Contents	Click this button to view the Word Help Index.
Search	Click this button to search for information on a specific word or phrase.
Back	Click this button to return to the last topic you displayed.
History	Click this button to view a list of the last topics you displayed. Then double click the topic you want to view again.
<<	Click this button to move backward through related topics.
>>	Click this button to move forward through related topics.

FILES AND DIRECTORIES

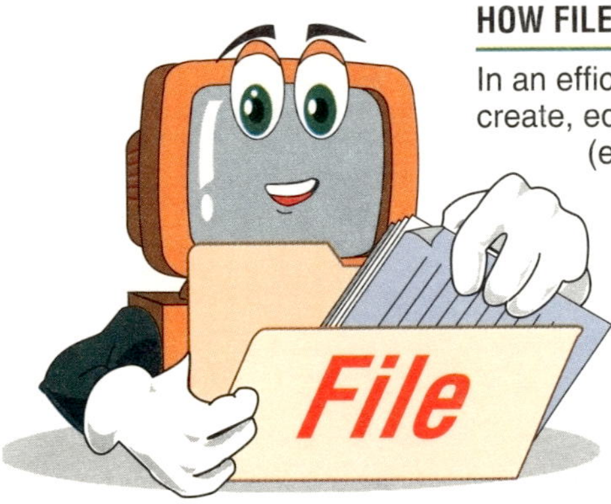

HOW FILES ARE SPECIFIED

In an efficient and productive office environment, people create, edit, review and organize paper documents (example: letters, worksheets, reports, etc.). These documents are stored in folders, which in turn are placed in cabinets. To retrieve a specific document, you must identify it by location (cabinet and folder) and then by name.

Computers work the same way. After creating a document in Word, it must be named and saved. During the save process, you must tell Word the drive (cabinet) and directory (folder) the file is to reside in.

Word uses a multilevel directory filing system to store and retrieve your programs and data files. The first level of this directory structure is called the root directory. From this directory other subdirectories may be created. A typical multilevel filing system is illustrated on the next page.

Note: The terms "directory" and "subdirectory" are used interchangeably. The "root directory" is the only directory that cannot be called a "subdirectory".

File Specification

A file is specified by describing its drive, path, and name (filename and extension).

c: **\winword\winword.cbt** **sales** **.doc**

DRIVE

Tells Word the drive the file is in.

PATH

Tells Word the path through the directory structure to get to the file location.

FILENAME

The filename can contain up to 8 characters.

EXTENSION

The extension can contain up to 3 characters. In some cases, it is omitted.

Note: The first backslash (\) specifies the path to the root directory. Subsequent backslashes (\) are used to separate directories and the filename.

The following characters are allowed:

- The letters A to Z, upper or lower case
- The digits 0 through 9
- The symbols ! @ # $ % ^ & - ( ) _ { } ~
- The filename cannot contain a **.** (period) or blank spaces

Using Directories to Organize Your Files

■ Directories can contain files and/or paths to other directories. In this example, the root directory has paths to three subdirectories.

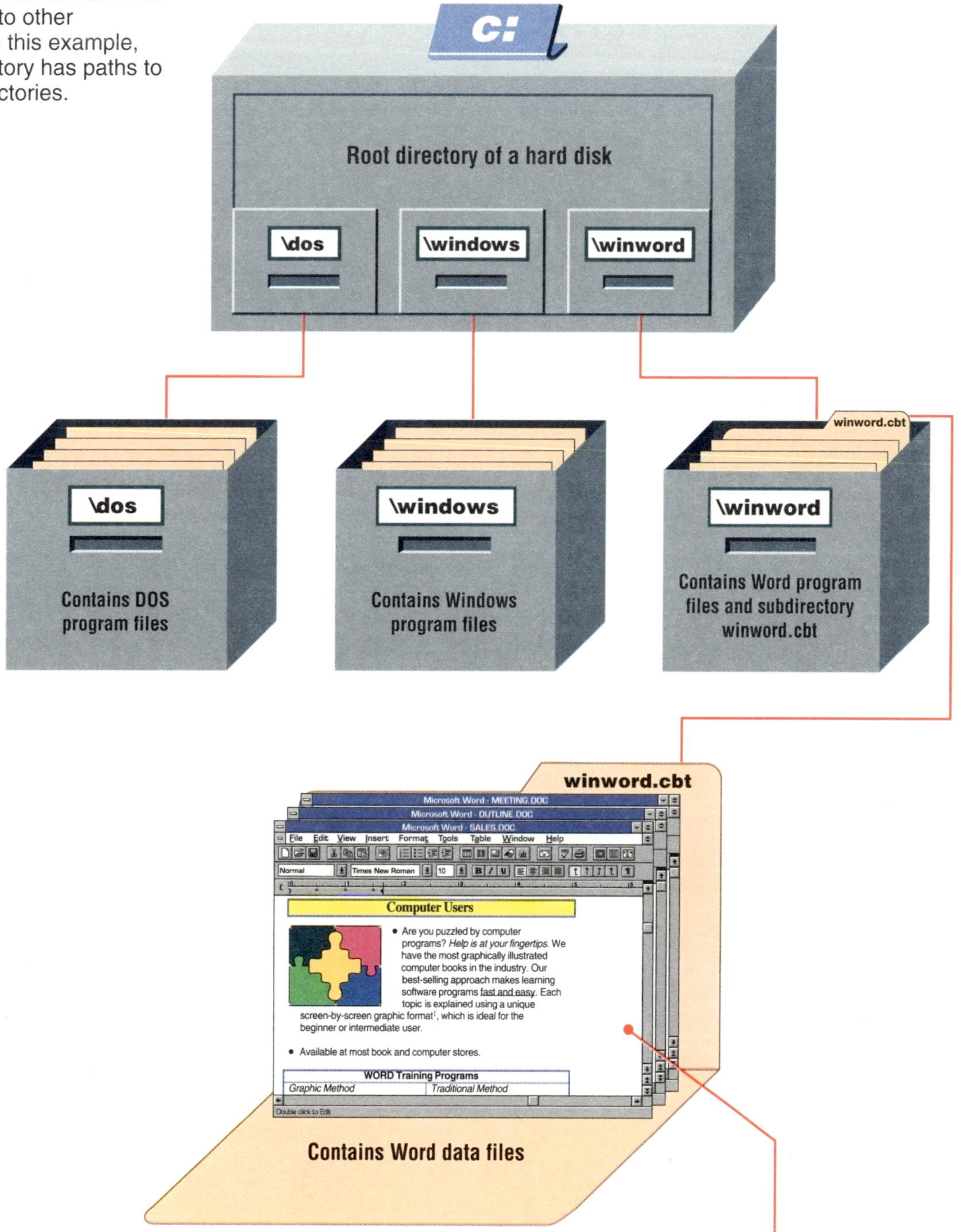

The file specification for this data file is:

c:\winword\winword.cbt\sales.doc

SAVE A NEW DOCUMENT

Save a New Document

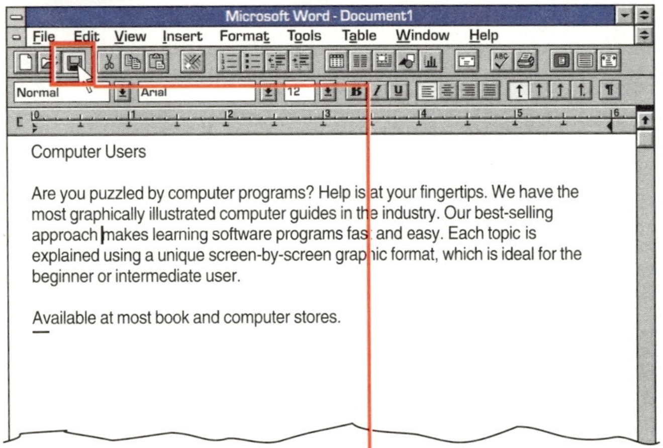

A document must be saved before exiting Word if it is required for future use.

1 Click the **Save** button and the **Save As** dialog box appears.

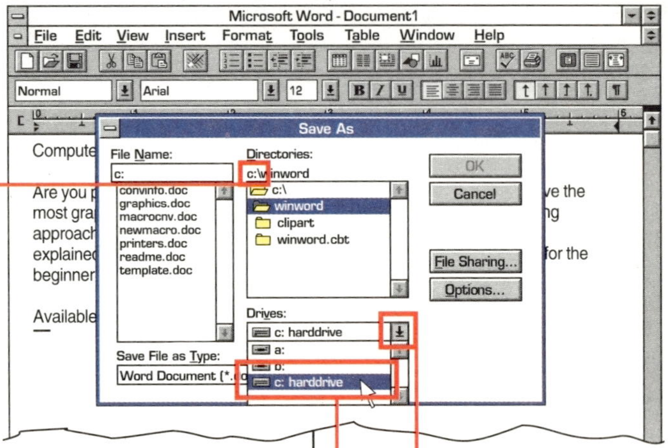

Most of the time you will save your work to the hard drive (example: c:).

Note: You should backup your work regularly to a floppy drive (a: or b:).

■ The document will be saved in the current drive (example: **c:**).

2 To change the current drive, click the arrow beside the **Drives:** box and a list of the available drives appears.

3 Click the drive you want to make current (example: **c:**).

SAVE A REVISED DOCUMENT

You should save regularly to prevent losing work due to power failure or hardware malfunctions.

1 Click the **Save** button to replace the previously saved version of the document with the current one.

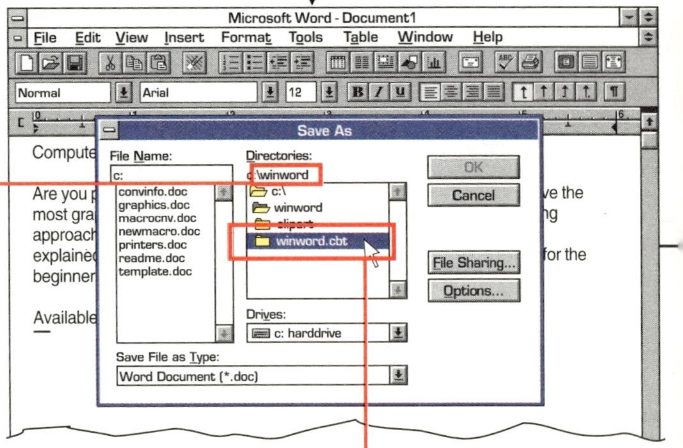

To better organize your documents, separate them from the program files located in the winword directory.

■ The document will be saved in the current directory (example: **winword**).

4 To change the current directory, double click the name of the directory you want to make current (example: **winword.cbt**).

*Note: The **winword.cbt** directory was created during the install procedure. If you do not have this directory, or wish to make a new directory, refer to your Microsoft Windows manual.*

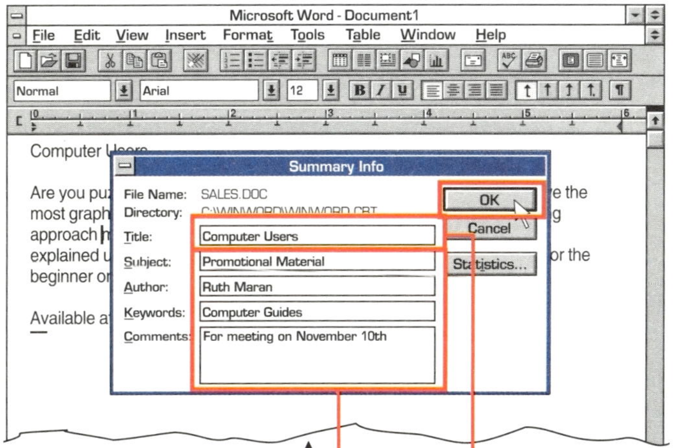

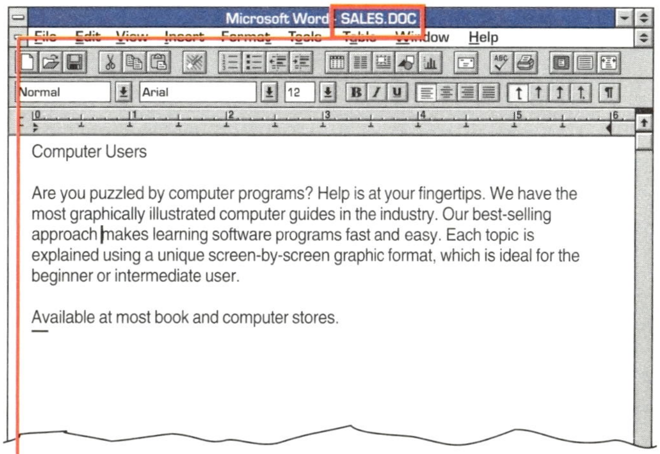

■ Word lets you describe the contents of the file. This can later be useful in locating the file.

*Note: If you do not want to enter summary information, click the **OK** button.*

7 Type a title for the document. Then press **Tab** to move to the next heading.

8 Type the remaining data, pressing **Tab** after each entry.

9 Click the **OK** button, or press **Enter**.

■ The document is saved (example: **SALES.DOC**).

*Note: If an extension is not specified, Word automatically adds the extension **.DOC**.*

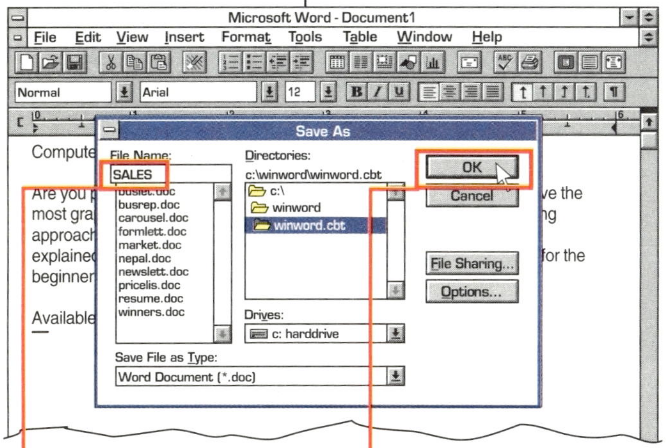

5 Click in the **File Name:** box, then type a name for your document (example: **SALES**).

6 Click the **OK** button, and the **Summary Info** dialog box appears.

DISPLAY DOCUMENT STATISTICS

1 Click the **Statistics** button in the **Summary Info** dialog box to display information about the document (example: Number of words).

*Note: Click the **OK** button to return to the **Summary Info** dialog box.*

CHANGE SUMMARY INFORMATION AFTER SAVING A DOCUMENT

1 Click **File** to open its menu.

2 Click **Summary Info**.

3 Press **Tab** until the information you want to change is highlighted. Then type the new text.

Repeat this step until you have made all the desired changes.

4 Click the **OK** button.

CLOSE A DOCUMENT AND EXIT WORD

OPEN A SAVED DOCUMENT

Close a Document

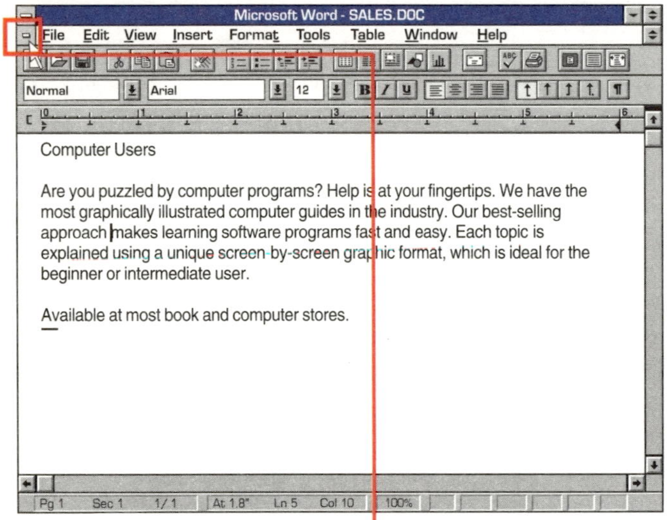

Once you are finished working with a document, close the document to simplify your workspace.

1 Double click the **Control-menu** box of the document you want to close.

Exit Word

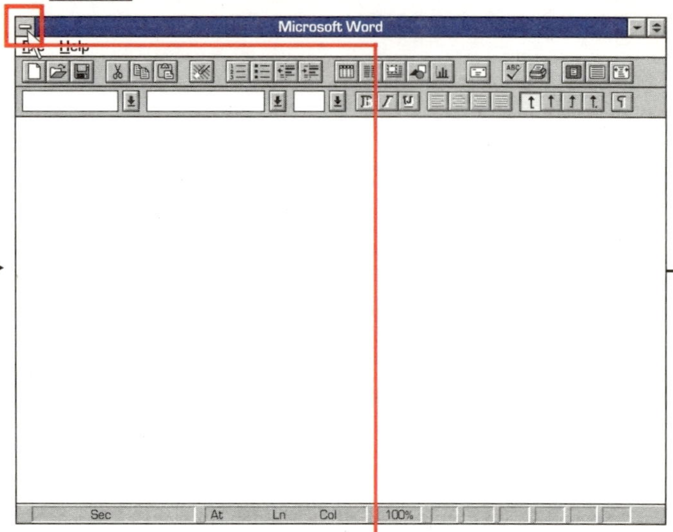

■ The document is closed.

1 To exit Word, double click its **Control-menu** box.

Open a Saved Document

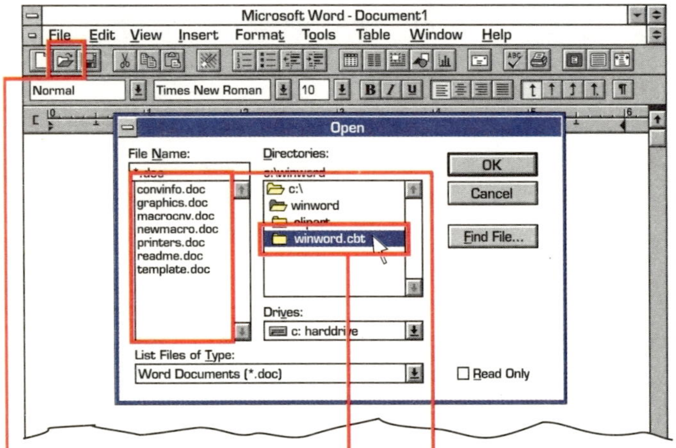

1 Click the **Open** button and the **Open** dialog box appears.

■ The files in the current drive and directory are displayed.

2 To open a file that resides in another directory, double click the name of the directory you want to change to (example: **winword.cbt**).

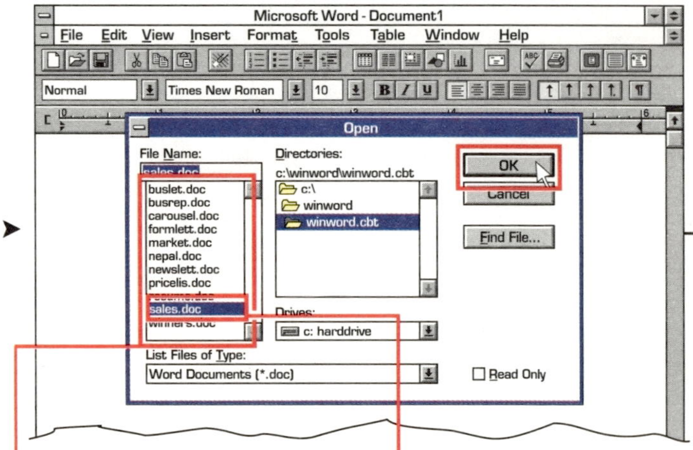

■ The files in the current drive and directory are displayed.

*Note: To open a file located in another drive, click the arrow beside the **Drives:** box ⬇. Then click the drive you want to change to.*

3 Click the name of the file you want to open (example: **sales.doc**).

4 Click the **OK** button, or press **Enter**.

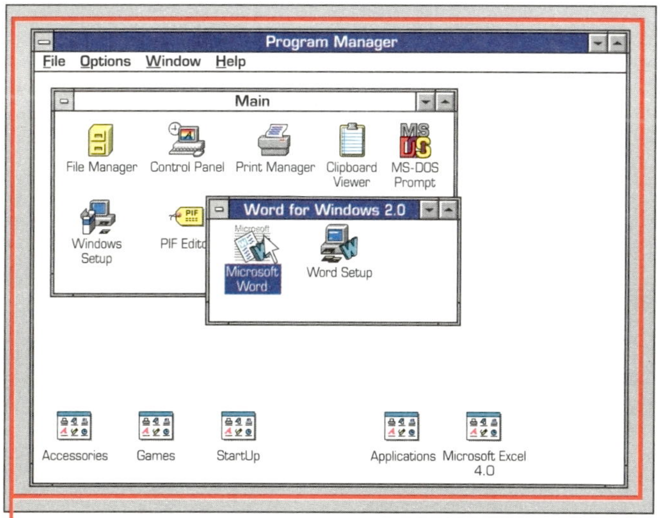

■ The **Program Manager** window is displayed.

Note: To start Word for Windows, refer to page 4.

If this dialog box appears when trying to close a document or exit Word, you have not saved the changes you made to the document.

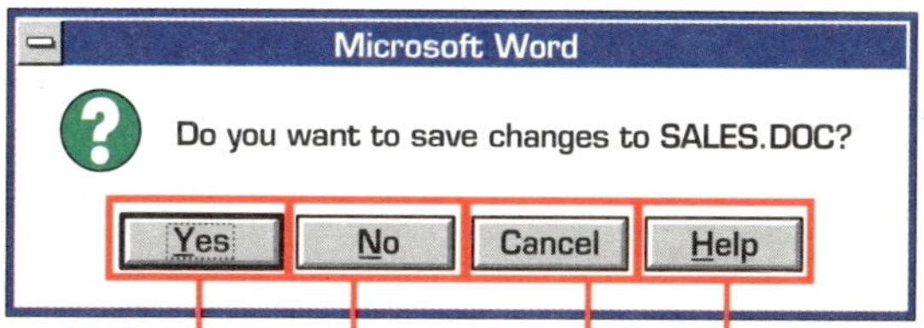

Click the **Yes** button to save the changes.

Note: The document will replace the previously saved document.

Click the **No** button if you do not want to save the changes.

Click the **Cancel** button to cancel the Close or Exit command.

Click the **Help** button to receive help.

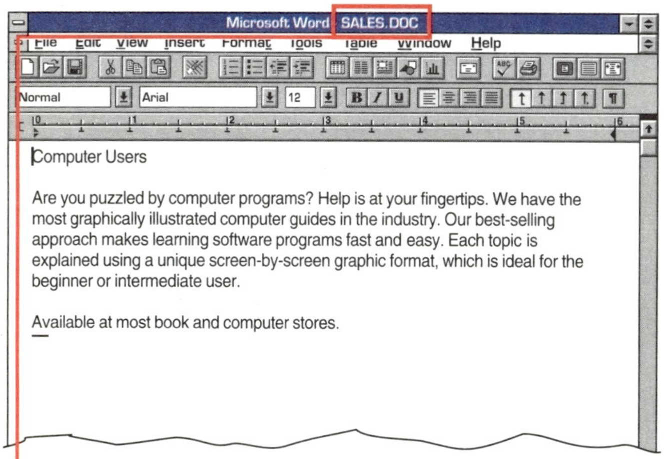

■ The file is opened (example: **SALES.DOC**).

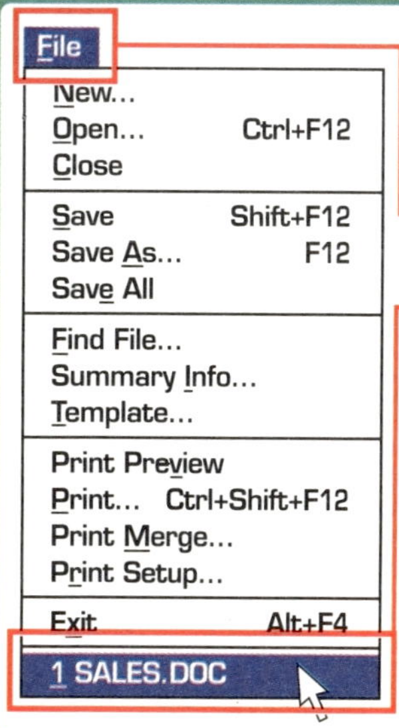

Word displays the names of the last four documents you opened. To open one of these documents:

1 Click **File** to open its menu.

2 Click the name of the file you want to open (example: **SALES.DOC**).

FIND A FILE

View Contents of Files

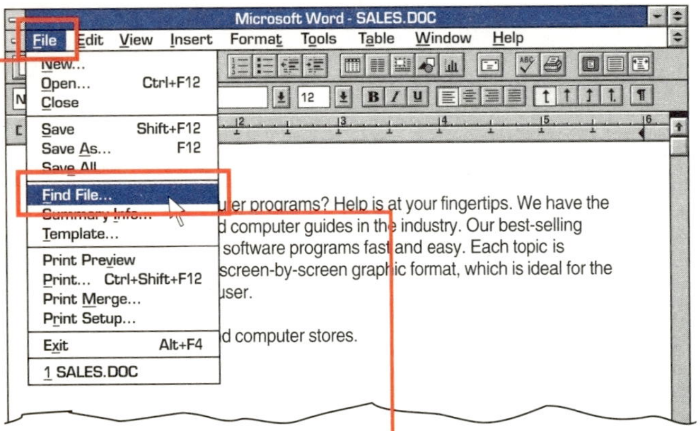

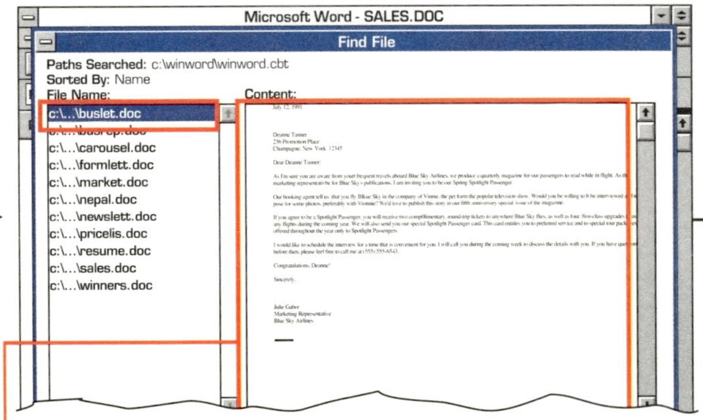

The Find File command allows you to quickly view the contents of files without having to open each one.

1 Click **File** to open its menu.

2 Click **Find File** and the **Find File** dialog box appears.

■ The contents of the highlighted file (example: **buslet.doc**) are displayed in the **Content:** box.

Search... Search for a File

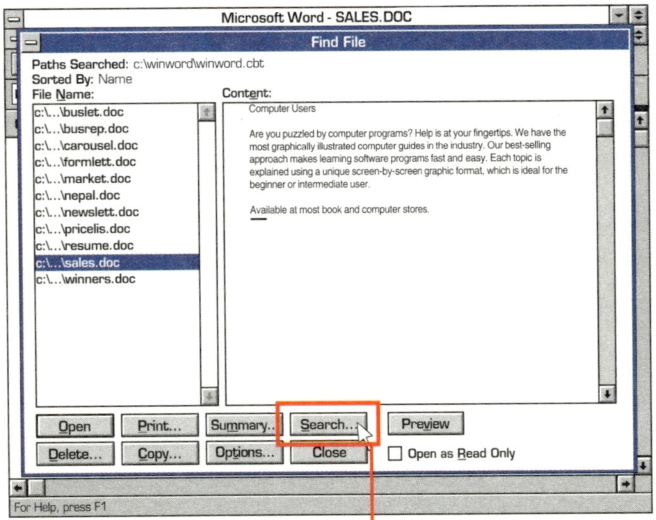

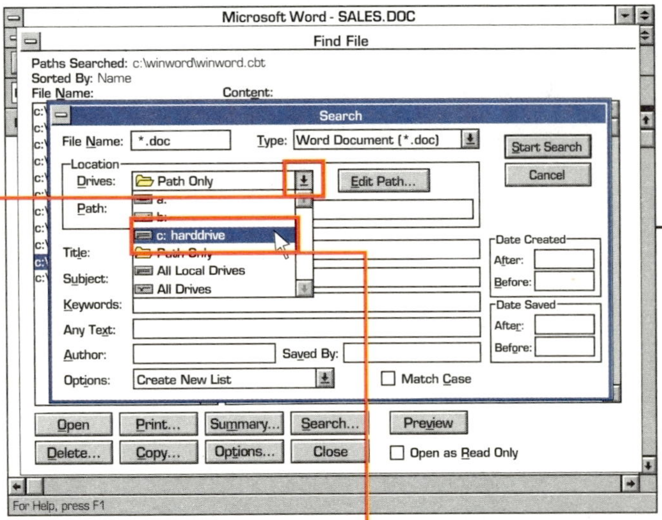

The Find File feature is useful if you cannot remember the name or location of the file you want to open.

1 To search for a file, click the **Search** button and the **Search** dialog box appears.

*Note: To open the **Find File** dialog box, click **Find**, then click **Find File**.*

2 If you do not know which directory the file resides in, click the arrow beside **Drives:**.

3 Click the drive you want to search (example: **c:**).

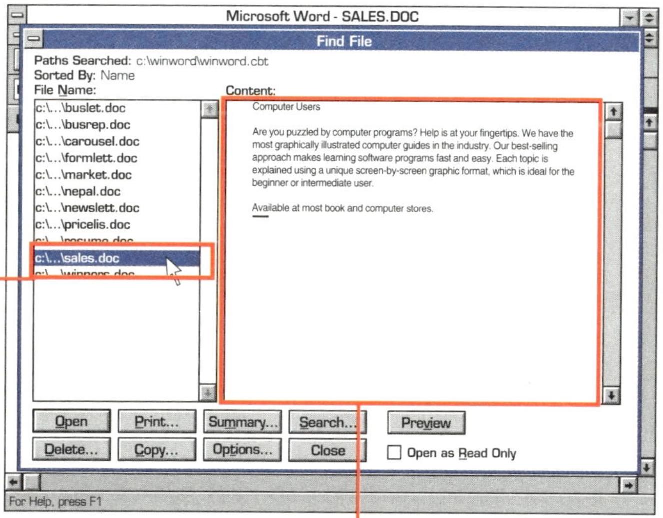

3 To view the contents of another file, click the file's name (example: **sales.doc**).

■ The contents of the file are displayed.

Open — OPEN A FILE FROM THE FIND FILE DIALOG BOX

1 In the **File Name:** box, click the name of the file you want to open.

2 Click the **Open** button.

Summary... — DISPLAY SUMMARY INFORMATION

1 In the **File Name:** box, click the name of the file that has the summary information you want to display.

2 Click the **Summary** button.

*Note: Press **Enter** to return to the **Find File** dialog box.*

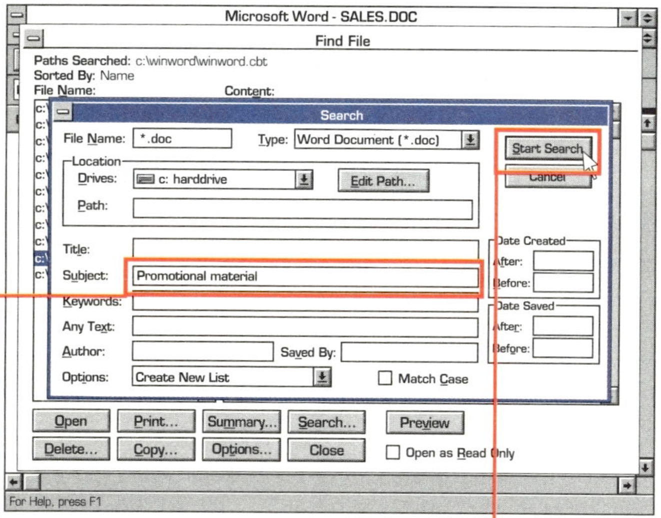

■ Word lets you enter information about the file you want to find.

4 Click in the box beside a heading you want to enter search text into (example: **Subject**).

5 Type the text that will match the summary information of the file you want to find.

Note: You can type search text into as many categories as desired.

6 Click the **Start Search** button.

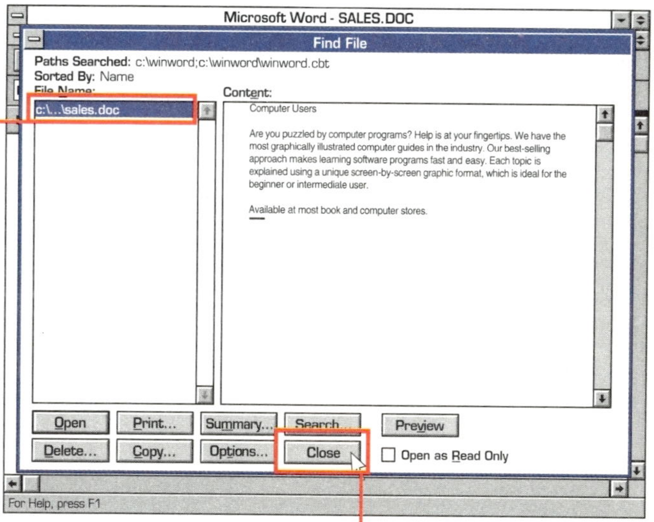

■ The files that match the criteria are displayed.

*Note: To once more list all files, click the **Search** button to open the **Search** dialog box. Then erase the criteria you typed in step **5**, and press **Enter**.*

7 To close the **Find File** dialog box, click the **Close** button.

SAVE FILE UNDER NEW NAME

DELETE A FILE

Save File under New Name

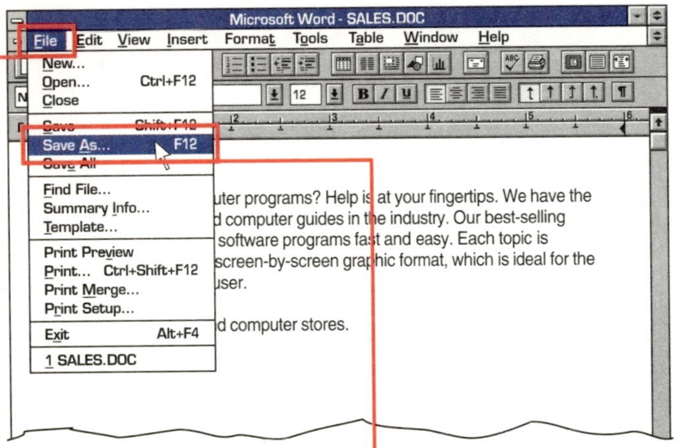

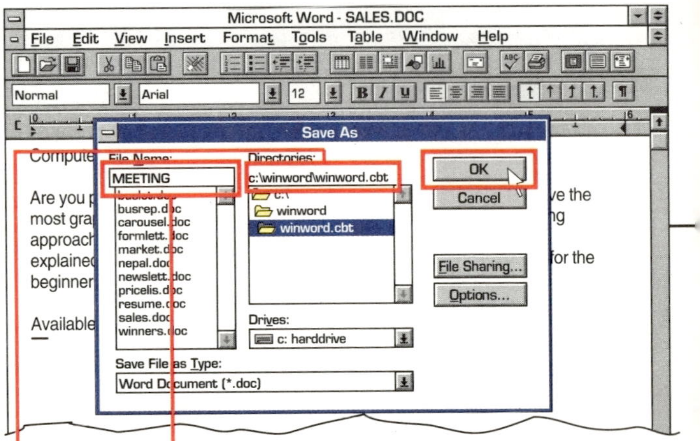

This feature is useful when you want to save several versions of the same document.

1 Click **File** to open its menu.

2 Click **Save As** and the **Save As** dialog box appears.

■ The document will be saved in the current drive and directory (example: **c:\winword\winword.cbt**).

Note: To change the current directory, double click the name of the directory you want to make current.

3 Type a name for your document (example: **MEETING**).

4 Click the **OK** button, and the **Summary Info** dialog box appears.

Delete... Delete a File

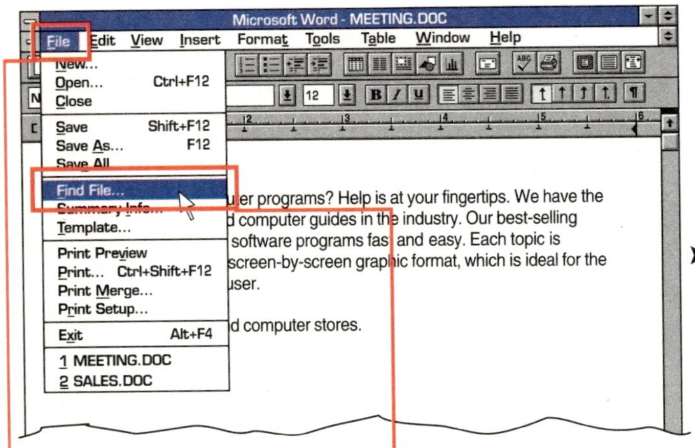

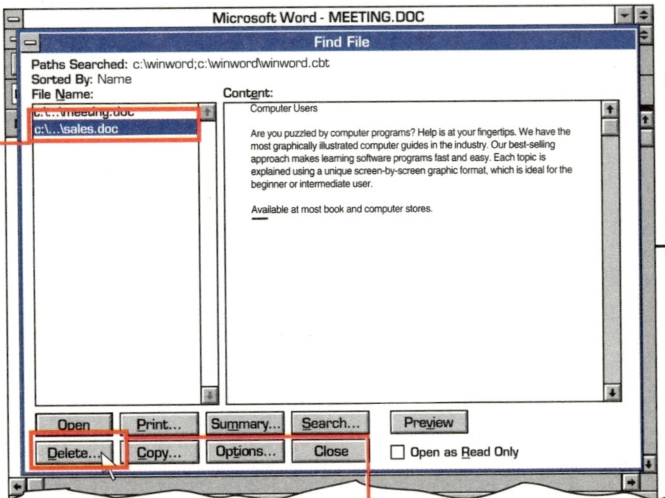

1 Click **File** to open its menu.

Note: You cannot delete a file that is currently open. To close a file, double click its ***Control-menu*** *box* ⊟.

2 Click **Find File** and the **Find File** dialog box appears.

3 Click the name of the file you want to delete (example: **sales.doc**).

Note: If the file you want to delete is not displayed, refer to 'Search for a File' on page 20.

4 Click the **Delete** button.

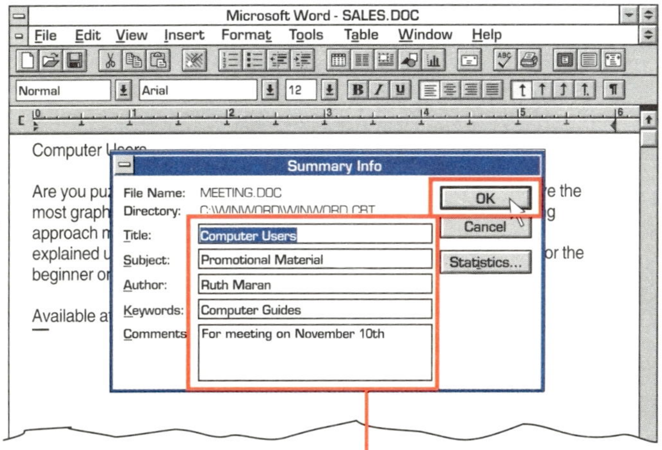

■ Word lets you change the file's summary information. This data can later be useful in locating the file.

Note: If you do not want to change the summary information, click the ***OK*** *button.*

5 To change the summary information, press **Tab** until the information you want to change is highlighted. Then type the new text.

Repeat this step until all desired changes are complete.

6 Click the **OK** button.

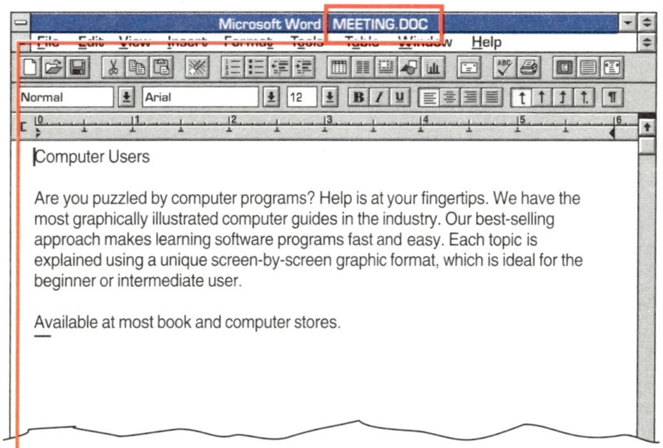

■ The document is saved (example: **MEETING.DOC**).

Note: If an extension is not specified, Word automatically adds the extension ***.DOC****.*

Note: The document ***SALES.DOC*** *is still on the hard drive.*

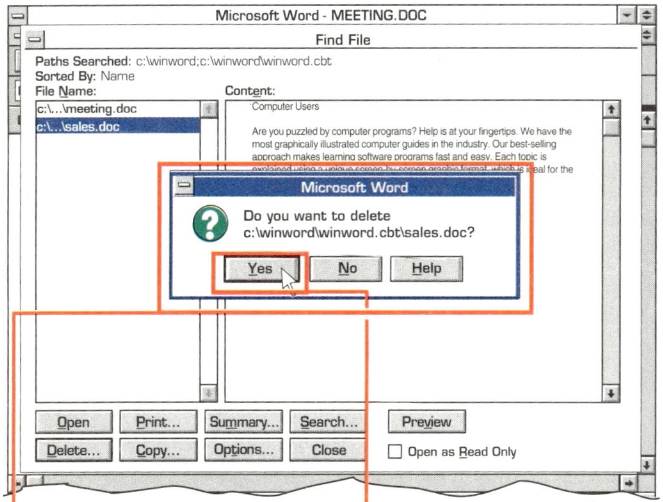

■ This dialog box appears offering you one last chance to change your mind.

5 To delete the file, click the **Yes** button.

Note: If you do not want to delete the file, click the ***No*** *button.*

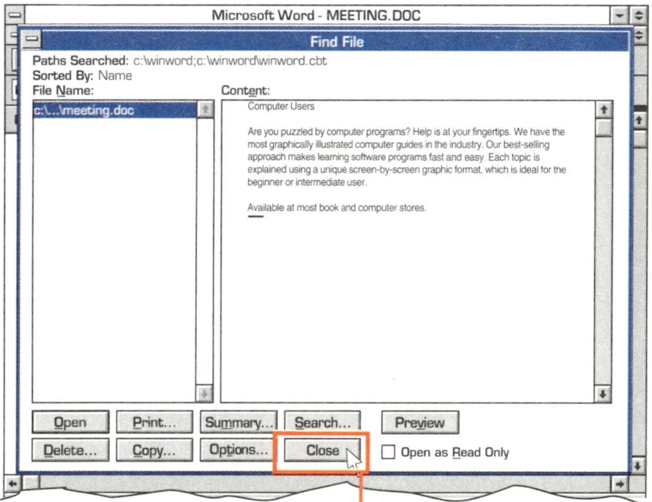

■ The file is deleted (example: **sales.doc**).

6 To close the **Find File** dialog box, click the **Close** button.

Open a New Document

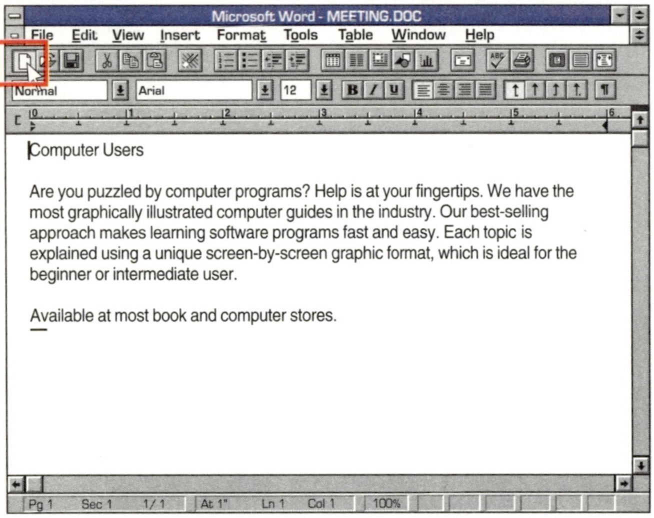

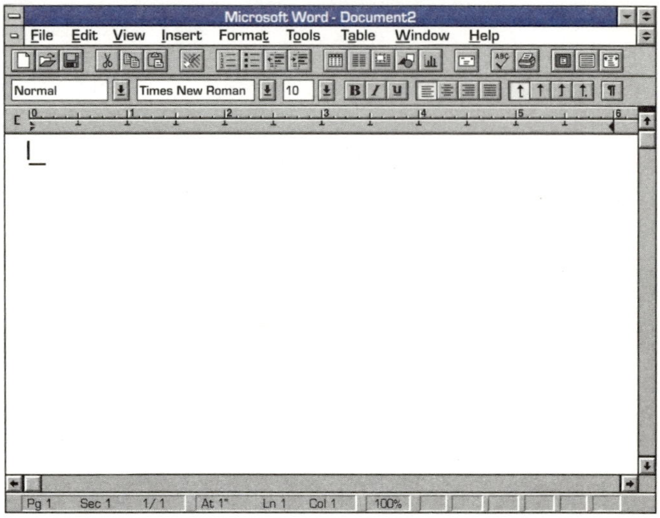

1 Click the **New** button.

■ A new document appears.

Switch Between Documents

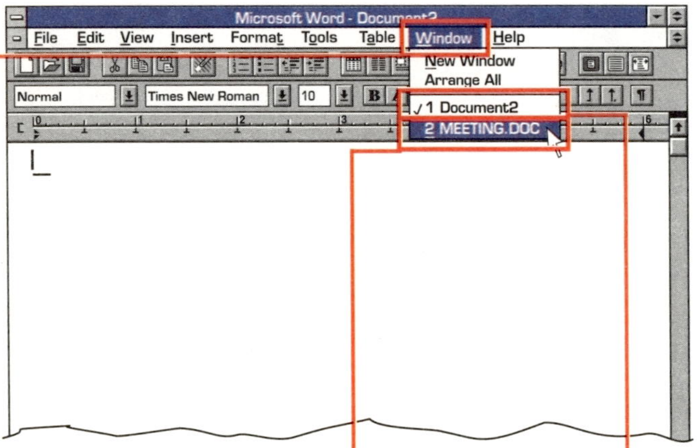

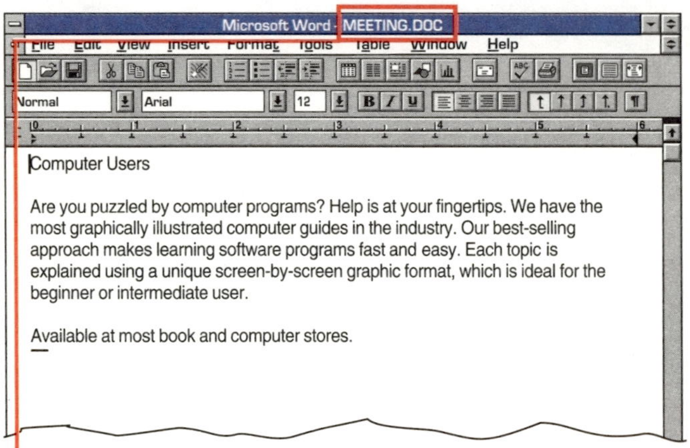

Currently open documents can be viewed by selecting their name from the Window menu.

1 Click **Window** to open its menu.

■ The active window displays a check mark ✓ beside it (example: **Document2**).

2 Click the name of the document you want to view (example: **MEETING.DOC**).

■ The document is displayed (example: **MEETING.DOC**).

SHORTCUT

Press **Ctrl+F6** repeatedly to switch between all open documents.

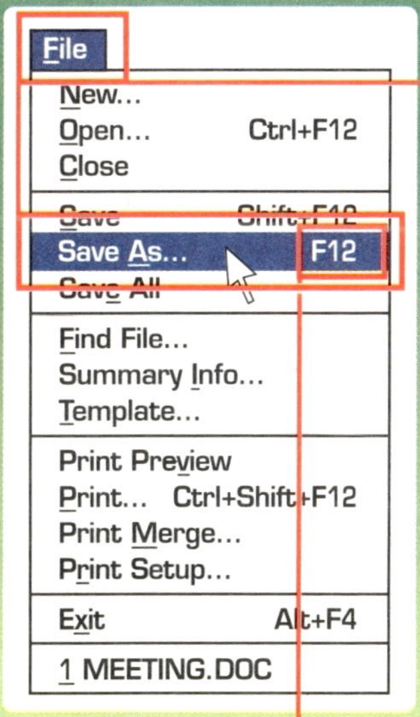

KEYBOARD SHORTCUT TO SELECT MENU COMMANDS

■ To select a menu command (example: **Save As**), press **Alt**, **F**, **A**.

F is the underlined letter for the **File** menu.

A is the underlined letter for the **Save As** command.

*Note: Word commands are not case sensitive. You can press **Alt**, **F**, **A** or **Alt**, **f**, **a**.*

If a dimmed command appears, this means it is not currently operational.

■ Some commands display alternative keyboard shortcuts. For example, to select the **Save As** command, press **F12**.

Arrange Documents

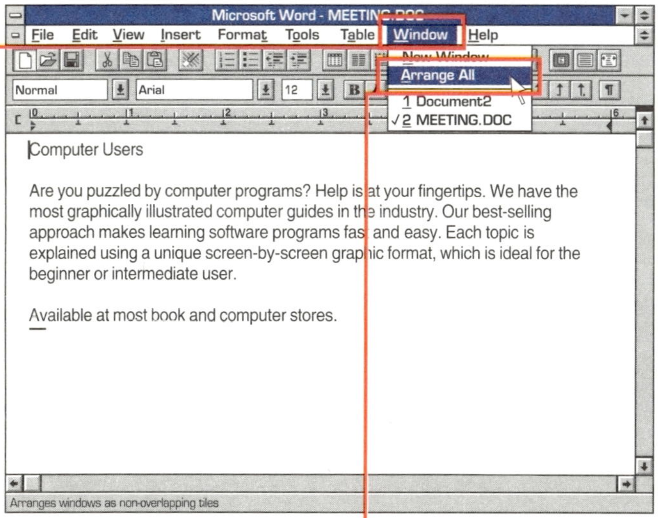

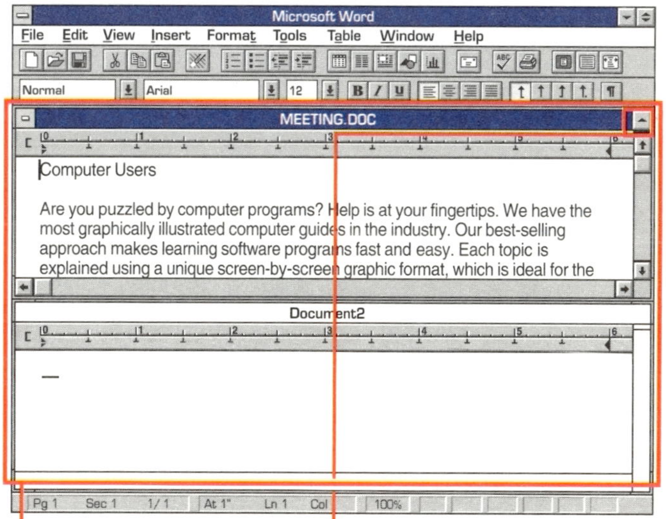

You can view all open documents at the same time.

1 Click **Window** to open its menu.

2 Click **Arrange All**.

■ The documents are arranged on the screen, allowing you to view all documents at the same time.

3 To maximize a document, click anywhere in the document to make it active.

4 Click the document's **Maximize** button.

INSERT AND REPLACE TEXT

Insert a Blank Line

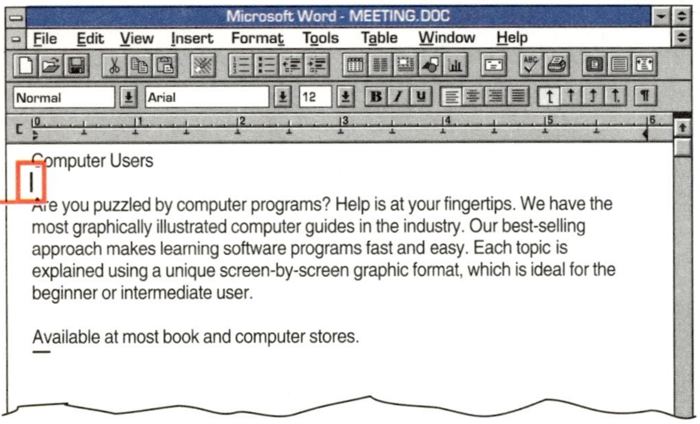

1 Position the insertion point at the location where you want to insert a blank line.

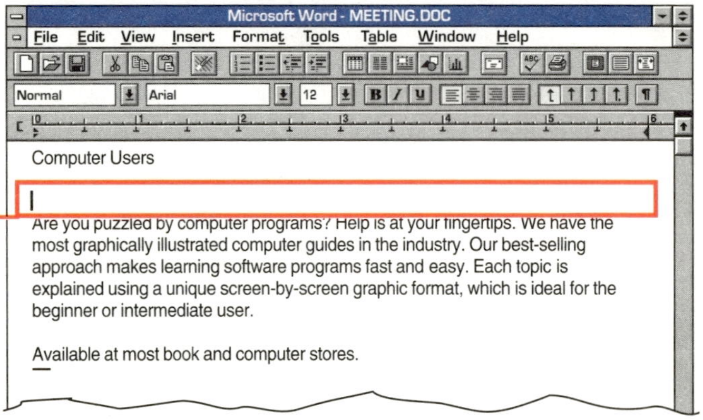

2 Press **Enter** to insert a blank line.

Split and Join Paragraphs

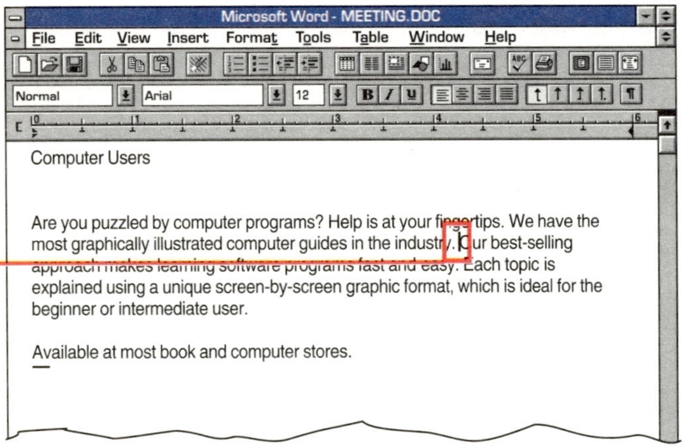

1 Position the insertion point at the location where you want to split a paragraph into two.

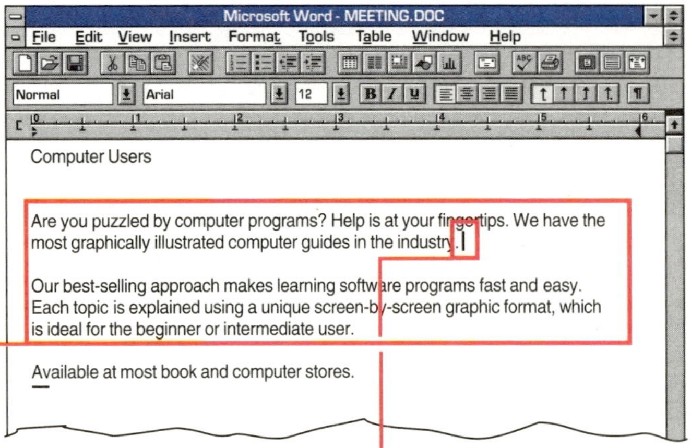

2 Press **Enter** and the paragraph is split into two.

3 To leave a blank line between the two paragraphs, press **Enter** again.

4 To join two paragraphs, position the insertion point at the end of the first paragraph. Then press the **Delete** key (example: press **twice**) until the paragraphs are joined.

Insert Text

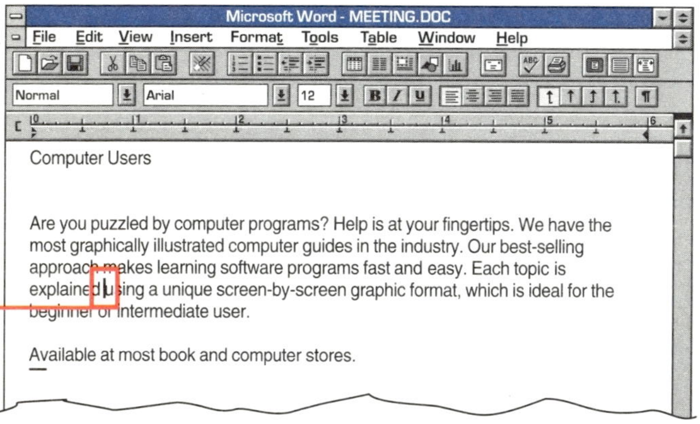

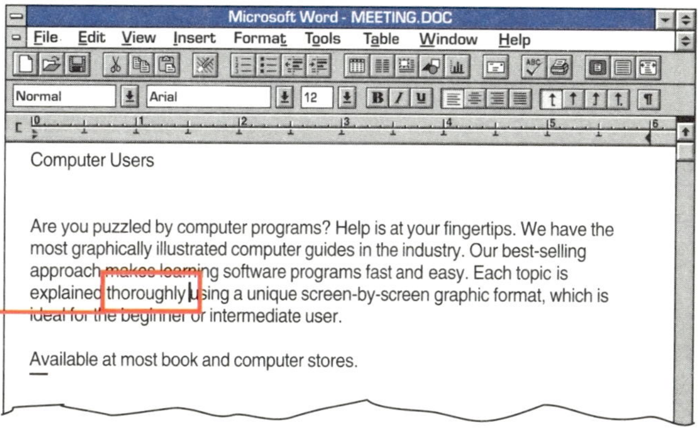

1 Position the insertion point at the location where you want to insert text.

*Note: If OVR is displayed at the bottom right corner of the screen, press the **Insert** key. This turns off the Overtype mode and allows new characters to be inserted.*

2 Type the text you want to insert (example: **thoroughly**).

3 To insert a blank space, press the **Spacebar**.

Note: The words to the right of the inserted text are pushed forward.

Replace Text

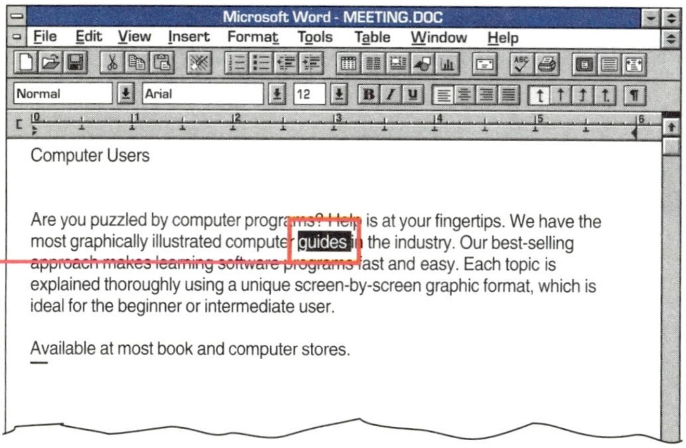

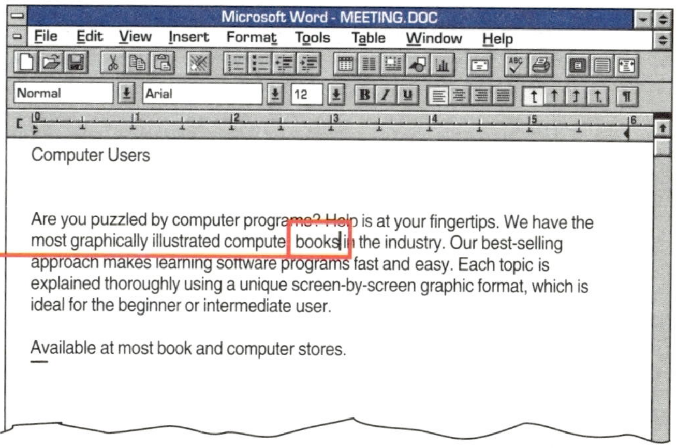

1 Select the text you want to replace with new text (example: **guides**).

Note: To select text, refer to page 10.

2 Type the text you want to replace the existing text (example: **books**).

DELETE TEXT

UNDO

Delete — Delete a Blank Line

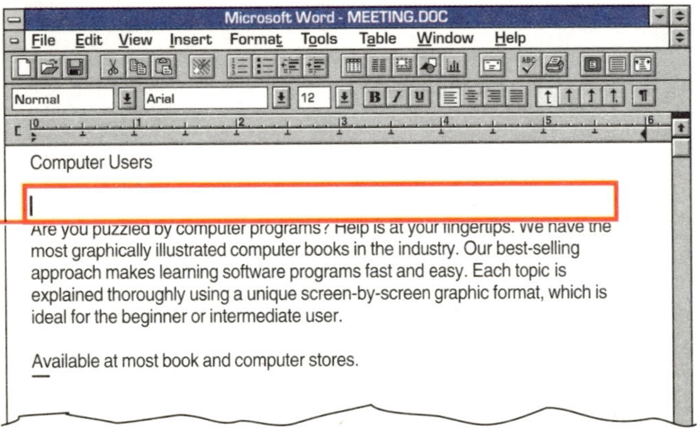

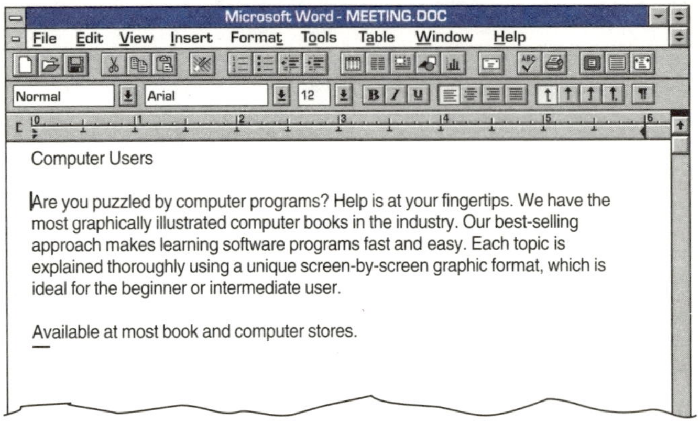

1 Position the insertion point on the blank line you want to delete.

2 Press the **Delete** key.

■ The blank line is deleted.

Delete — Delete One Character at a Time

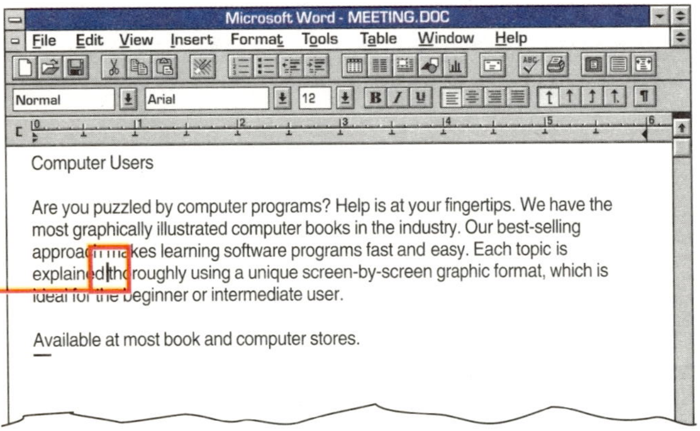

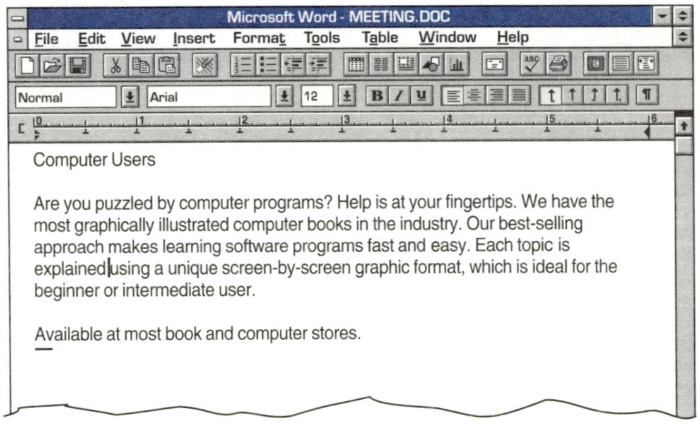

1 Position the insertion point to the left of the first character you want to delete (example: **t** in **t**horoughly).

2 Press the **Delete** key to delete one character.

3 Continue pressing the **Delete** key until the text you want to remove (example: **thoroughly**) is deleted.

■ The characters are deleted.

Note: A character can also be deleted by positioning the insertion point to the right of the character. Then press the ***Backspace*** *key.*

Delete Selected Text

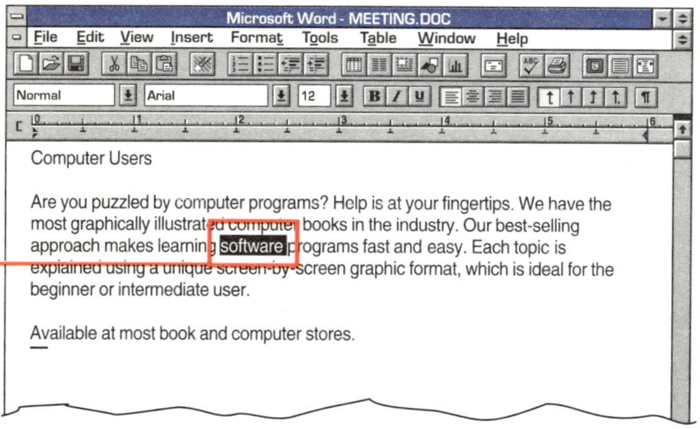

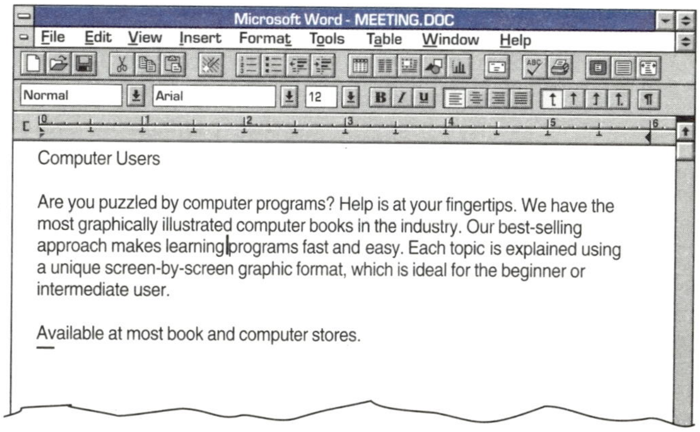

1 Select the text you want to delete (example: **software**).

Note: To select text, refer to page 10.

2 Press the **Delete** key.

■ The text is deleted.

Undo

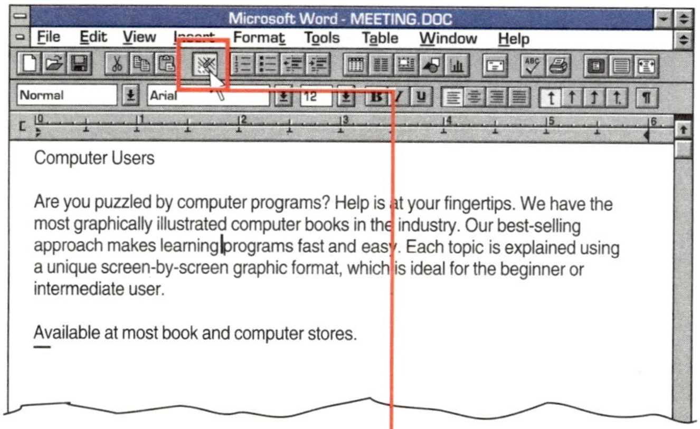

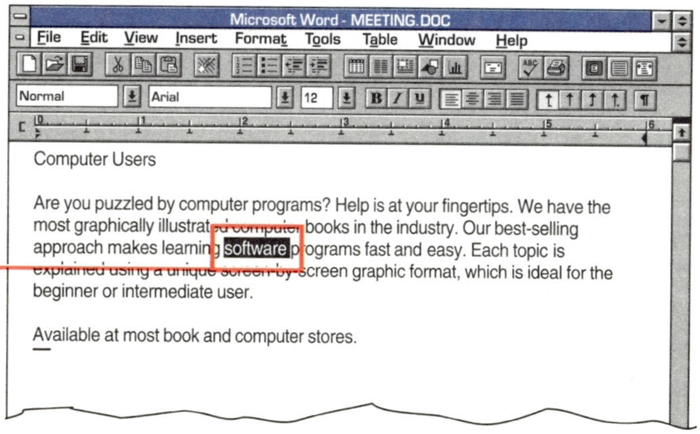

Undo cancels your last action. This only works immediately after performing the action.

1 Click the **Undo** button.

■ Your last action is cancelled (example: the word **software** reappears).

*Note: To cancel the **Undo** command you just performed, click the **Undo** button again.*

MOVE TEXT

Move Text Within the Same Document

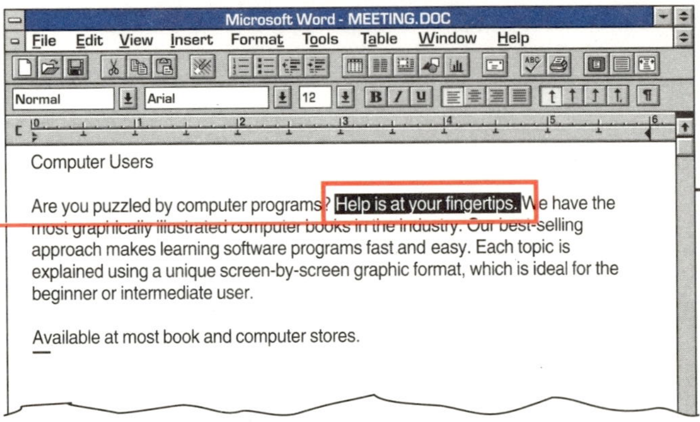

1 Select the text you want to move.

Note: To select text, refer to page 10.

Move Text to Another Document

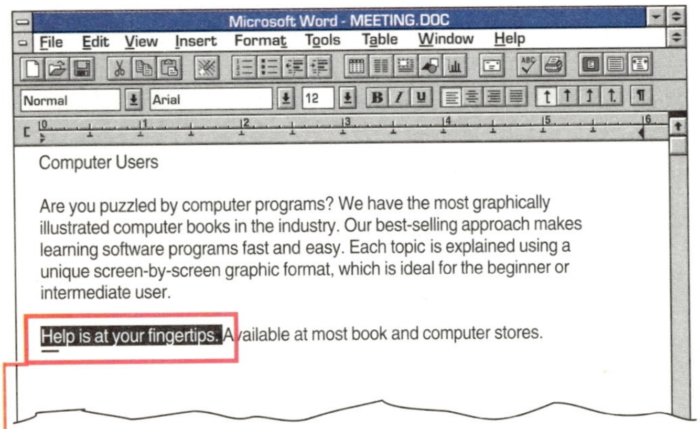

1 Select the text you want to move.

Note: To select text, refer to page 10.

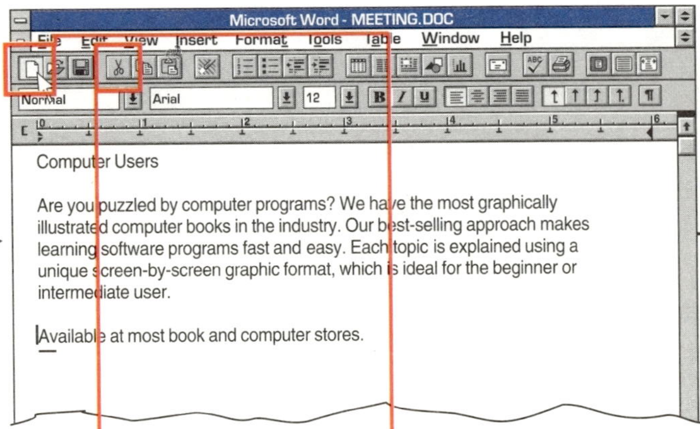

2 Click the **Cut** button and the text is removed from the screen and placed on the clipboard.

Note: The clipboard is a temporary storage area which stores the text to be moved.

3 To move the text to a new document, click the **New** button to open a new document.

Note: To move the text to a saved document, open that document. Refer to page 18.

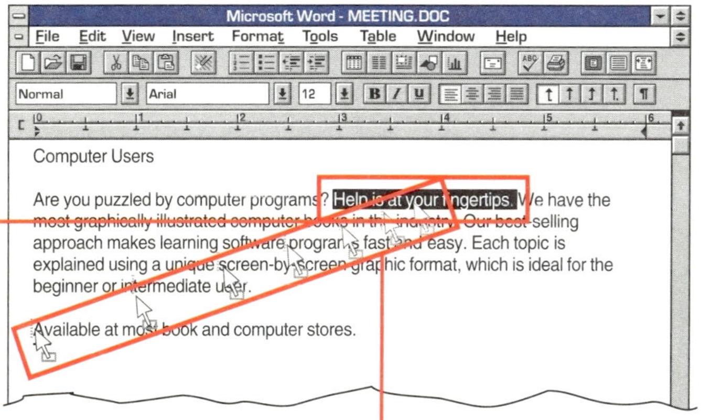

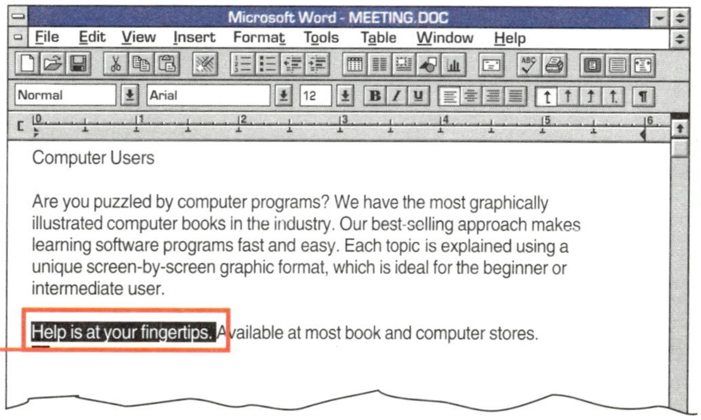

2 Move the mouse pointer I over the selected text and it changes to ↖.

3 Click and hold down the left mouse button as you drag the text to a new location.

Note: The dotted line ⁝ indicates where the text will be moved.

4 Release the mouse button and the text is moved.

Note: You cannot move text past the horizontal line ▬ displayed on the screen. To move this line, position the insertion point after the last character in the document. Then press ***Enter*** *several times.*

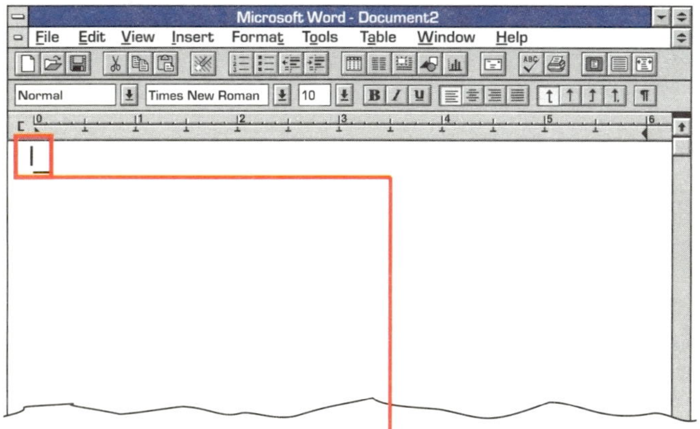

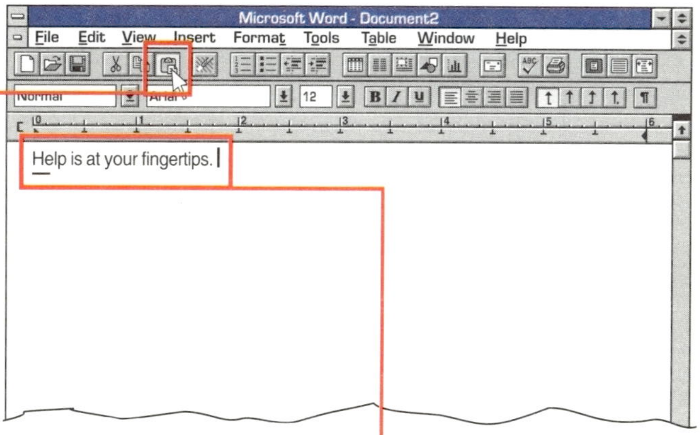

■ A new document appears.

Note: The ***MEETING.DOC*** *document is hidden behind the new document.*

4 Position the insertion point where you want the text to be moved.

5 Click the **Paste** button.

■ The text is moved.

COPY TEXT

Copy Text Within the Same Document

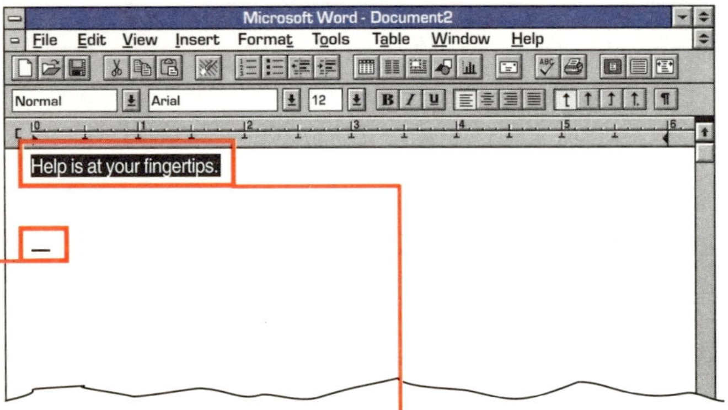

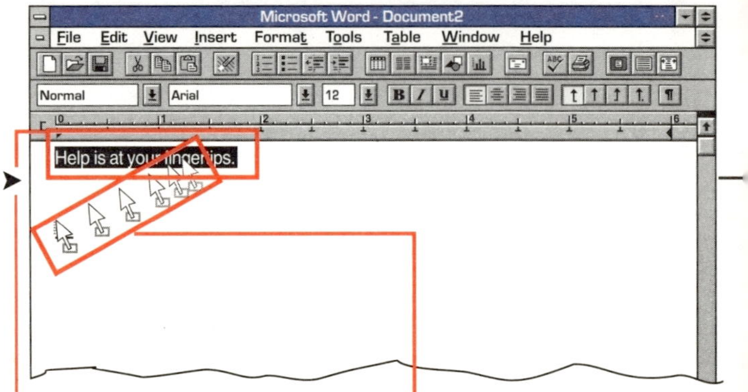

■ You cannot place a copy of selected text past the horizontal line — displayed on the screen.

1 To move the line, position the insertion point after the last character in the document. Then press **Enter** several times (example: **3 times**).

2 Select the text you want to copy.

Note: To select text, refer to page 10.

3 Move the mouse pointer I over the selected text and it changes to ↖.

4 Press and hold down the **Ctrl** key.

5 Click and hold down the left mouse button as you drag the text to a new location.

Note: The dotted line ⁝ indicates where the text will be copied.

Copy Text to Another Document

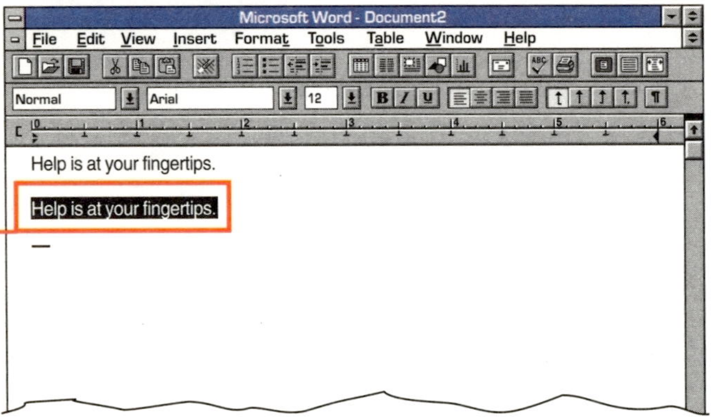

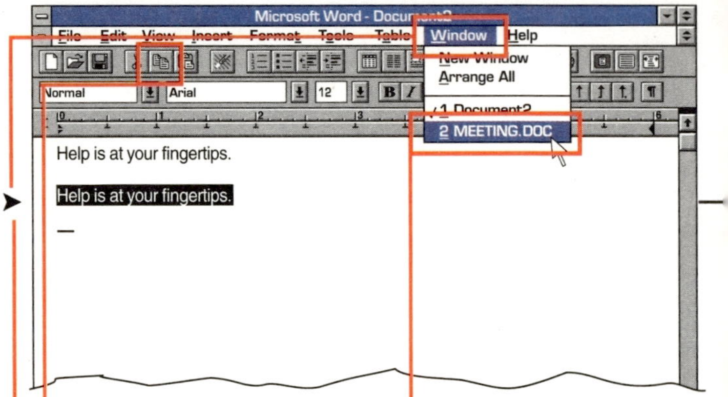

1 Select the text you want to copy.

Note: To select text, refer to page 10.

2 Click the **Copy** button and the text is placed on the clipboard.

Note: The clipboard is a temporary storage area which stores the text to be copied.

3 To copy the text to another open document, click **Window** to open its menu.

4 Click the document's name (example: **MEETING.DOC**).

*Note: To copy the text to a new document, click the **New** button.*

To copy the text to a saved document, open that document. Refer to page 18.

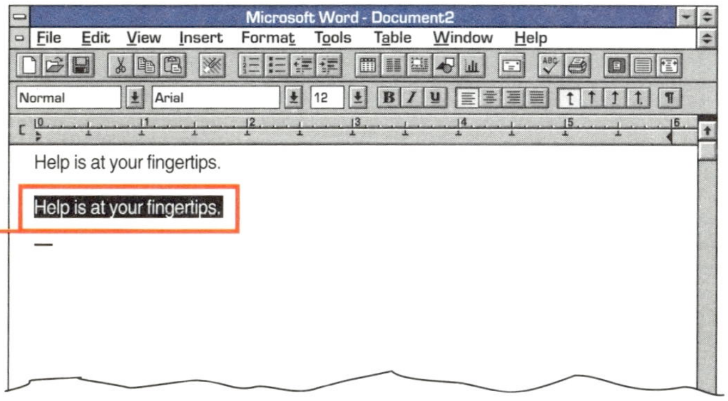

6 Release the mouse button, then the **Ctrl** key. The text is copied.

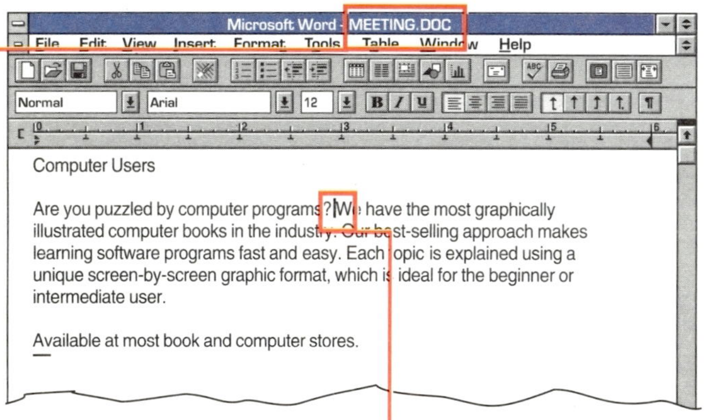

■ The document appears (example: **MEETING.DOC**).

5 Position the insertion point where you want the text to be copied.

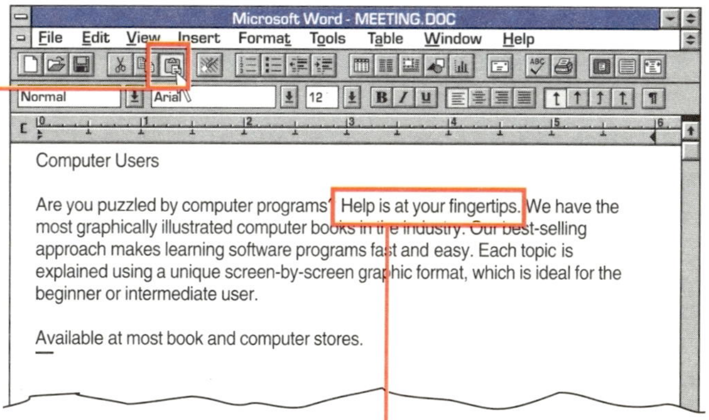

6 Click the **Paste** button.

■ The text is copied.

SPELL CHECK A DOCUMENT

Spell Check a Document

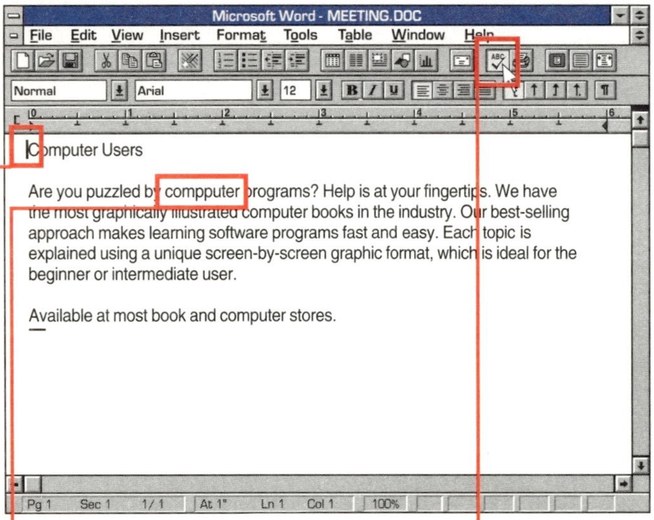

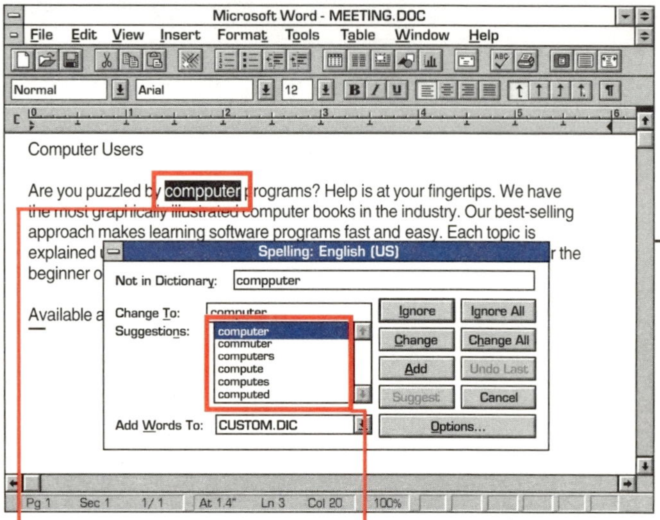

■ For this example, the spelling of 'computer' was changed to 'com**p**puter'.

1 Position the insertion point where you want the spell check to begin.

Note: To only spell check a section of text, select the text.

2 Click the **Spelling** button.

■ When spell checking a document, Word compares each word in your document with a list of words in the Word dictionary. If no match is found, the word is considered to be misspelled.

■ Word stops at the first misspelled word that it finds (example: **compputer**).

■ Suggestions for the correct spelling are displayed.

F7 CHECK THE SPELLING OF ONE WORD

1 Click anywhere on the word you want to spell check.

2 Press the **F7** key.

SPELLING OPTIONS

Ignore Click this button if you do not want to change the spelling of the word.

Add Click this button to add the word to the dictionary so it is later recognized as a correctly spelled word.

Change Click this button to replace the misspelled word with the correctly spelled word.

Ignore All Click this button if you do not want to change the spelling of the word for the rest of the document.

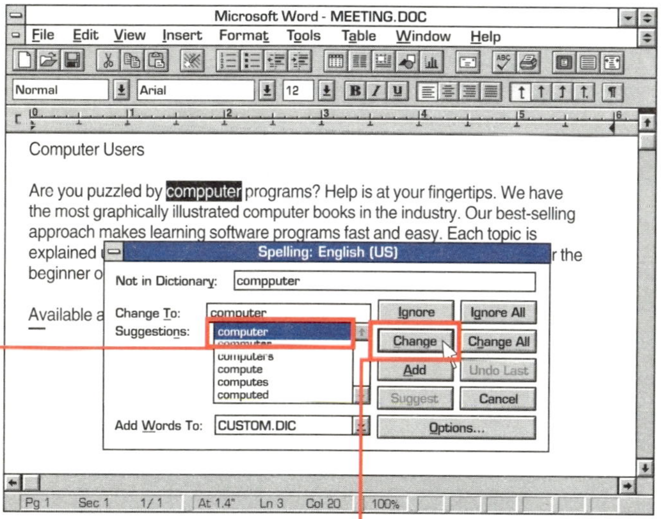

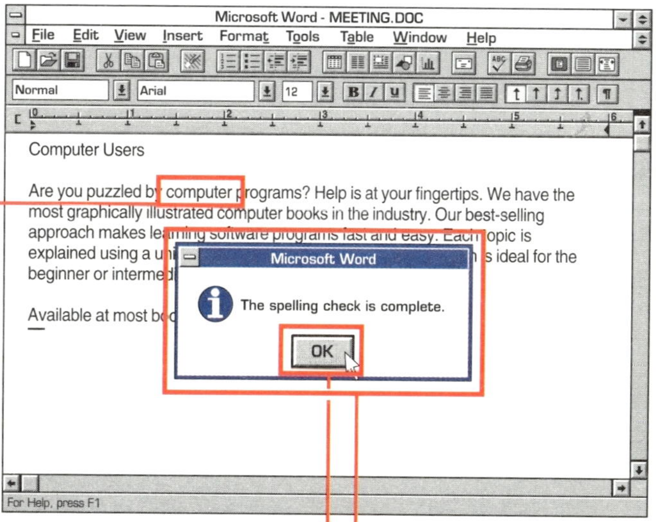

3 To change the spelling of the word, click the correct spelling in the **Suggestions:** box (example: **computer**).

*Note: You can also change the spelling of the word by double clicking in the box beside **Change To:**. Then type the correct spelling.*

4 Click the **Change** button to replace the misspelled word.

*Note: If you do not want to change the spelling of the word, click the **Ignore** button.*

■ The misspelled word is corrected and Word searches for the next misspelled word.

■ When the spell check is complete, the above dialog box appears.

5 To return to the document, click the **OK** button.

Change All Click this button to correct the misspelled word for the rest of the document.

Undo Last Click this button to reverse the last change.

Cancel Click this button to stop the spell check and return to the document.

This dialog box appears if the insertion point was not at the beginning of the document when you started the spell check.

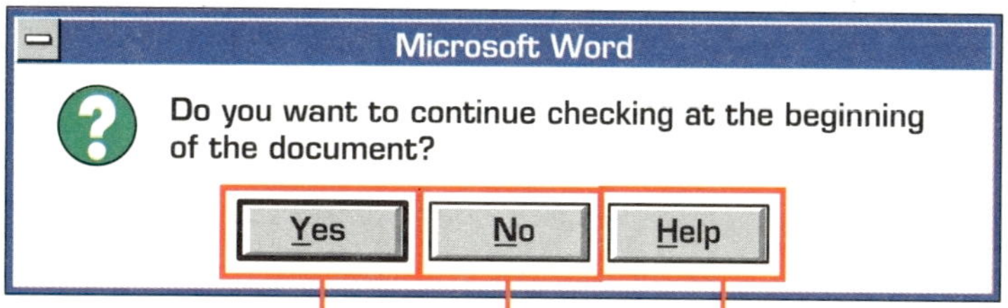

■ Click this button to continue spell checking from the beginning of the document.

■ Click this button to return to the document.

■ Click this button to receive help.

THESAURUS

TOOLBAR, RIBBON, AND RULER DISPLAY

Thesaurus

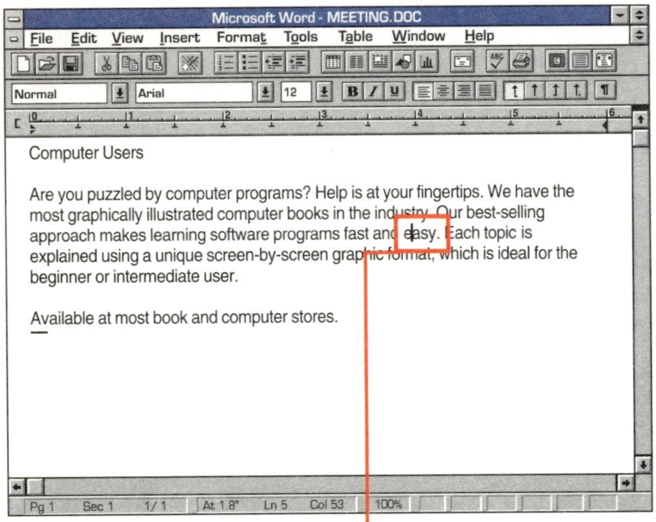

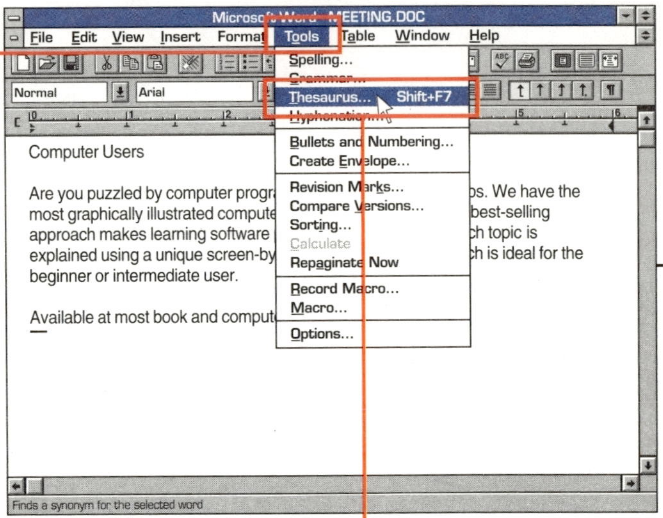

The Thesaurus searches for words with the same meaning (synonyms).

1 Click anywhere on the word you want a synonym for (example: **easy**).

2 Click **Tools** to open its menu.

3 Click **Thesaurus**.

Toolbar, Ribbon, and Ruler Display

You can hide the Toolbar, Ribbon, or Ruler when working in a document to provide a larger working area.

Toolbar

Ribbon

Ruler

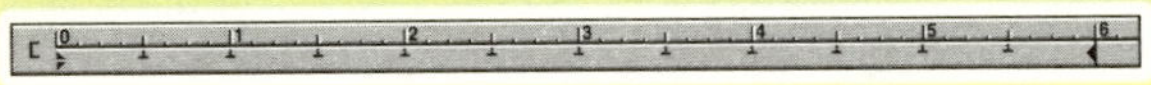

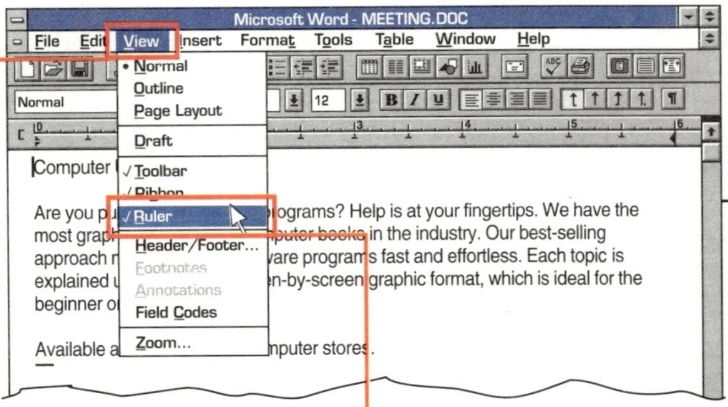

1 Click **View** to open its menu.

■ A check mark ✓ in front of an item indicates it is currently displayed.

2 Click the item you want to hide (example: **Ruler**).

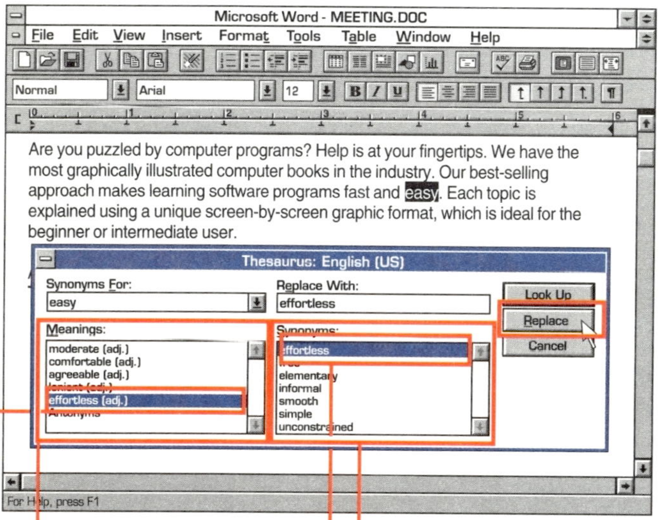

■ Different meanings for the word are displayed in the **Meanings:** box.

4 To display synonyms for a word displayed in the **Meanings:** box, click the word (example: **effortless**).

■ Synonyms for the highlighted word are displayed in the **Synonyms:** box.

5 Click the term you want to replace the word from your document (example: **effortless**).

6 Click the **Replace** button.

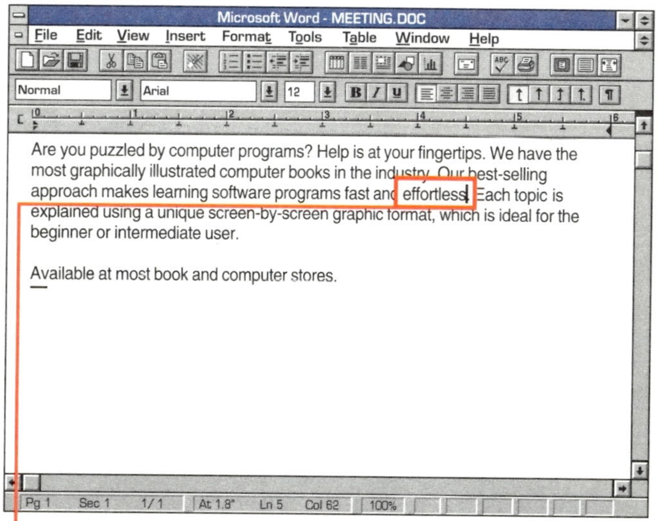

■ The word from your document (example: **easy**) is replaced by the word from the Thesaurus (example: **effortless**).

*Note: To quickly move to the top of the document, press **Ctrl+Home**.*

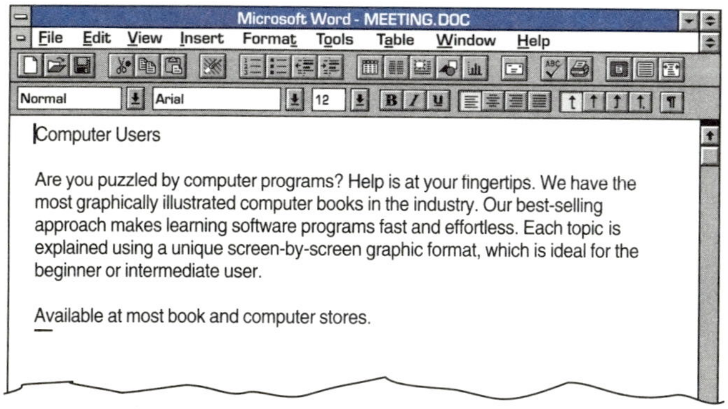

■ The item is hidden (example: **Ruler**).

*Note: To display an item, repeat steps **1** and **2**.*

FIND TEXT

FIND AND REPLACE TEXT

Find Text

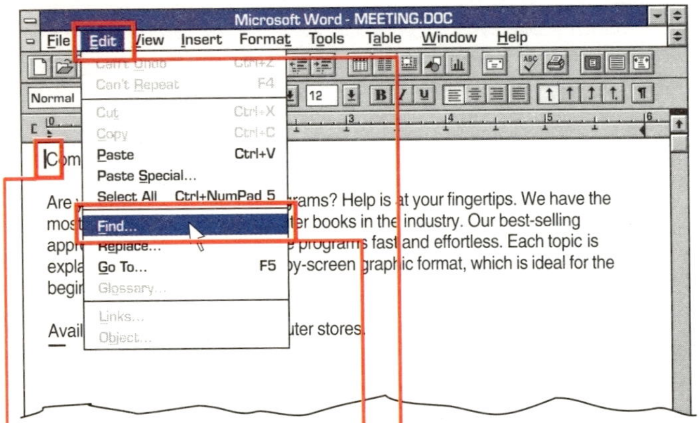

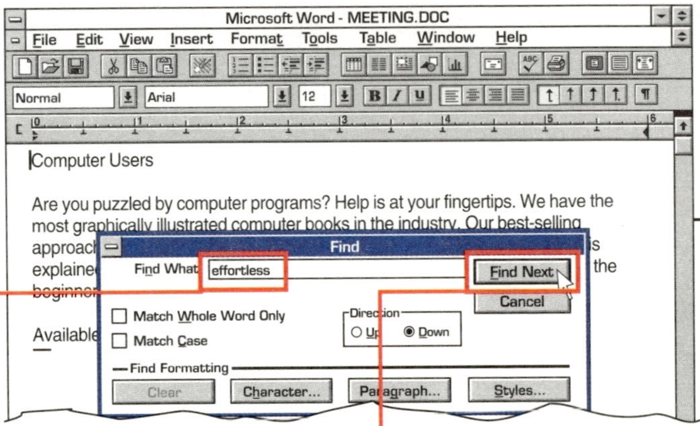

Find moves you quickly to a word or phrase in your document.

1 Position the insertion point where you want Word to start the search.

Note: To only search a section of the document, select the text. Refer to page 10.

2 Click **Edit** to open its menu.

3 Click **Find** and the **Find** dialog box appears.

4 Type the text you want to find (example: **effortless**).

5 Click the **Find Next** button.

Find and Replace Text

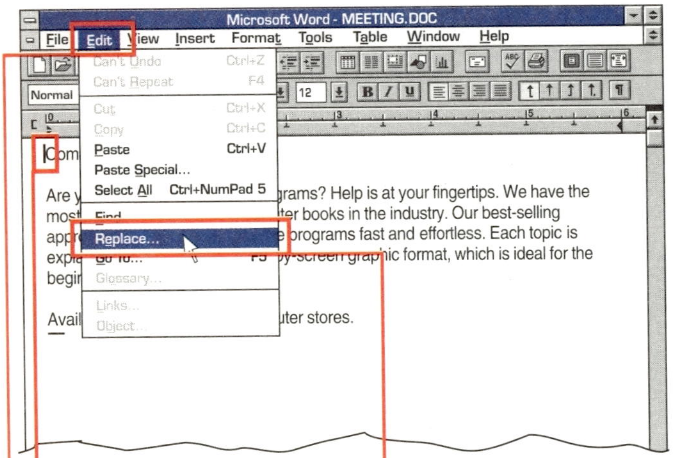

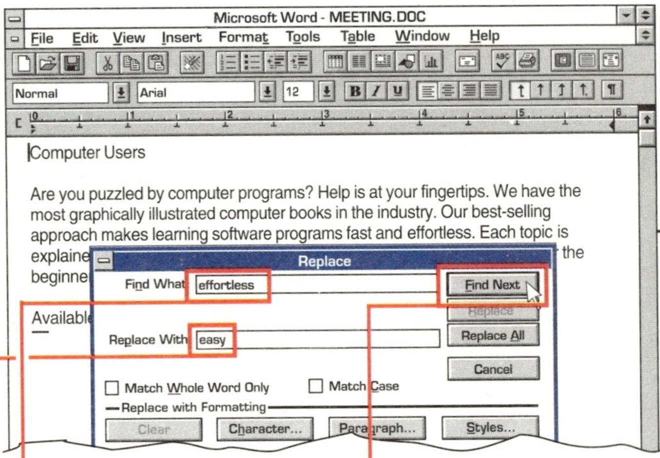

1 Position the insertion point where you want Word to start the search.

2 Click **Edit** to open its menu.

3 Click **Replace** and the **Replace** dialog box appears.

4 Type the text you want to search for (example: **effortless**).

5 Double click in the box beside **Replace With:**. Then type the text you want to replace the searched term (example: **easy**).

6 Click the **Find Next** button to stop at each word to be replaced. You can then decide which of the selected words you want to replace.

*Note: Click the **Replace All** button to replace all matching words at the same time.*

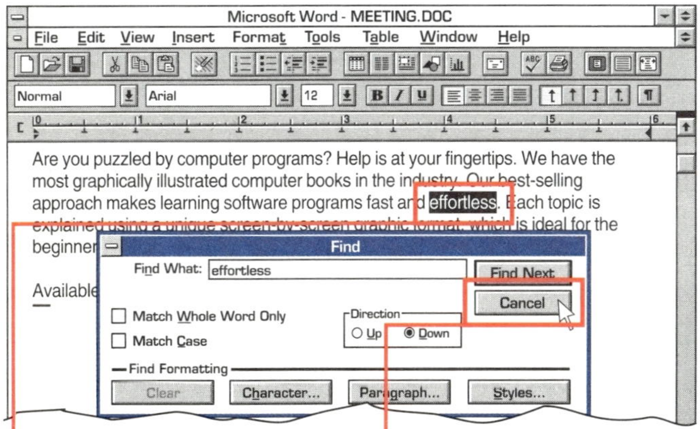

■ The first matching word is found.

Note: To find the next matching word, click the ***Find Next*** *button again.*

6 To close the **Find** dialog box, click the **Cancel** button.

The following two options can speed up your search. The options appear in the Find and the Replace dialog boxes.

☒ Match Whole Word Only

■ Click this box if you do not want to find the word if it is part of a larger word (example: **jog** will not find **jog**ging).

☒ Match Case

■ Click this box if you only want to find words with exactly matching upper and lower case characters (example: **Jog** will only find **Jog**).

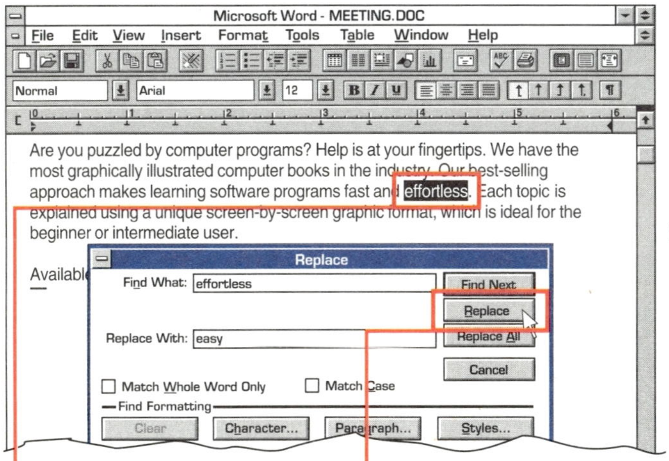

■ The first matching word is found.

7 To replace the word, click the **Replace** button.

Note: If you do not want to replace the word, click the ***Find Next*** *button to find the next matching word.*

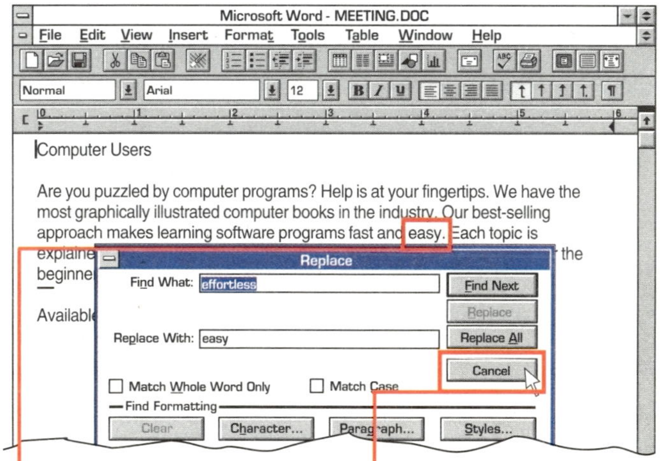

■ The word is replaced, and Word searches for the next matching word.

8 To close the **Replace** dialog box, click the **Cancel** button.

CHANGE FONTS AND POINT SIZES

Change Font

You can change the font (type style) of characters on the screen. Here are some examples:

Arial

CG Times

Courier

Letter Gothic

Times New Roman

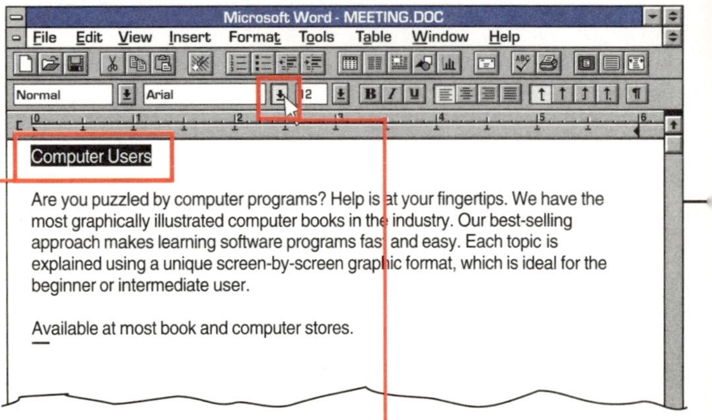

1 Select the text you want to change to a new font.

Note: To change the font of text you are about to type, position the insertion point where you are about to type the text.

2 Click the arrow beside the **Font** box and a list of the available fonts appears.

Change Point Size

You can change the point size (height) of characters on the screen. For example, the Times New Roman font is displayed below in 8 different point sizes:

Times New Roman

Times New Roman

Times New Roman

Times New Roman

Times New Roman

Times New Roman

Times New Roman

Times New Roman

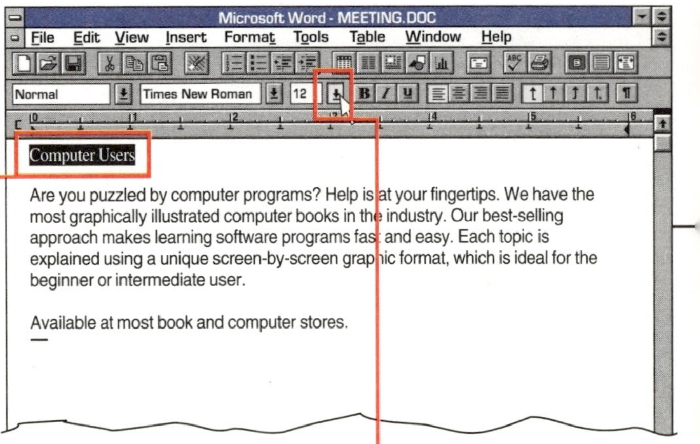

1 Select the text you want to change to a new point size.

Note: To change the point size of text you are about to type, position the insertion point where you are about to type the text.

2 Click the arrow beside the **Point Size** box and a list of the available point sizes appears.

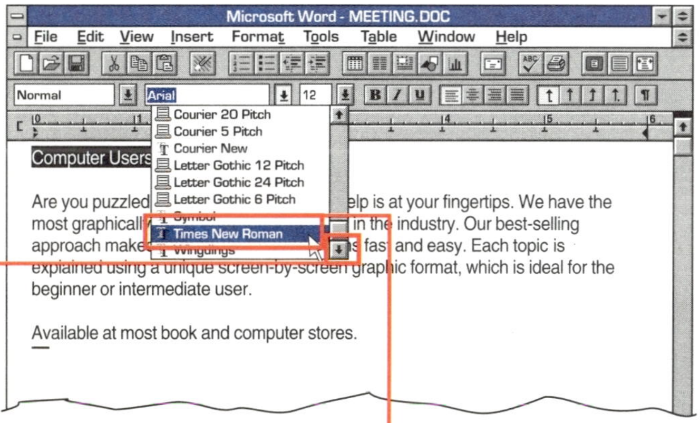

3 To view more fonts, click the down scroll arrow.

Note: The available fonts depend on your printer, and Microsoft Windows set up.

4 Click the desired font name (example: **Times New Roman**).

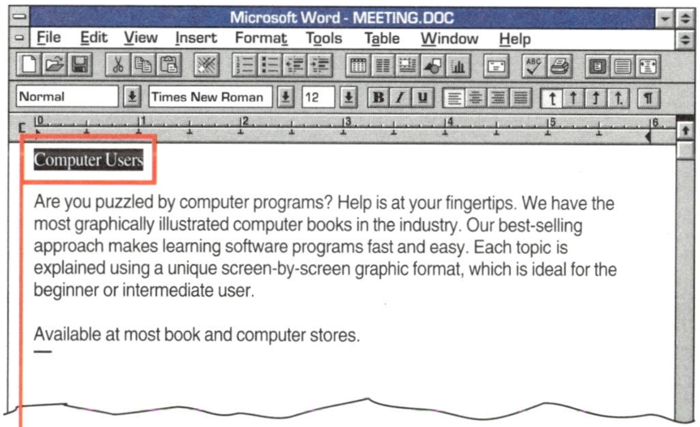

■ The text is displayed with the new font.

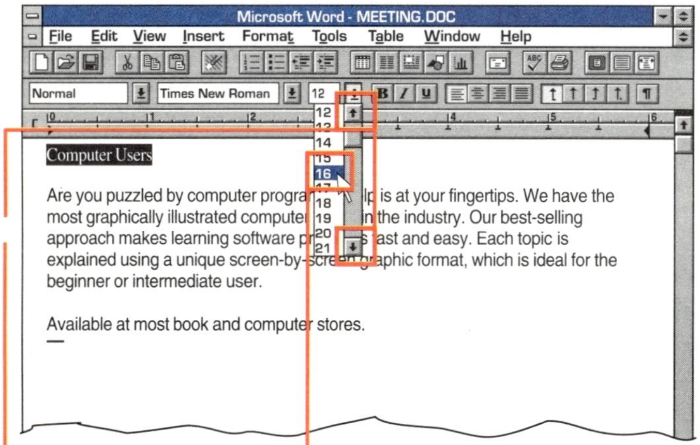

3 To view more point sizes, click the up or down scroll arrow.

Note: The available point sizes depend on your printer, and Microsoft Windows set up.

4 Click the desired point size (example: **16**).

Note: 36 points is 1/2 an inch.

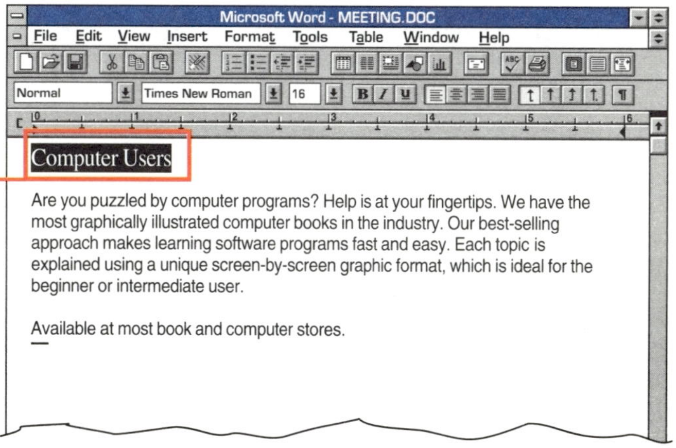

■ The text is displayed with the new point size.

ALIGN TEXT

BOLD, ITALIC AND UNDERLINE

Left | Center | Right | Justify Text

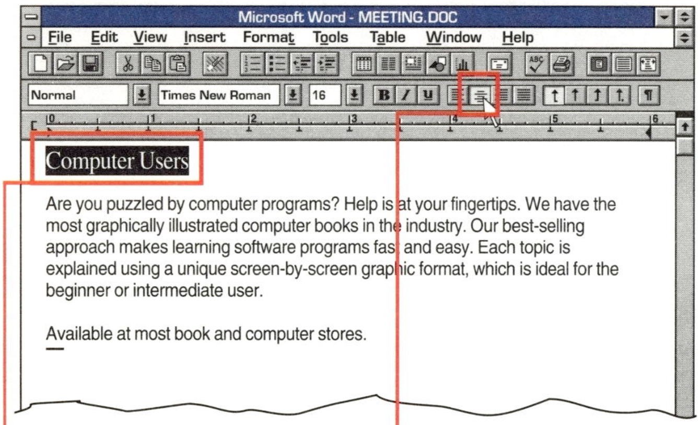

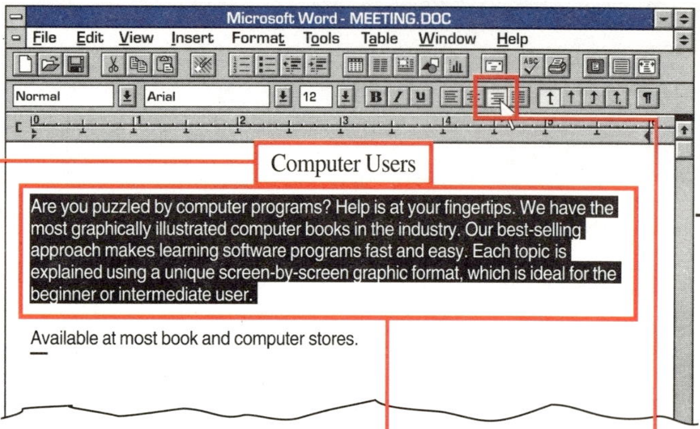

1 Select the text you want to align.

Note: To align text you are about to type, position the insertion point where you are about to type the text.

2 Click an alignment button (example: **Center**).

■ The text is aligned (example: **centered**).

3 Select the next text area you want to align.

4 Click an alignment button (example: **Right**).

Bold

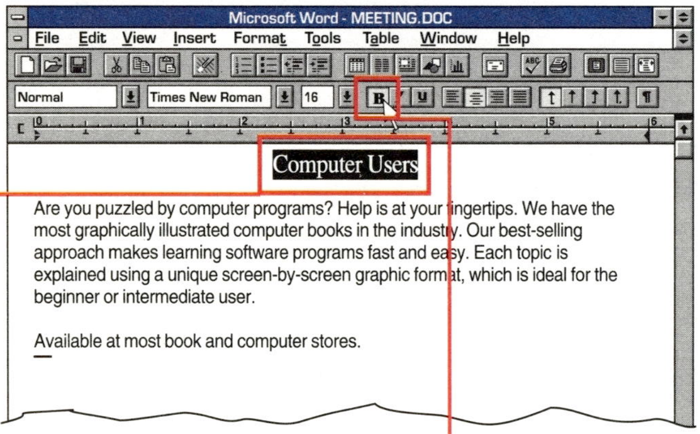

1 Select the text you want to make bold.

Note: To bold text you are about to type, position the insertion point where you are about to type the text.

2 Click the **Bold** button.

*Note: To remove the bold formatting from selected text, click the **Bold** button again.*

Italic

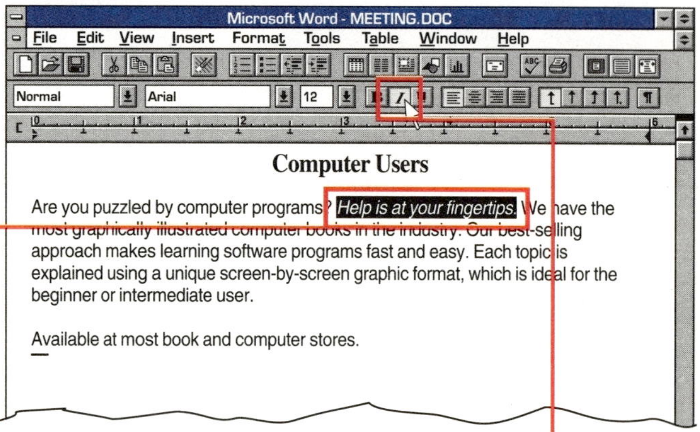

1 Select the text you want to make italic.

Note: To italicize text you are about to type, position the insertion point where you are about to type the text.

2 Click the **Italic** button.

*Note: To remove the italic formatting from selected text, click the **Italic** button again.*

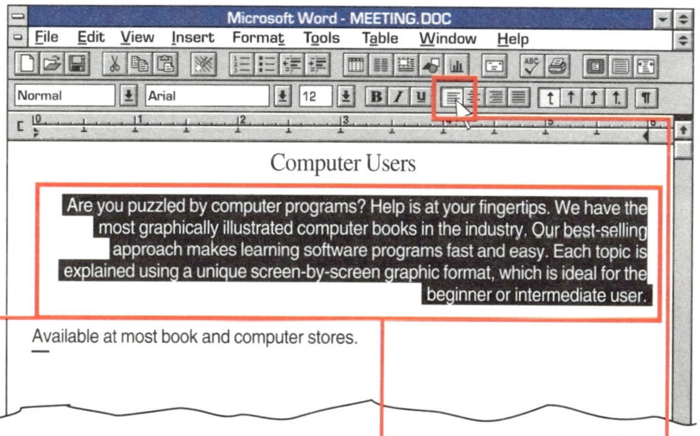

■ The text is aligned (example: right aligned).

5 Select the next text area you want to align.

6 Click an alignment button (example: **Left**).

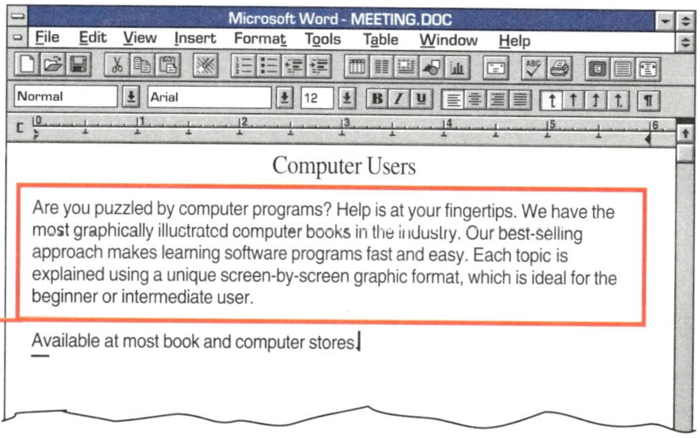

■ The text is aligned (example: left aligned).

Note: To deselect text, click anywhere on the screen.

Underline

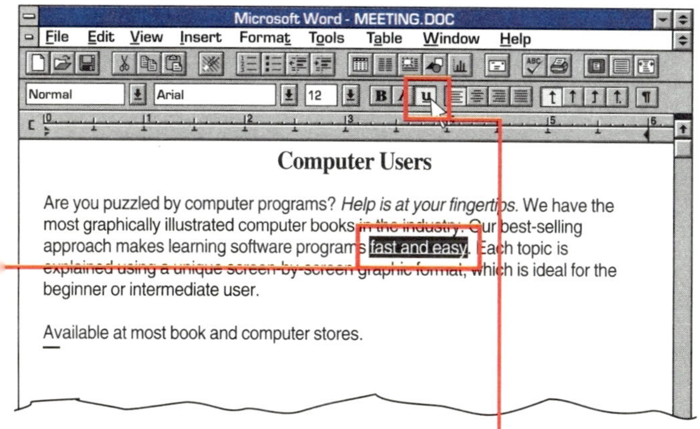

1 Select the text you want to underline.

Note: To underline text you are about to type, position the insertion point where you are about to type the text.

2 Click the **Underline** button.

*Note: To remove the underline formatting from selected text, click the **Underline** button again.*

SET TABS

When you first open a document, Word has a tab stop ⊥ placed at every half inch.

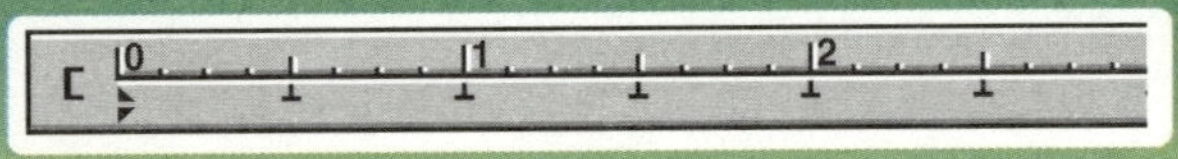

You can create your own tab stops using the following four tab buttons:

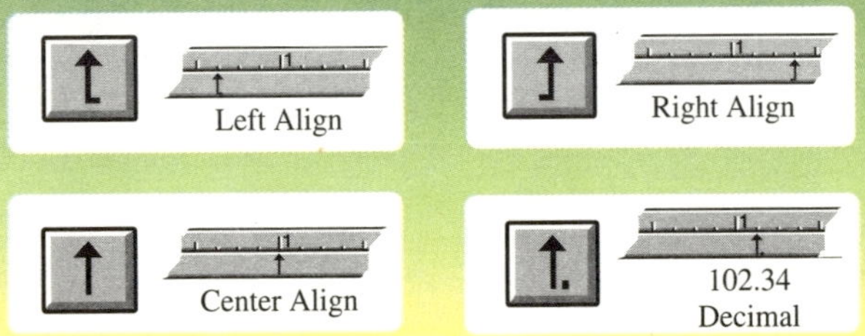

Add a Tab Stop

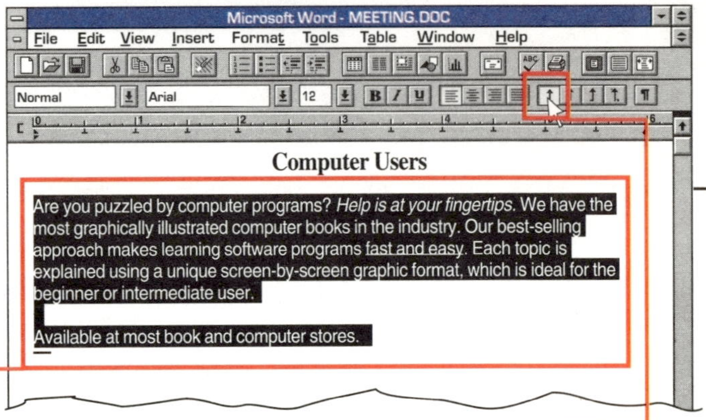

1 Select the text you want to add a tab stop to.

Note: To add a tab stop to text you are about to type, position the insertion point where you are about to type the text.

2 Click the desired tab button (example: **Left align**).

Move a Tab Stop

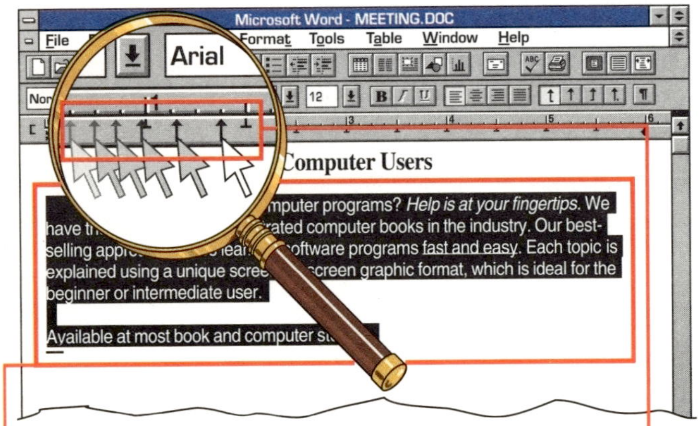

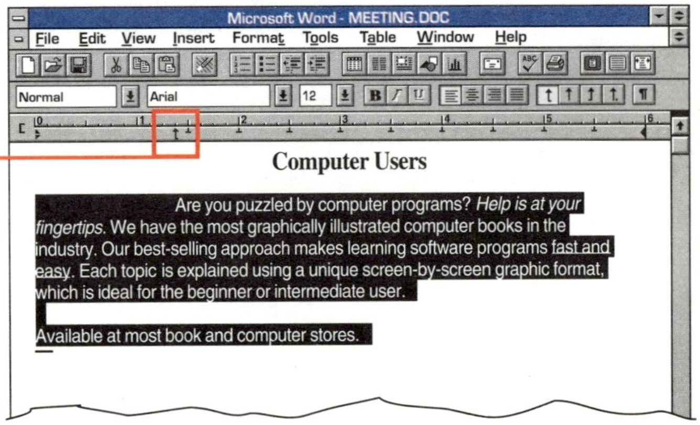

1 Select the text that contains the tab stop you want to move.

Note: To move a tab stop for text you are about to type, position the insertion point where you are about to type the text.

2 Position the mouse pointer ↖ over the tab stop you want to move.

3 Click and hold down the left mouse button as you drag the tab stop to a new location.

4 Release the mouse button and the tab stop is moved.

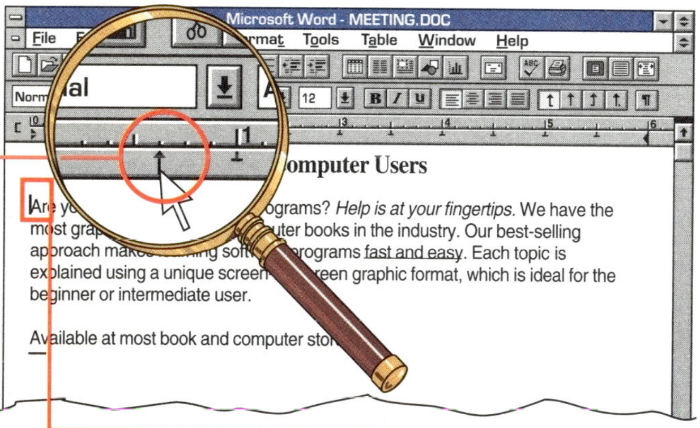

3 Click the position on the ruler where you want to place the tab. The tab is added to the ruler.

Note: Make sure you click on the lower half of the ruler.

4 Position the insertion point at the beginning of the text you want to tab over.

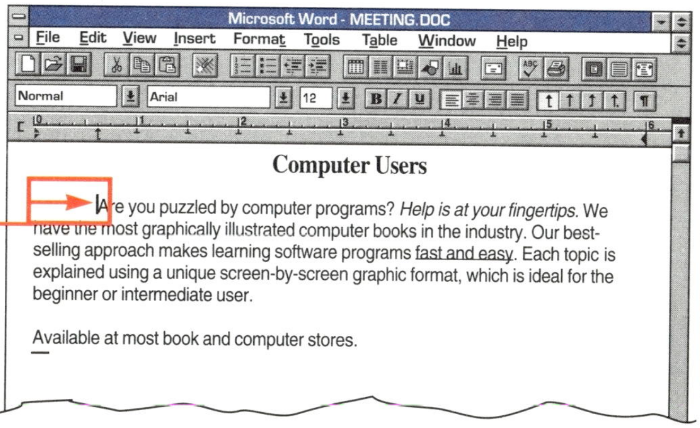

5 Press the **Tab** key and the text is moved to the first tab stop.

Remove a Tab Stop

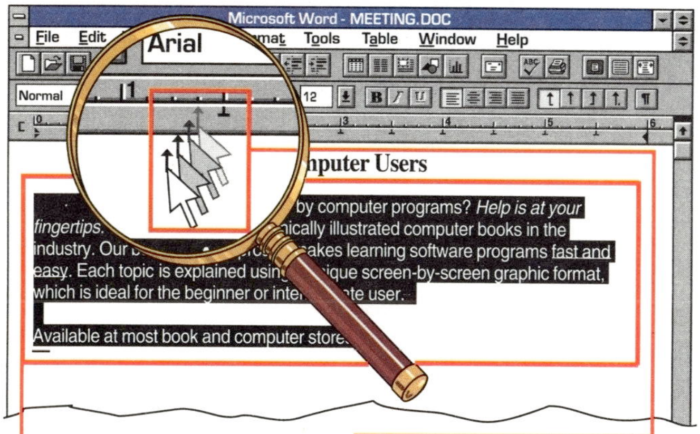

1 Select the text that contains the tab stop you want to remove.

Note: To remove a tab stop for text you are about to type, position the insertion point where you are about to type the text.

2 Position the mouse pointer ↖ over the tab stop you want to remove from the ruler.

3 Click and hold down the left mouse button as you drag the tab stop off the ruler.

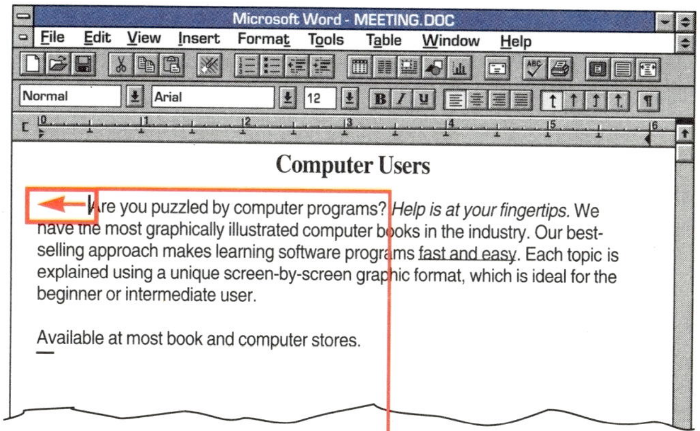

4 Release the mouse button and the tab stop is removed.

5 To move a paragraph one tab stop to the left, position the insertion point at the beginning of the paragraph. Then press the **Backspace** key.

INDENT PARAGRAPHS

Indent and Unindent Using the Toolbar

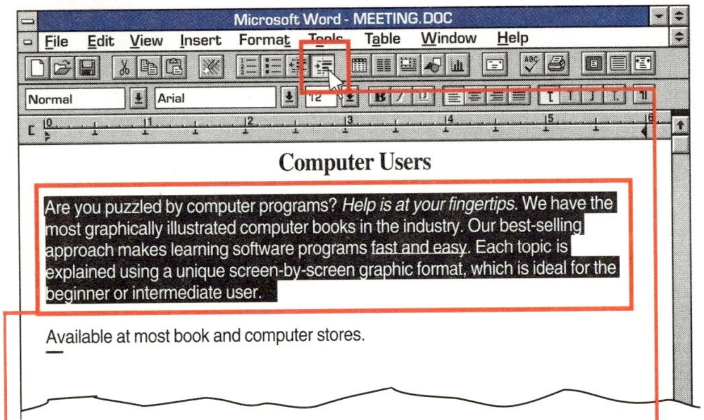

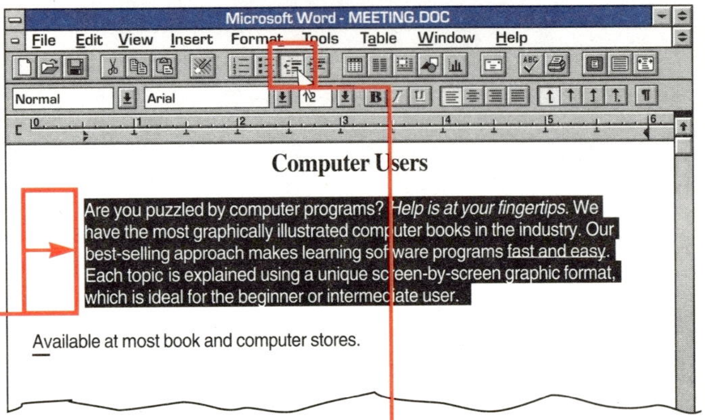

1 Select the paragraphs you want to indent.

Note: To change the indents of text you are about to type, position the insertion point where you are about to type the text.

2 Click the **Indent** button to move the entire paragraph one tab stop to the right.

■ The paragraph is indented one tab stop to the right.

3 Click the **Unindent** button to move the entire paragraph one tab stop to the left.

Indent Left Edge of Paragraph

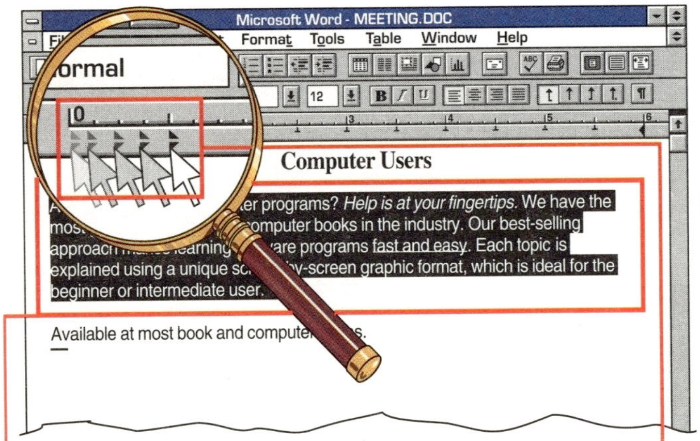

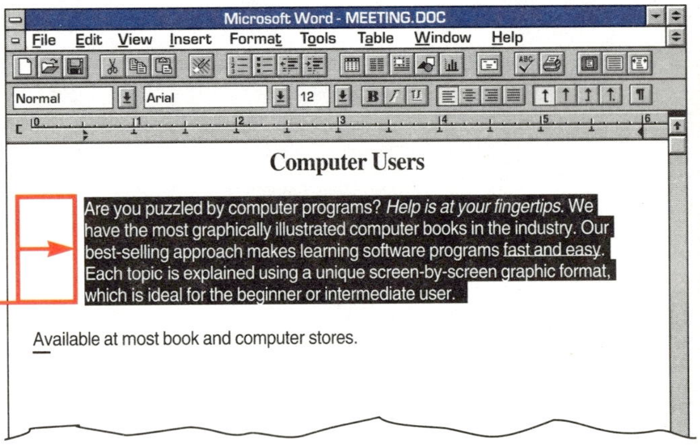

1 Select the paragraphs you want to indent.

Note: To change the indents of text you are about to type, position the insertion point where you are about to type the text.

2 Position the mouse pointer over the **Left Indent** marker.

Note: Make sure you position the mouse pointer over the bottom half of the symbol.

3 Click and hold down the left mouse button as you drag the marker to a new location.

4 Release the mouse button and the entire left edge of the paragraph is indented.

Indent Right Edge of Paragraph

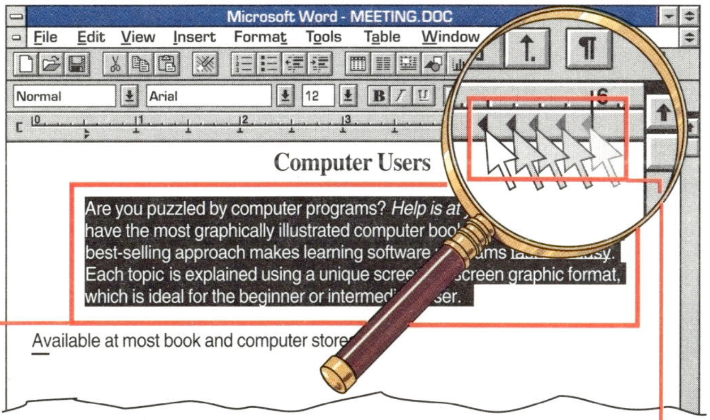

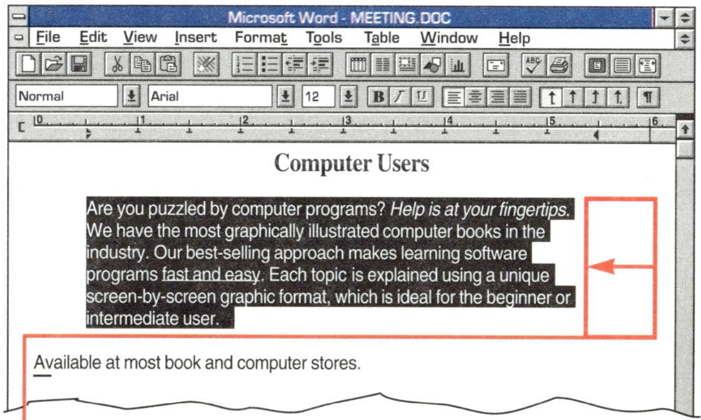

1 Select the paragraphs you want to indent.

Note: To change the indents of text you are about to type, position the insertion point where you are about to type the text.

2 Position the mouse pointer ⇖ over the **Right Indent** marker ◀.

3 Click and hold down the left mouse button as you drag the marker to a new location.

4 Release the mouse button and the entire right edge of the paragraph is indented.

Indent First Line of Paragraph

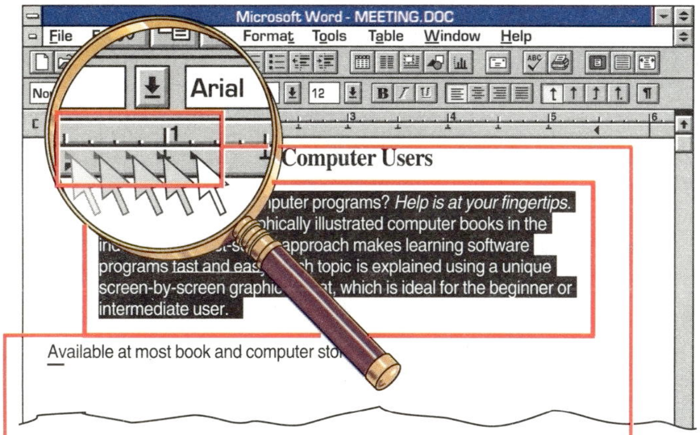

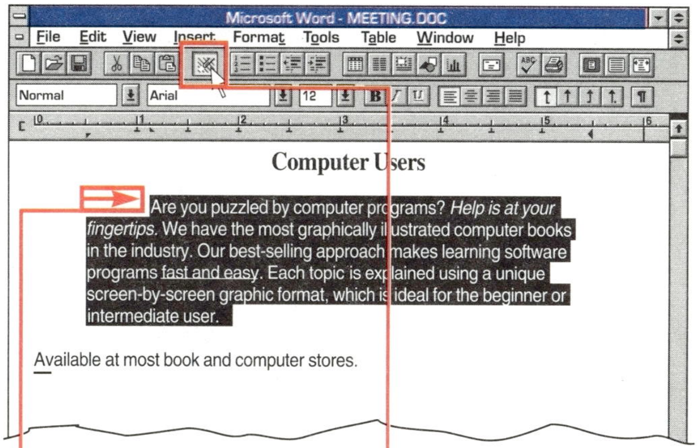

1 Select the paragraphs you want to indent.

Note: To change the indents of text you are about to type, position the insertion point where you are about to type the text.

2 Position the mouse pointer ⇖ over the **First-Line Indent marker** ◣.

Note: Make sure you position the mouse pointer over the top half of the ▸ symbol.

3 Click and hold down the left mouse button as you drag the marker to a new location.

4 Release the mouse button and only the first line of the paragraph is indented.

5 To undo the indent changes you made, click the **Undo** button.

Note: This only works immediately after changing the indents.

Create a Style

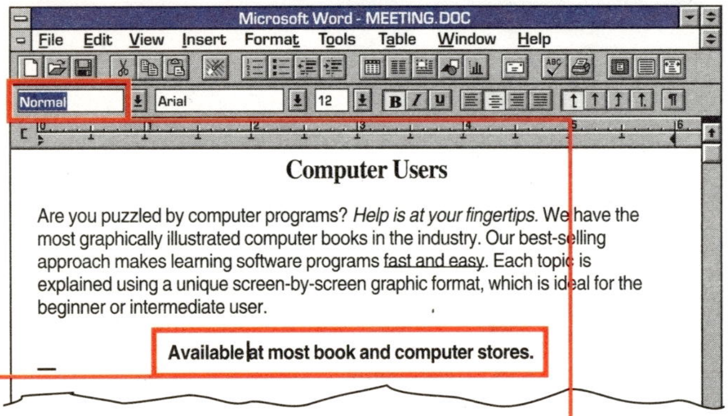

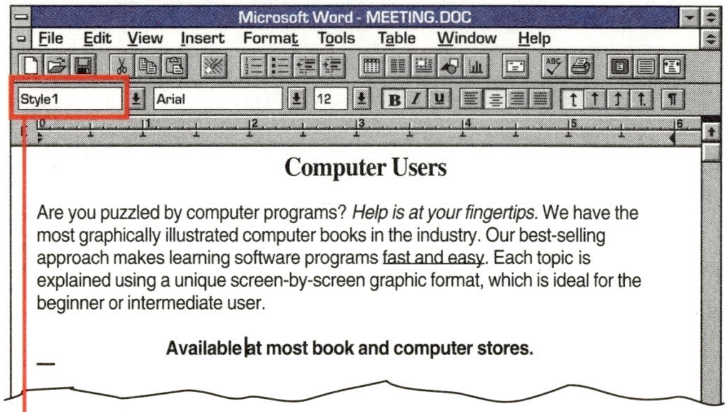

A style is a set of format commands (example: bold, center) that you name and save.

You can apply a style to any part of a document. This can save time and keep your text format consistent.

1 Format a paragraph with the formats you like (example: bold, center).

2 Position the insertion point anywhere in the paragraph.

3 Double click in the **Style** box.

4 Type a name for the style (example: **Style1**).

5 Press **Enter** and the style is created.

Change an Existing Style

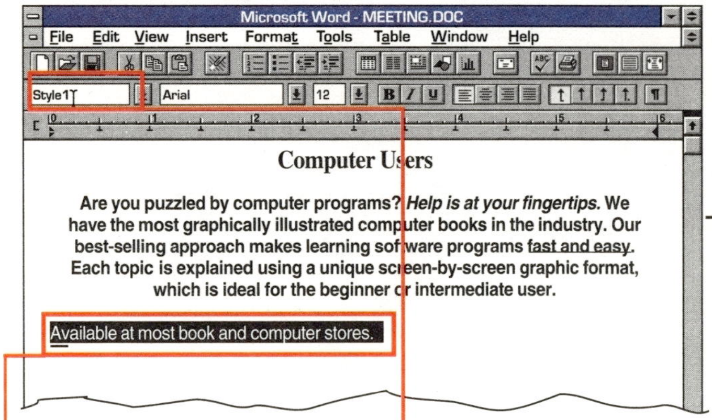

If you change an existing style, all paragraphs with that style are changed.

1 Select the paragraph that has the style you want to change.

2 Make the desired format changes to the paragraph (example: left align, not bold).

3 Click in the style box. Then press **Enter**.

Apply a Style

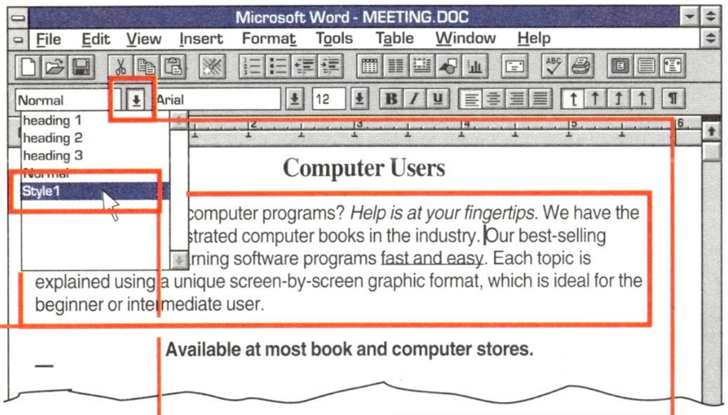

1 Position the insertion point anywhere in the paragraph you want to apply the style to.

Note: To apply the style to more than one paragraph, select the paragraphs.

2 Click the arrow beside the **Style** box and a list of the available styles appears.

3 Click the desired style (example: **Style1**).

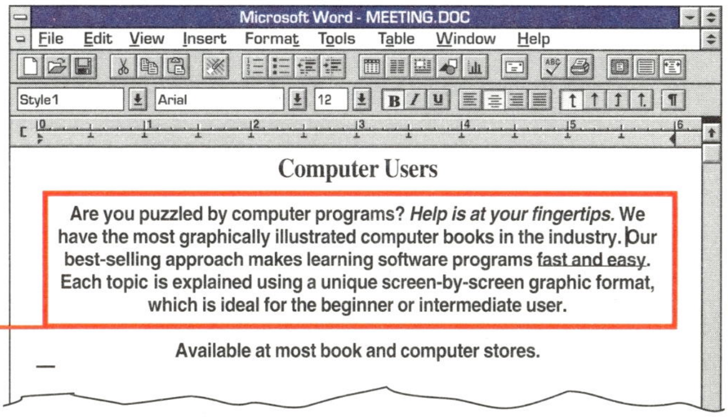

■ The paragraph displays the new style.

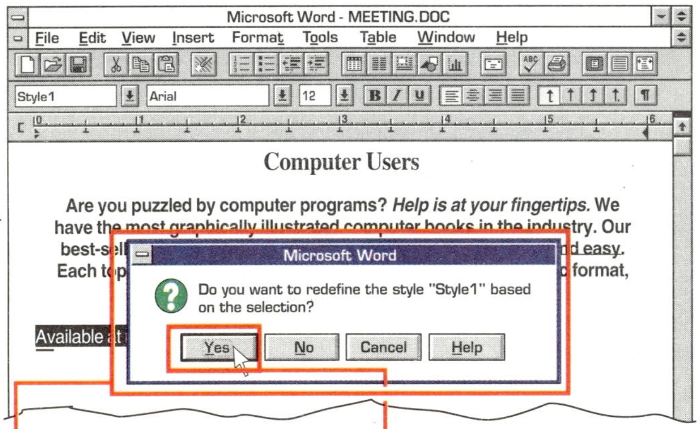

■ This dialog box appears asking if you want to redefine the style using the new formats.

4 Click the **Yes** button to redefine the style.

Note: Click the ***No*** *button if you do not want to redefine the style.*

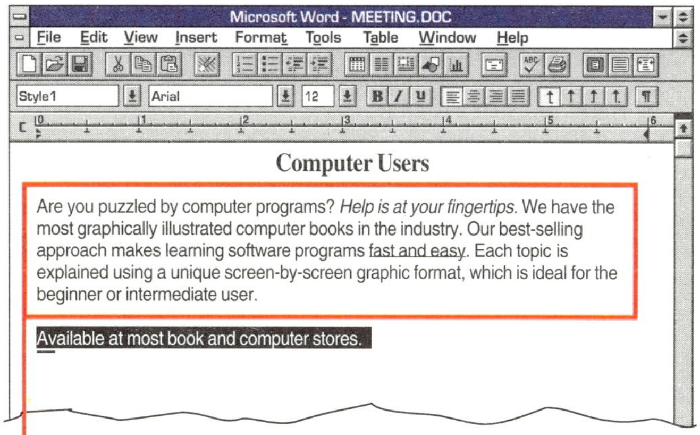

■ All paragraphs you had earlier applied the style to display the style changes.

ADD NUMBERS OR BULLETS

Add Numbers

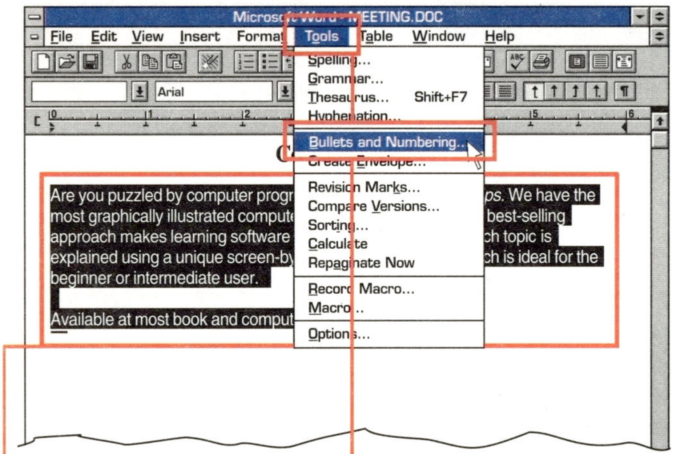

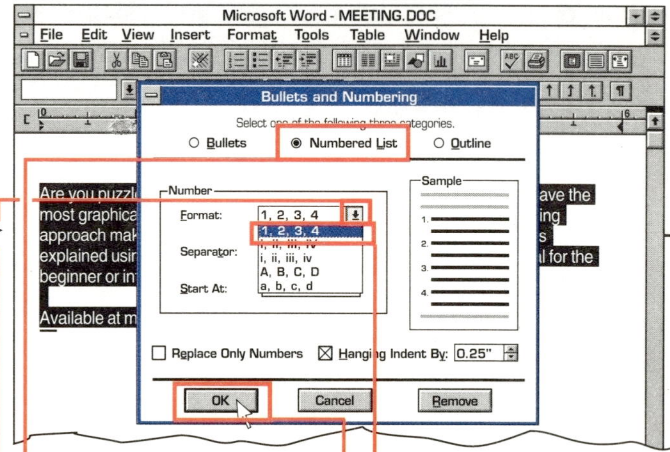

Word can number paragraphs to create a numbered list.

1 Select the paragraphs you want to add numbers to.

2 Click **Tools** to open its menu.

3 Click **Bullets and Numbering** to open its dialog box.

4 Click the circle beside **Numbered List**.

5 Click the arrow beside **Format:** and a list of the available number formats appears.

6 Click the desired number format.

*Note: To remove a numbered list from a document, click the **Remove** button.*

7 Click the **OK** button.

Add Bullets

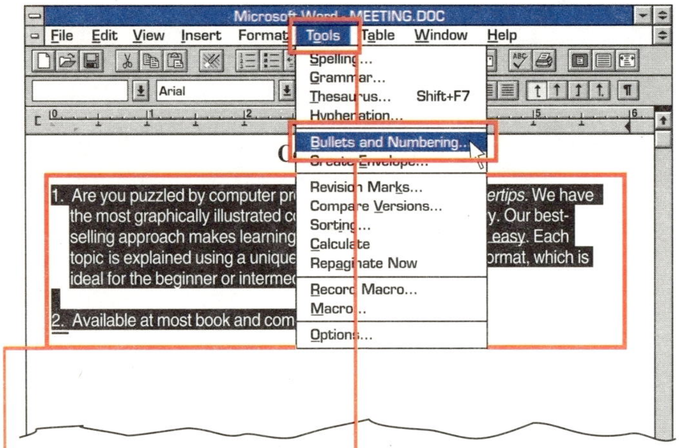

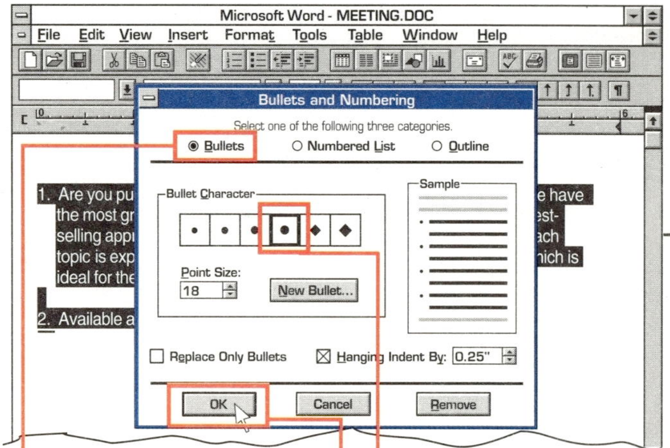

Bullets can be added to a document to visually separate groups of information.

1 Select the paragraphs you want to add bullets to.

2 Click **Tools** to open its menu.

3 Click **Bullets and Numbering** and its dialog box appears.

4 Click the circle beside **Bullets**.

5 Click the desired bullet type.

*Note: To remove bullets from a document, click the **Remove** button.*

6 Click the **OK** button.

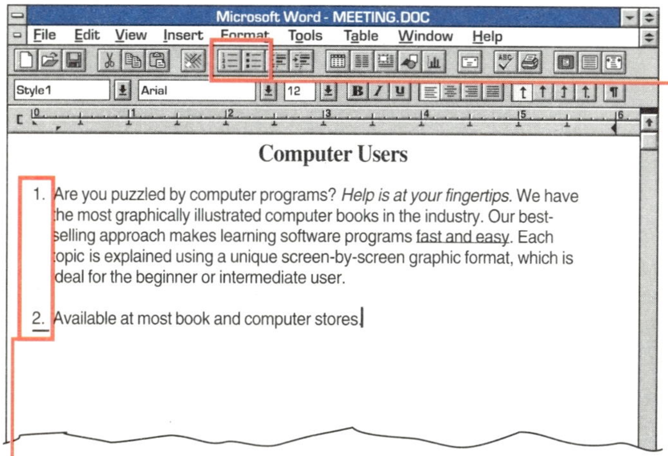

■ The paragraphs are numbered.

Note: To deselect text, click anywhere on the screen.

TO QUICKLY ADD NUMBERS

1 Select the paragraphs you want to add numbers to.

2 Click the **Numbered List** button.

TO QUICKLY ADD BULLETS

1 Select the paragraphs you want to add bullets to.

2 Click the **Bulleted List** button.

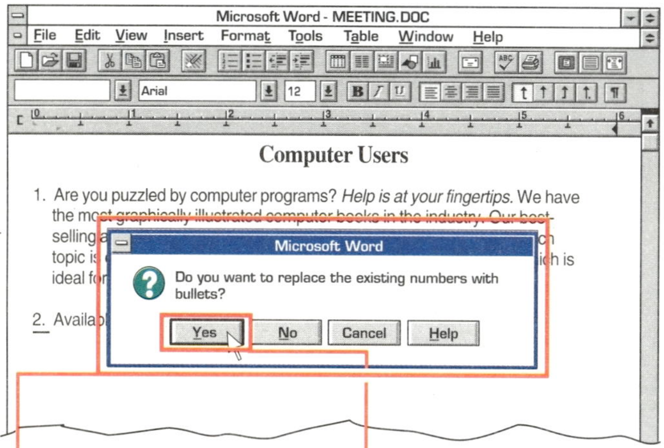

■ This dialog box appears asking if you want to replace the existing numbers with bullets.

7 Click the **Yes** button to replace the numbers.

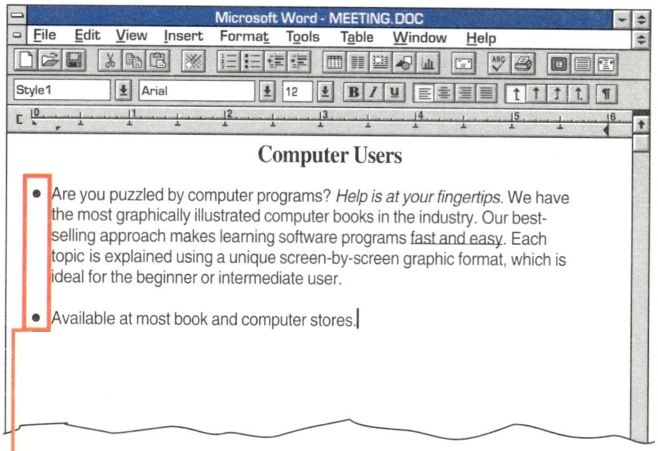

■ The paragraphs are displayed with bullets.

Note: To deselect text, click anywhere on the screen.

CHANGE LINE SPACING

ADD BORDERS

Change Line Spacing

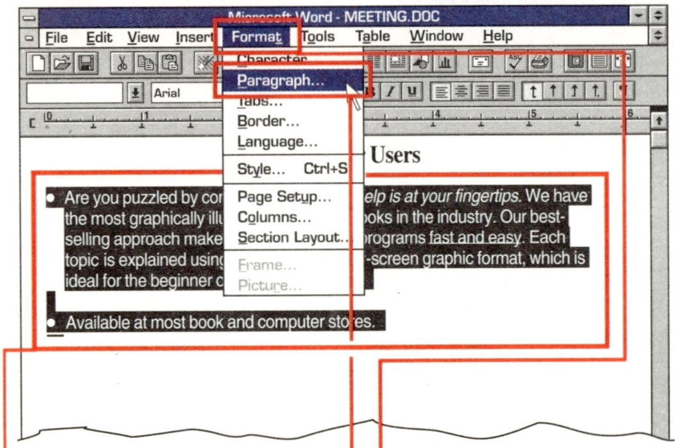

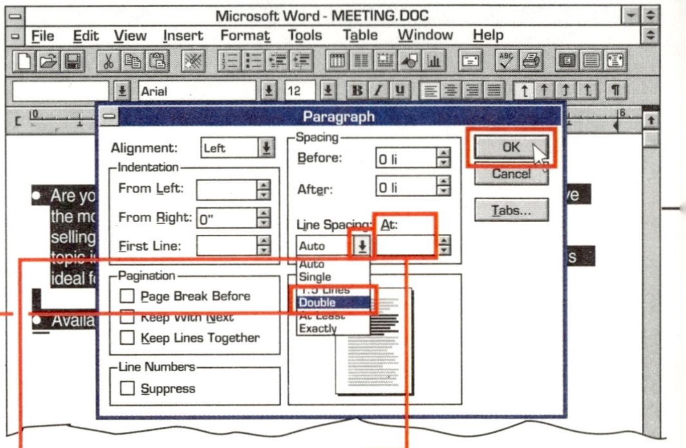

1 Select the text you want to apply the new line spacing to.

Note: To change the line spacing of text you are about to type, position the insertion point where you are about to type the text.

2 Click **Format** to open its menu.

3 Click **Paragraph** and its dialog box appears.

4 Click the arrow under **Line Spacing:** and a list of the available line spacing options appears.

5 Click the desired line spacing (example: **Double**).

6 If you selected **At Least** or **Exactly** in step **5**, click in the **At:** box. Then type the desired spacing.

7 Click the **OK** button, or press **Enter**.

Add Borders

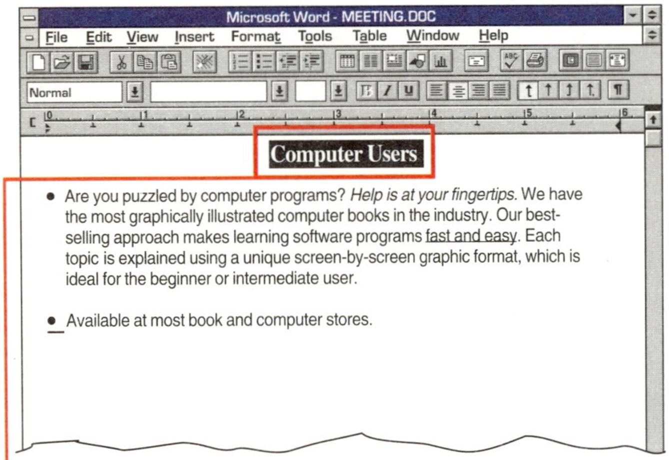

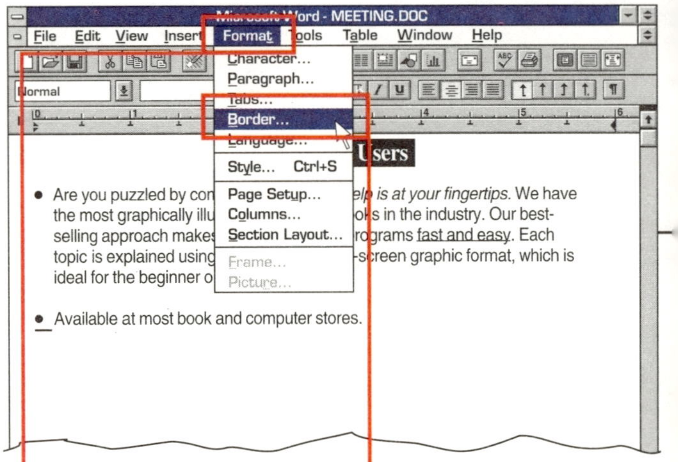

1 Select the text you want to add borders to.

2 Click **Format** to open its menu.

3 Click **Border** and the **Border Paragraphs** dialog box appears.

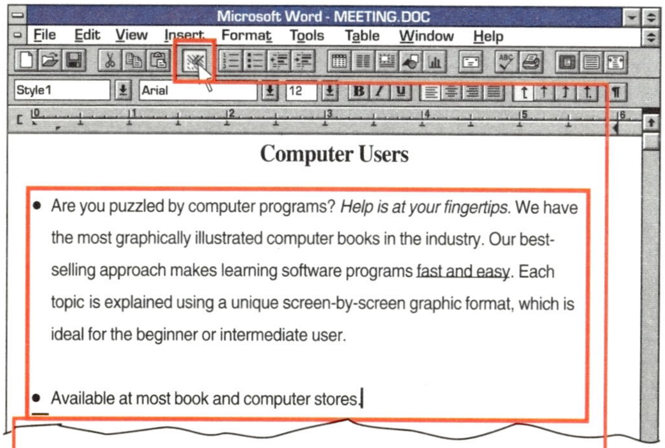

The line spacing is changed.

Note: To deselect text, click anywhere on the screen.

8 To undo the line spacing change, click the **Undo** button.

Note: This only works immediately after the line spacing is changed.

LINE SPACING OPTIONS	DESCRIPTION
Auto	Word selects the best line spacing.
Single	Single spacing.
1.5 Lines	One-and-one-half spacing.
Double	Double spacing.
At Least	Enter your own line spacing. Word will increase the spacing if necessary.
Exactly	Enter your own line spacing. Word will never change the spacing.

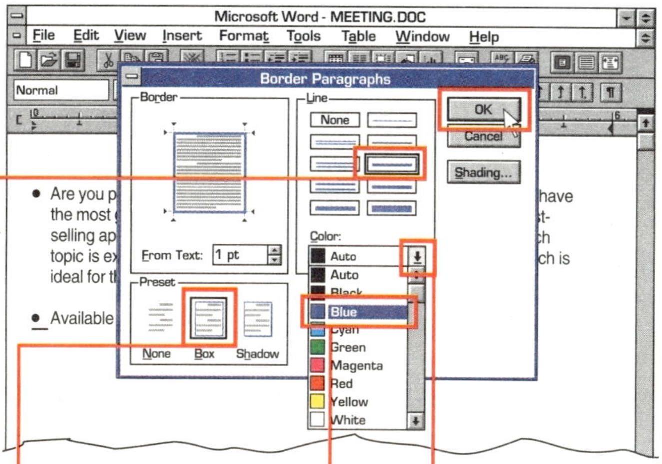

4 Click the desired border type (example: **Box**).

*Note: To remove borders, click **None**.*

5 Click the desired line format.

6 To make a colored line, click the arrow beside **Color:**.

7 Click the desired color (example: **Blue**).

8 Click the **OK** button, or press **Enter**.

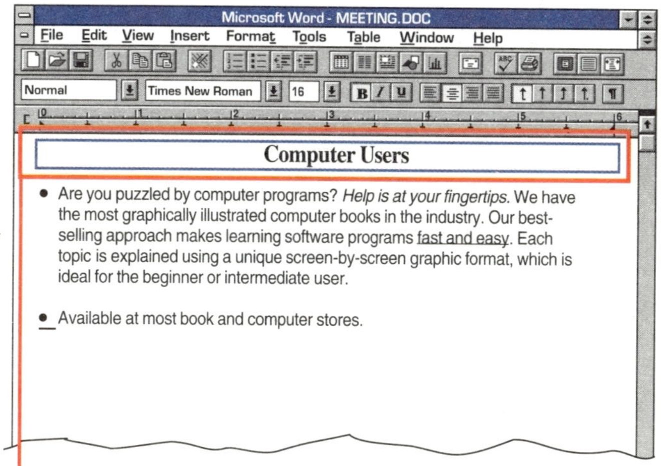

The border is displayed.

Note: To deselect text, click anywhere on the screen.

ADD SHADING

Add Shading

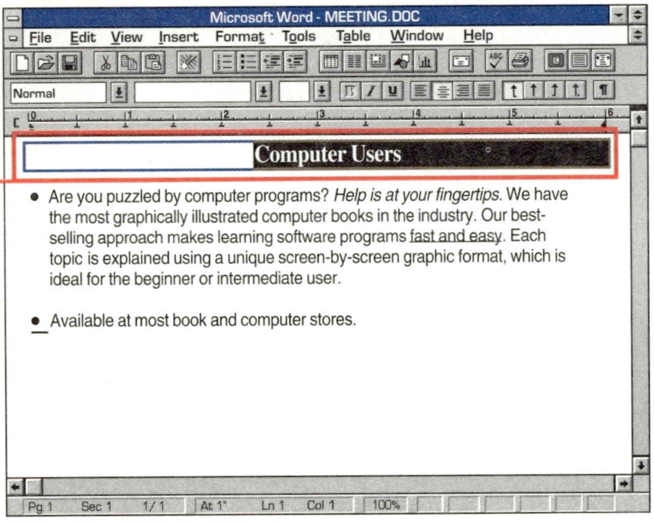

1 Select the text you want to display with shading.

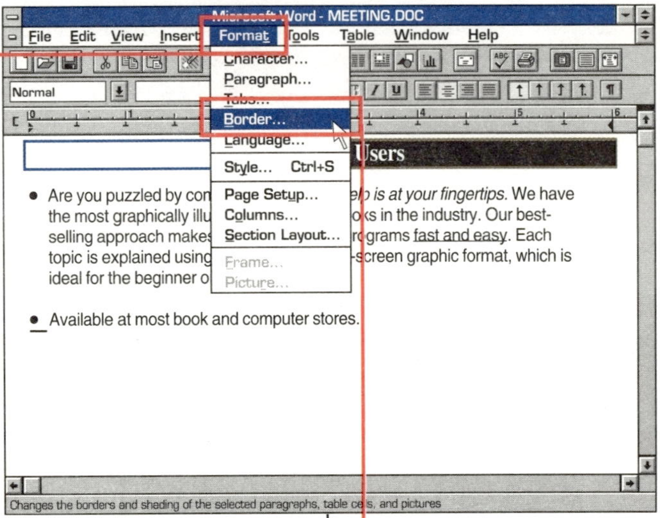

2 Click **Format** to open its menu.

3 Click **Border** and the **Border Paragraphs** dialog box appears.

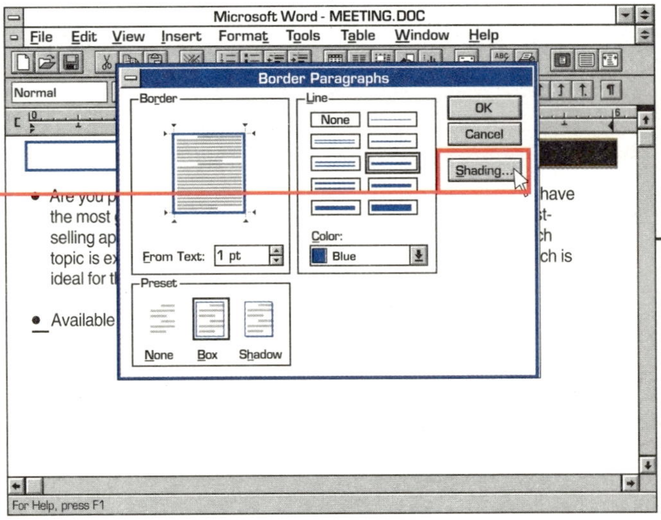

4 Click the **Shading** button and the **Shading** dialog box appears.

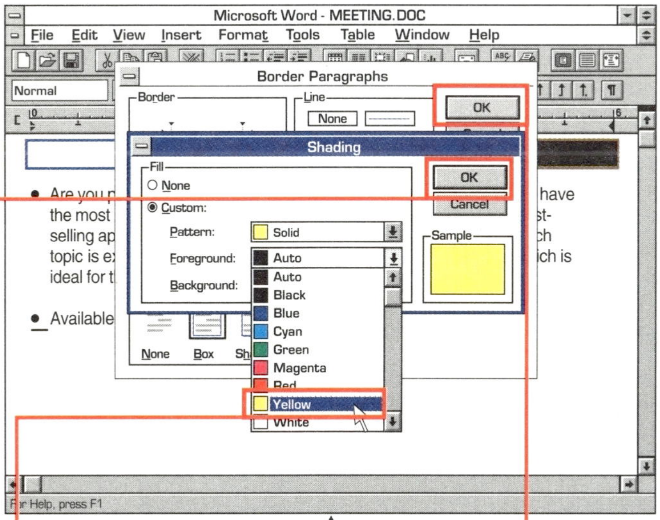

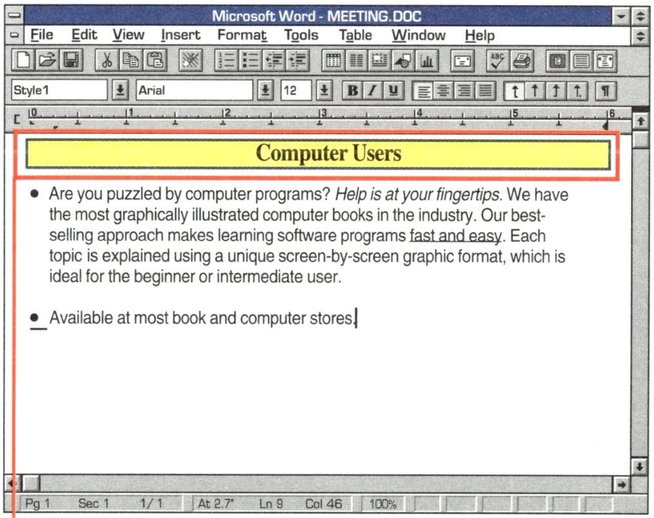

6 Click the desired color (example: **Yellow**).

7 Click this **OK** button to close the **Shading** dialog box.

8 Click this **OK** button to close the **Border Paragraphs** dialog box and return to the document.

■ The shading is displayed.

Note: To deselect text, click anywhere on the screen.

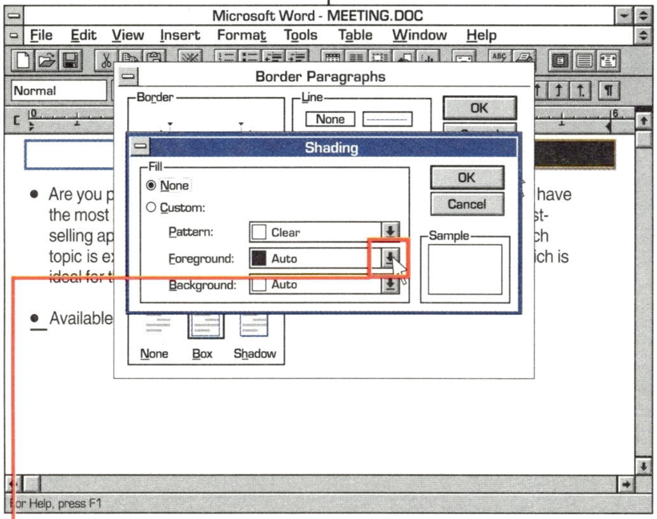

5 Click the arrow beside **Foreground:** and a list of the available shading colors is displayed.

*Note: To choose a pattern, click the arrow ⬇ beside **Pattern:**.*

*To choose a background color, click the arrow ⬇ beside **Background:**.*

*Note: To remove shading, click the circle beside **None**.*

CHANGE MARGINS

Change [Left Margin

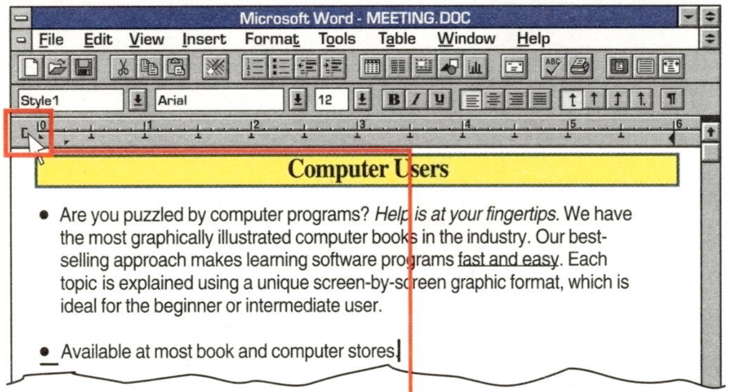

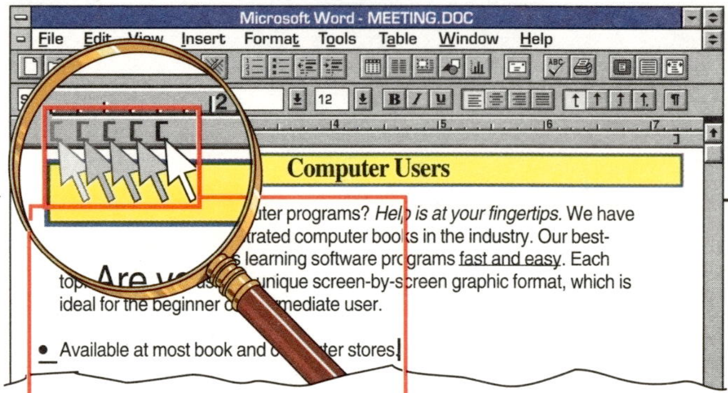

When you first open a document, there is a distance of 1.25 inches between the text and the left and right edges of the paper.

1 Click the **Margin Scale** symbol **[** to display the margin markers.

Note: To change the margins for only a part of the document, change the indentation. Refer to page 46.

2 To change the left margin, position the mouse pointer over the **Left Margin** marker **[**.

3 Click and hold down the left mouse button as you drag the margin to a new location.

Change Top and Bottom Margins

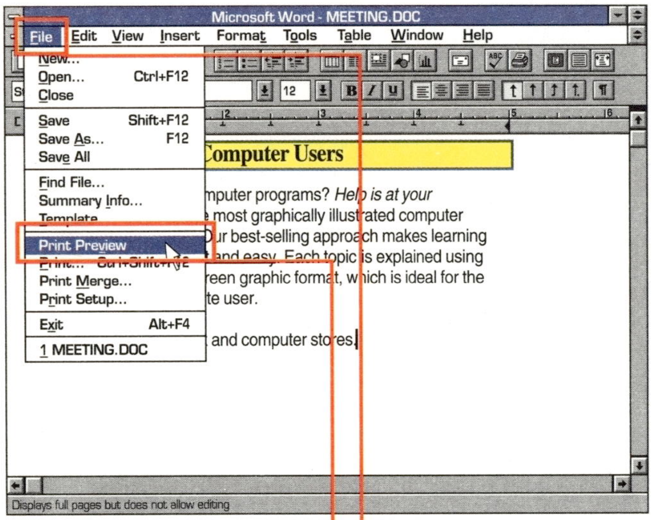

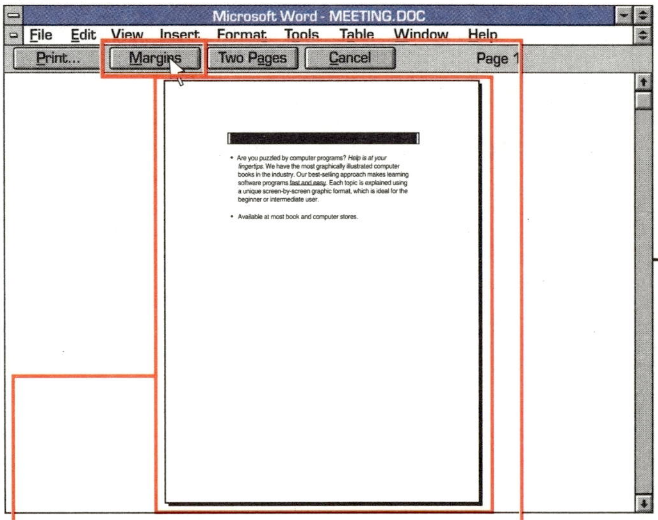

When you first open a document, there is a distance of 1 inch between the text and the top and bottom edges of the paper.

1 Click **File** to open its menu.

2 Click **Print Preview**.

This is how the document will look on a printed page.

Note: For more information on the Print Preview window, refer to page 76.

3 Click the **Margins** button to display the current margins.

Change] Right Margin

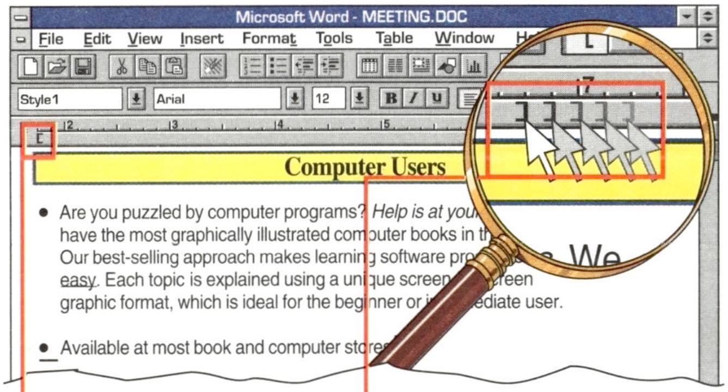

4 Release the mouse button and the margin is changed.

5 To change the right margin, position the mouse pointer over the **Right Margin** marker].

6 Click and hold down the left mouse button as you drag the margin to a new location.

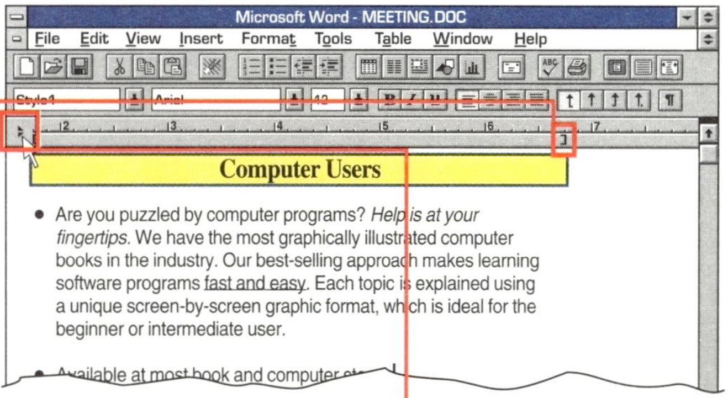

7 Release the mouse button and the margin is changed.

8 Click the **Indent Scale** symbol ▸ to once again display the indent markers.

Note: You can also change the left and right margins using the method described below.

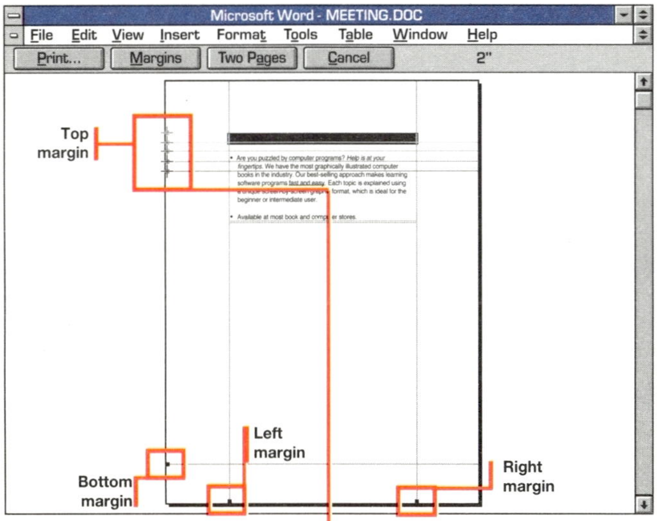

■ The margins are displayed.

4 Position the mouse pointer over the margin marker ■ you want to move and it changes to +.

5 Click and hold down the left mouse button as you drag the margin to a new location.

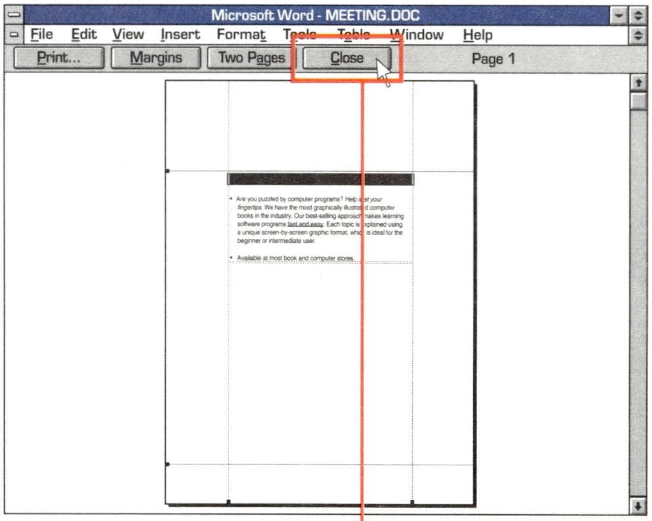

6 Release the mouse button.

7 Click anywhere off the page and the margin change is displayed.

8 Click the **Close** button to return to the document.

INSERT A PAGE BREAK

NUMBER PAGES

Insert a Page Break

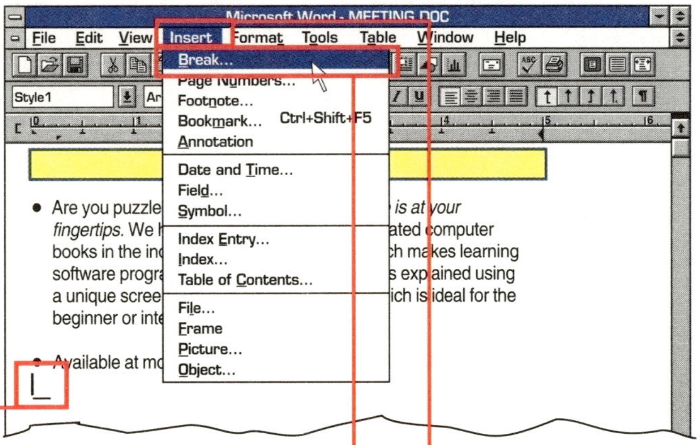

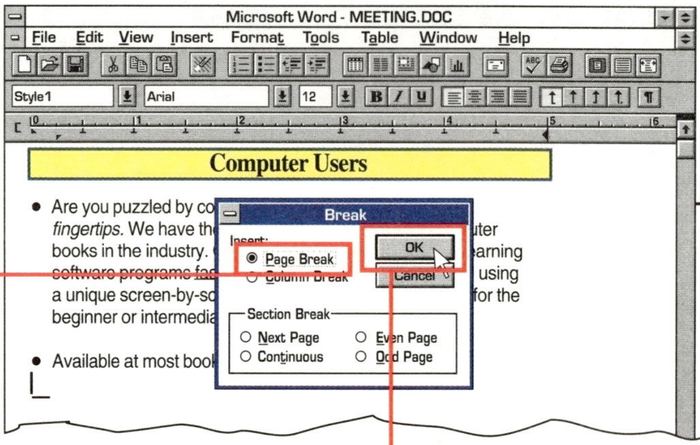

1 Position the insertion point where you want the page to end.

Note: You cannot position the insertion point past the horizontal line — displayed on the screen. To move this line, position the insertion point after the last character in the document. Then press ***Enter*** *several times.*

2 Click **Insert** to open its menu.

3 Click **Break** and the **Break** dialog box appears.

4 Click the circle beside **Page Break**.

5 Click the **OK** button.

Number Pages

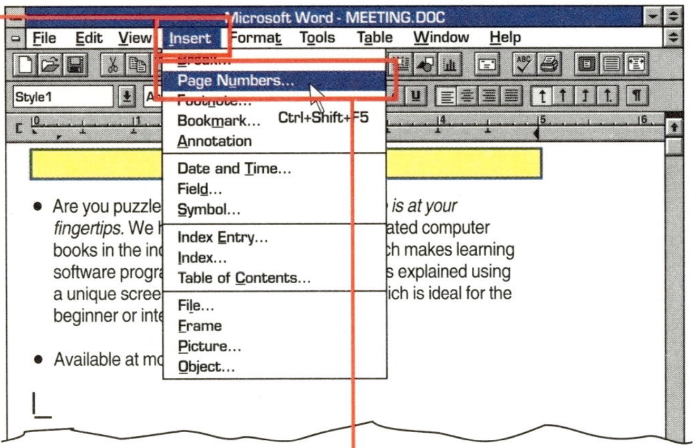

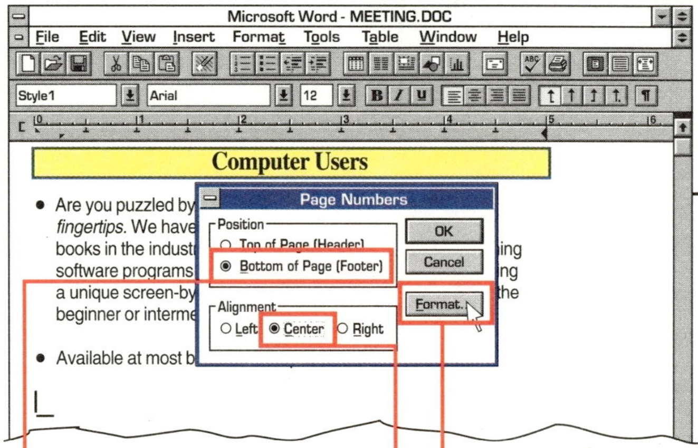

1 Click **Insert** to open its menu.

2 Click **Page Numbers** and its dialog box appears.

Note: Page numbering will appear on all pages, except the first one. To display a page number on the first page, use the Header/Footer command. Refer to page 60.

3 Click the circle beside the desired position of the page numbers (example: **Bottom of Page**).

4 Click the circle beside the desired alignment of the page numbers (example: **Center**).

5 To select a page number format, click the **Format** button.

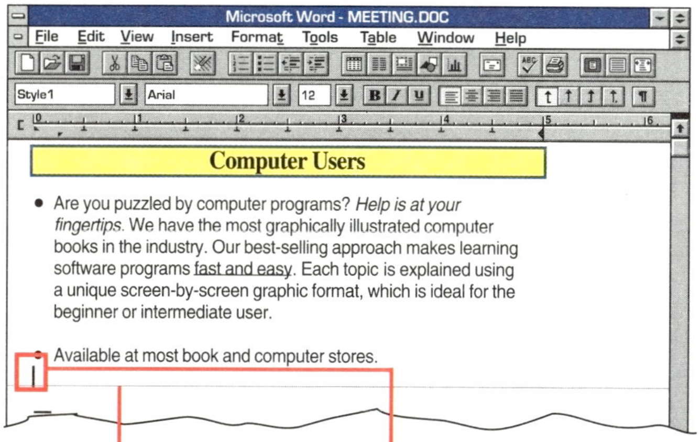

■ A dotted line appears which represents the end of the page.

6 To remove a page break, position the insertion point on the page break. Then press the **Delete** key.

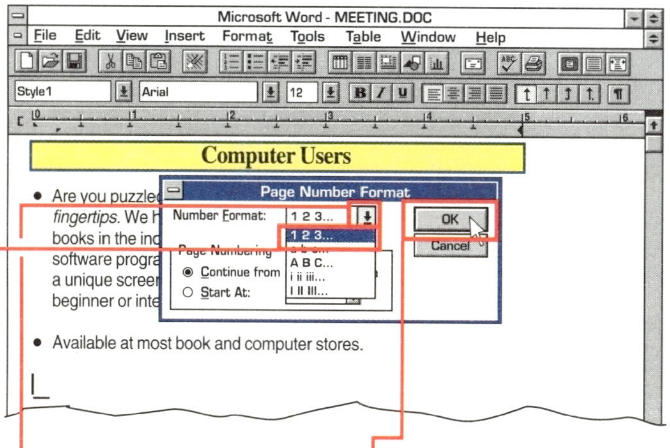

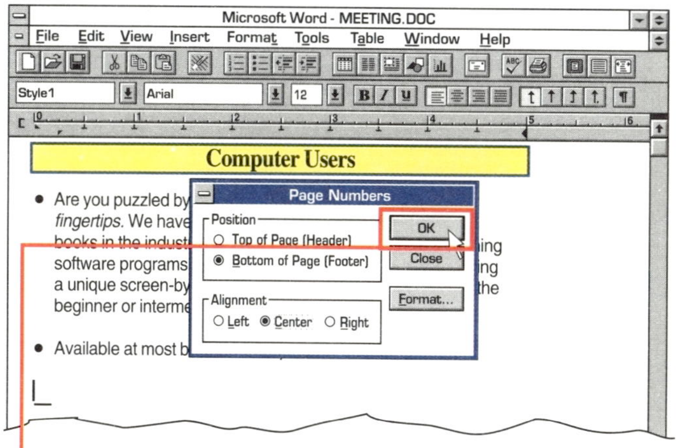

6 Click the arrow beside **Number Format:** and a list of the available formats appears.

7 Click the desired format (example: **1 2 3...**).

8 Click the **OK** button and the **Page Numbers** dialog box reappears.

9 Click the **OK** button to return to the document.

Note: Page numbers cannot be seen in the Normal view. To view the page numbers, change to the Page Layout view. Refer to page 62.

FOOTNOTES

HEADERS AND FOOTERS

Footnotes

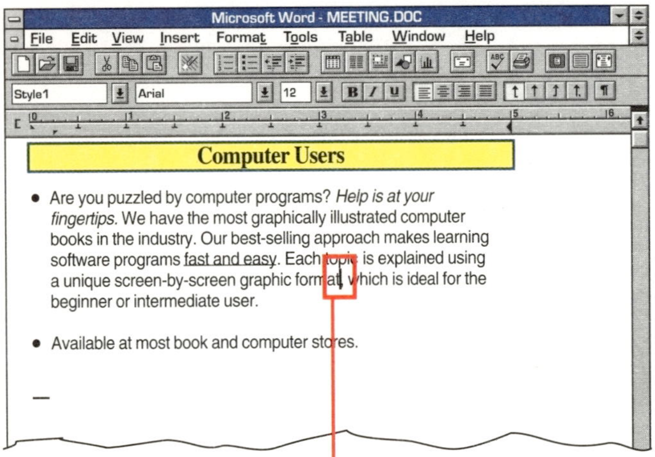

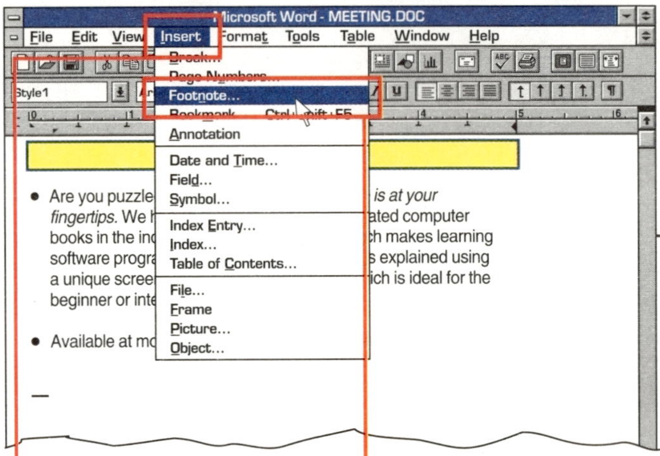

Footnotes provide additional information on an item in your text. They appear at the bottom of each page.

1 Position the insertion point where you want the number for the footnote to appear.

2 Click **Insert** to open its menu.

3 Click **Footnote** and its dialog box appears.

Headers and Footers

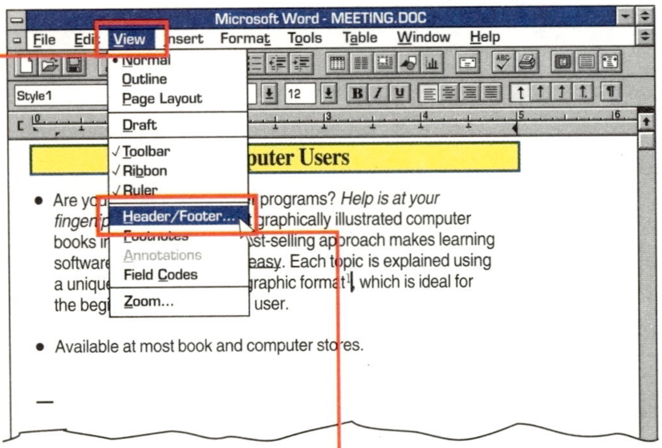

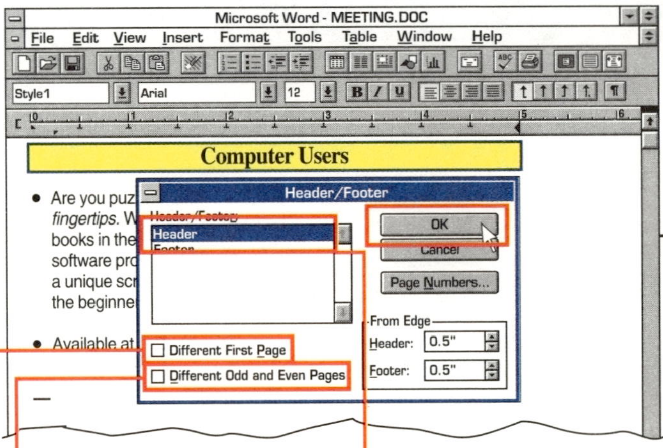

Headers are printed at the top of every page. Footers are printed at the bottom of every page.

1 Click **View** to open its menu.

2 Click **Header/Footer** and the **Header/Footer** dialog box appears.

3 Click this box to create a different header or footer for odd versus even pages.

4 Click this box to create a different header or footer for the first page of the document.

Note: ☒ indicates the option is on. ☐ indicates the option is off.

5 Click the type of header or footer you want to create (example: **Header**).

6 Click the **OK** button, and Word opens an area for you to type the header or footer.

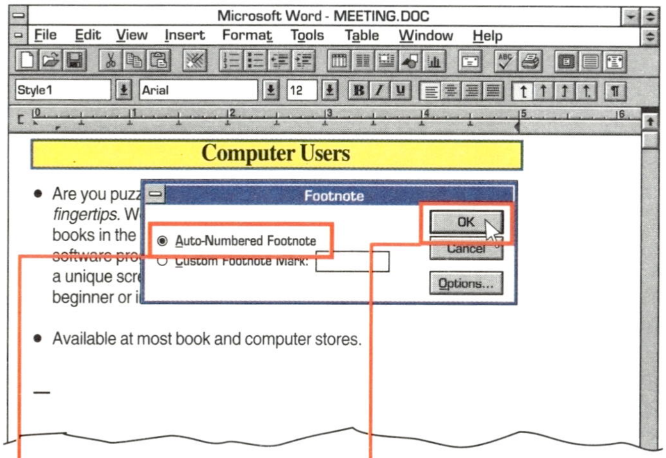

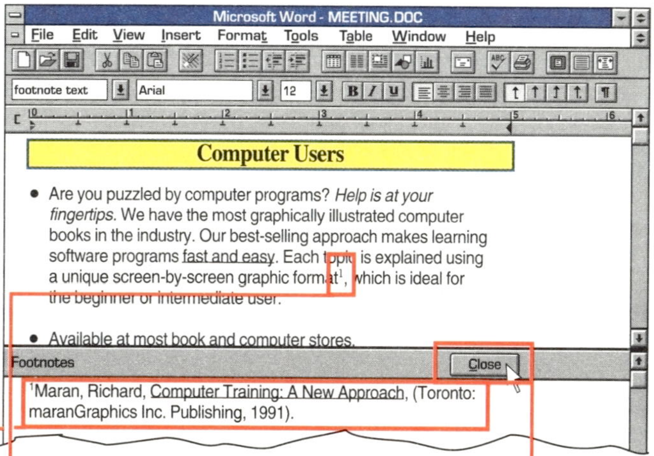

4 To automatically number the footnote, click the circle beside **Auto-Numbered Footnote**.

Note: To create your own footnote marker, click in the box beside ***Custom Footnote Mark:****. Then type the marker (example: **).*

5 Click the **OK** button, and Word opens an area for you to type the footnote.

■ The footnote number appears in the document.

6 Type the text for the footnote.

Note: You can format the footnote just as you would any other text in the document.

7 Click the **Close** button.

Note: Footnotes cannot be seen in the Normal view. To view and/or edit footnotes, change to the Page Layout view. Refer to page 62.

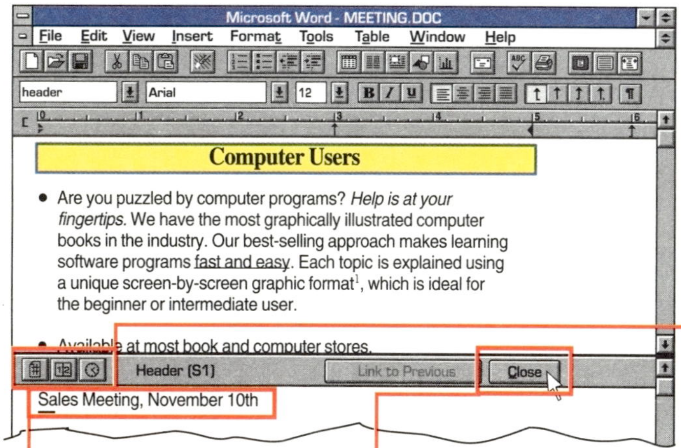

Click this button to insert the current page number in the header or footer.

Click this button to insert the current date in the header or footer.

Click this button to insert the current time in the header or footer.

7 Type the header or footer.

Note: You can format the text just as you would any other text in the document.

8 Click the **Close** button.

Note: Headers and Footers cannot be seen in the Normal view. To view and/or edit a Header or Footer, change to the Page Layout view. Refer to page 62.

CHANGE VIEWS

ZOOM THE SCREEN

Page Layout View

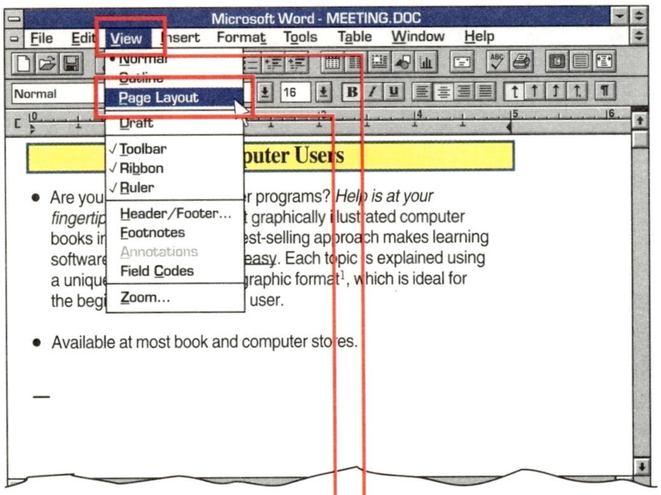

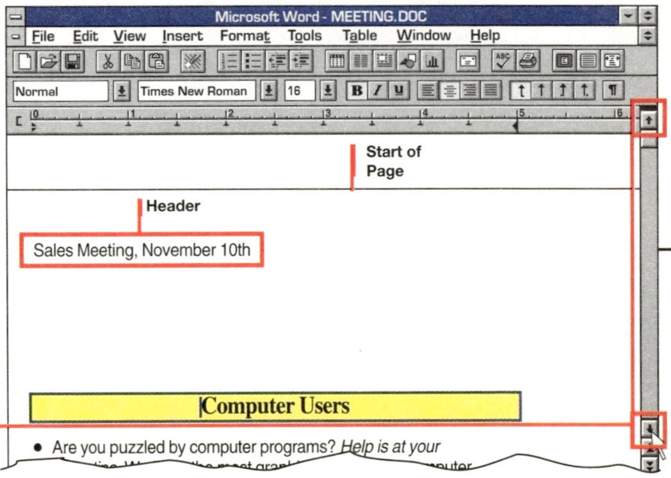

When you first start Word, the document is displayed in the Normal view. This is the best view for most tasks. However, some features are not displayed (example: headers, page numbers).

1 To display each page of the document as it will look when printed, click **View** to open its menu.

2 Click **Page Layout**.

■ The document is displayed in the Page Layout view.

3 Click the up or down scroll arrow to move through the document.

■ You can change the text using the same methods you learned when editing a document in the Normal view.

Note: Since the screens are more complicated, the computer is slower when changes are made.

Zoom the Screen

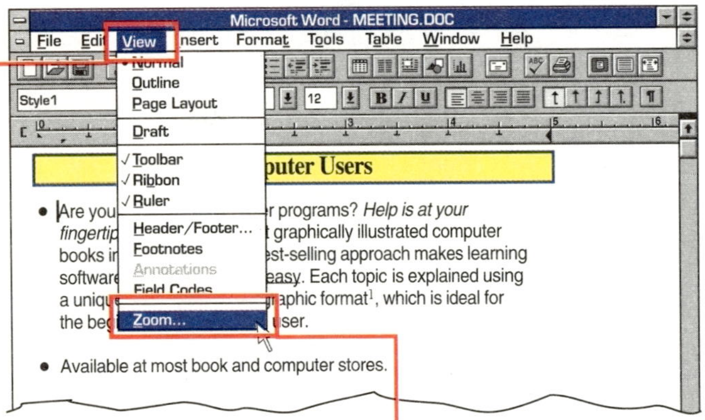

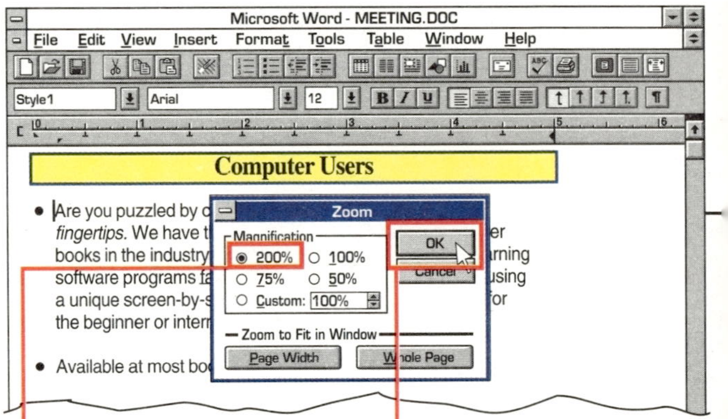

You can magnify or reduce the size of the displayed document.

1 Click **View** to open its menu.

2 Click **Zoom** and the **Zoom** dialog box appears.

3 Click the circle beside the desired magnification (example: **200%**).

4 Click the **OK** button.

Normal View

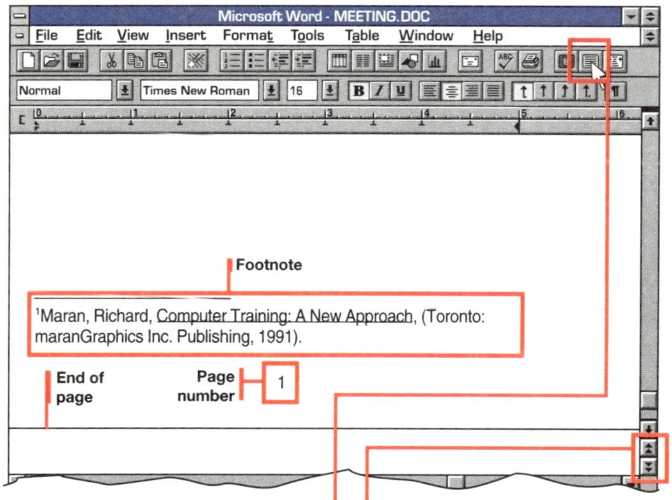

■ The bottom of the page is displayed.

4 If your document has more than one page, click ▼ to view the next page, or click ▲ to view the previous page.

5 To return to the Normal view, click this button.

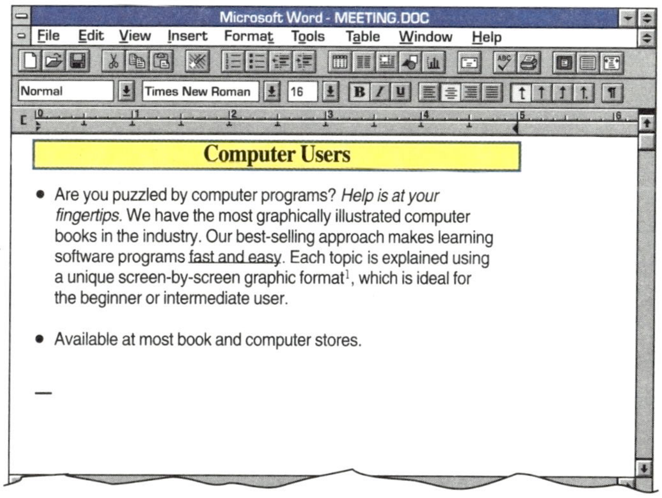

6 To quickly return to the top of the document, press **Ctrl+Home**.

■ The document is displayed at full size in the Normal view.

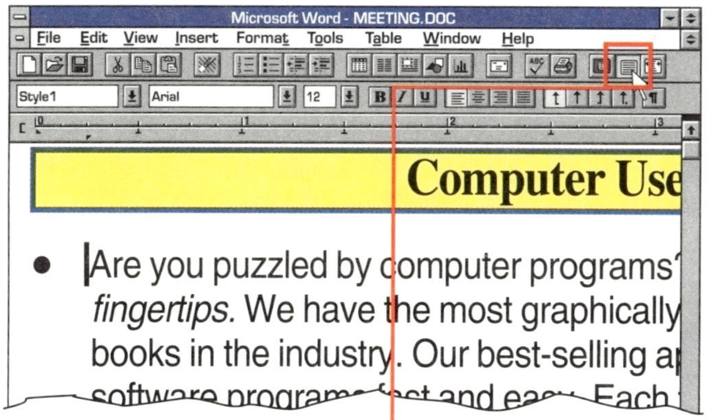

■ The document is magnified (example: 200 percent).

5 To view the document at full size in the Normal view, click this button.

To view the entire page in the Page Layout view:

1 Click the **Zoom Whole Page** button.

To view the entire width of the page:

1 Click the **Zoom Page Width** button.

Note: This is useful if the page has a width greater than 8.5 inches.

CREATE A TABLE

SELECT CELLS

ENTER TEXT IN A TABLE

Create a Table

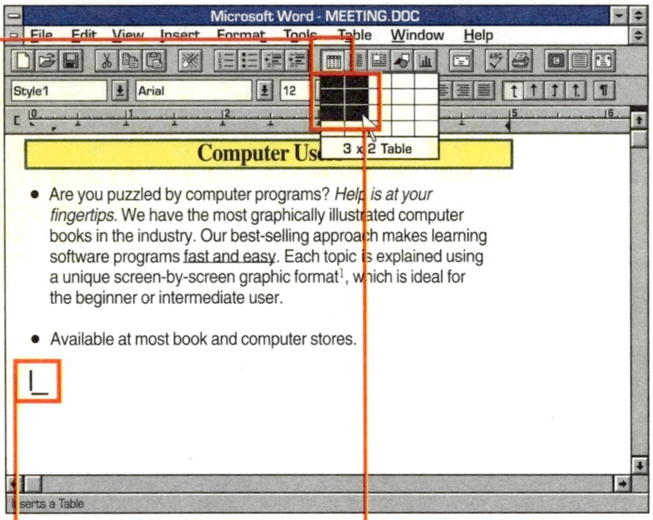

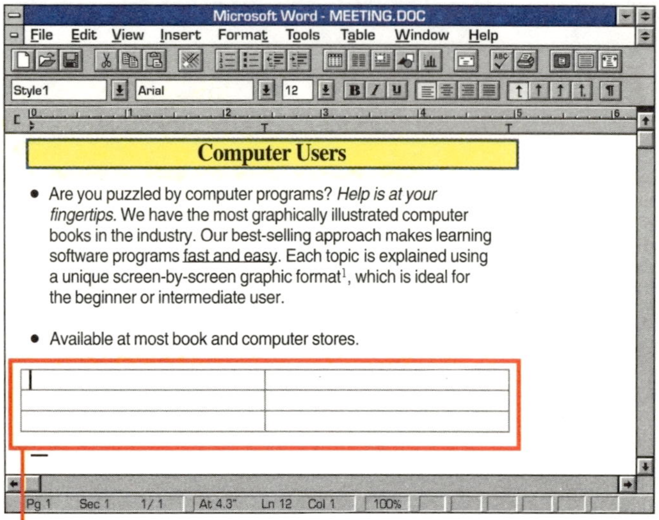

1 Position the insertion point where you want the table to appear.

2 Position the mouse pointer over the **Table** button.

3 Click and hold down the left mouse button as you drag the mouse pointer over the desired table size (example: **3 x 2**).

4 Release the mouse button and the table is created.

Select Cells

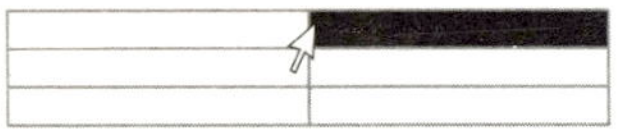

To select a cell

1 Position the mouse pointer over the far left part of the cell and it changes to ↗.

2 Click the left mouse button.

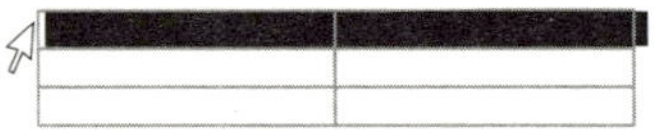

To select a row

1 Position the mouse pointer to the left of the row and it changes to ↗.

2 Click the left mouse button.

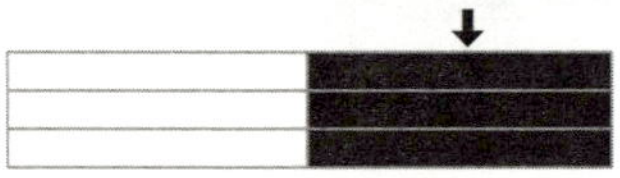

To select a column

1 Position the mouse pointer at the top of the column and it changes to ⬇.

2 Click the left mouse button.

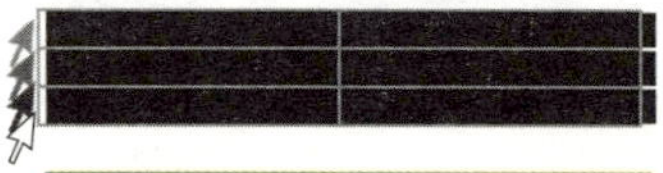

To select the entire table

1 Position the mouse pointer to the left of the first row and it changes to ↗.

2 Click and hold down the left mouse button as you drag the mouse pointer until the entire table is selected.

3 Release the mouse button.

To deselect cells

- Click anywhere outside the table.

Enter Text in a Table

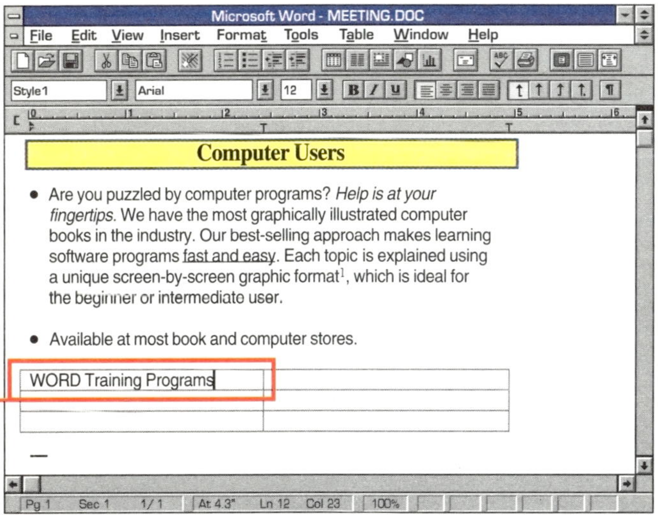

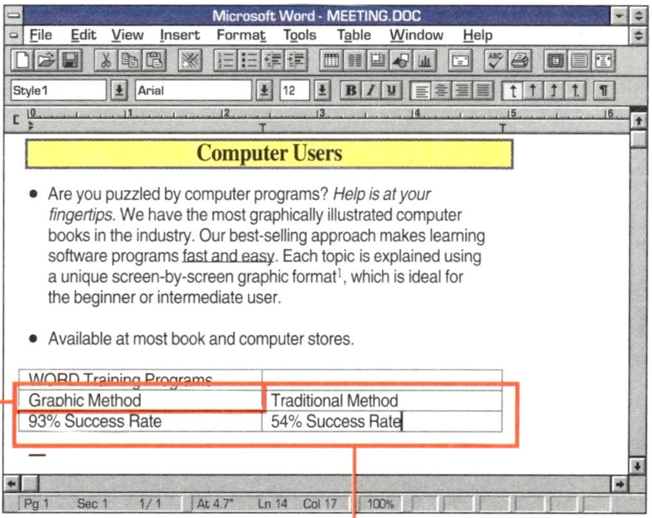

1. Click in the first cell you want to enter text into.
2. Type the text.

Note: If you make a mistake typing, press the ***Backspace*** *key, then type again.*

3. Click in the next cell you want to enter text into.
4. Type the text.
5. Type the remaining text.

Note: Do not press ***Enter*** *after typing text in a table. This will increase the row height. To immediately undo this action, press the* ***Backspace*** *key.*

MOVE THE INSERTION POINT ONE CELL IN ANY DIRECTION

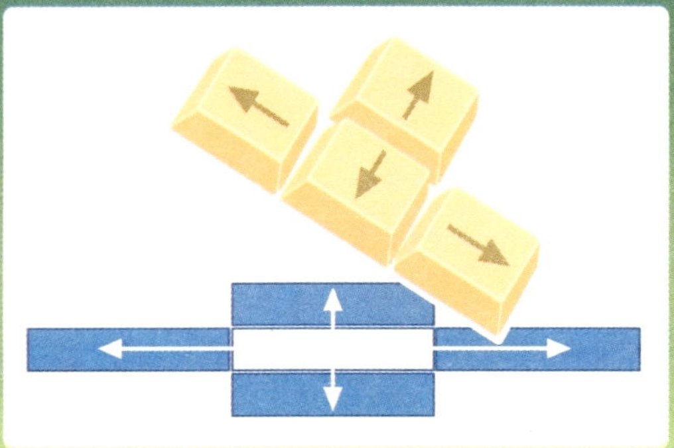

Press ↑ to move one cell up.

Press ← to move one cell left.

Press ↓ to move one cell down.

Press → to move one cell right.

INSERT OR DELETE A ROW

Insert a Row Within a Table

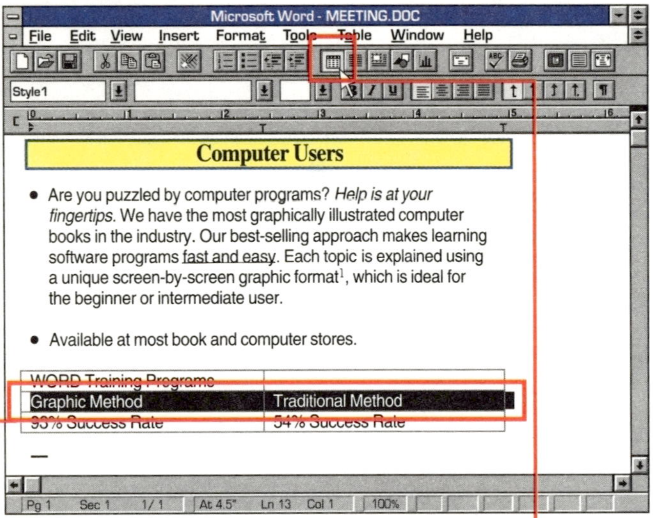

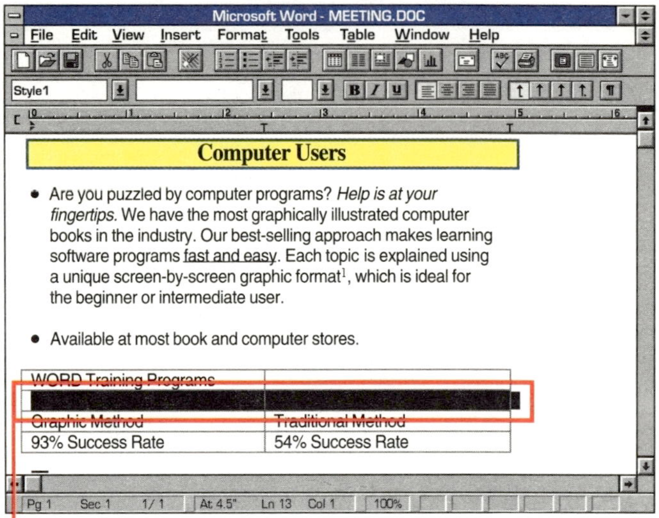

1 Select the row you want to move down to make room for a new row.

2 Click the **Table** button.

■ A new row is inserted.

Insert a Row at the End of a Table

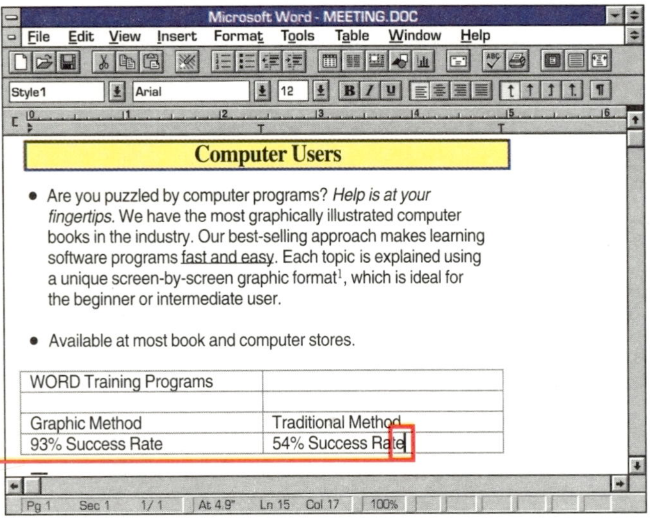

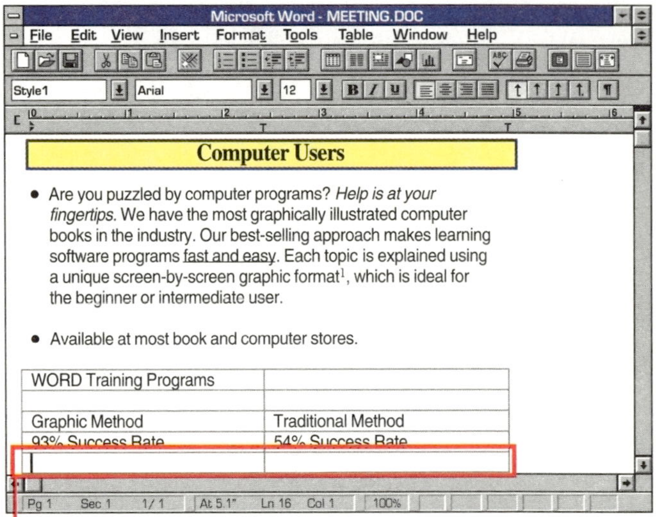

1 Position the insertion point in the last cell in the table.

2 Press the **Tab** key.

■ A new row is inserted.

DELETE TEXT FROM A TABLE

1 Select the cells that contain the text you want to delete.

2 Press the **Delete** key.

Delete a Row

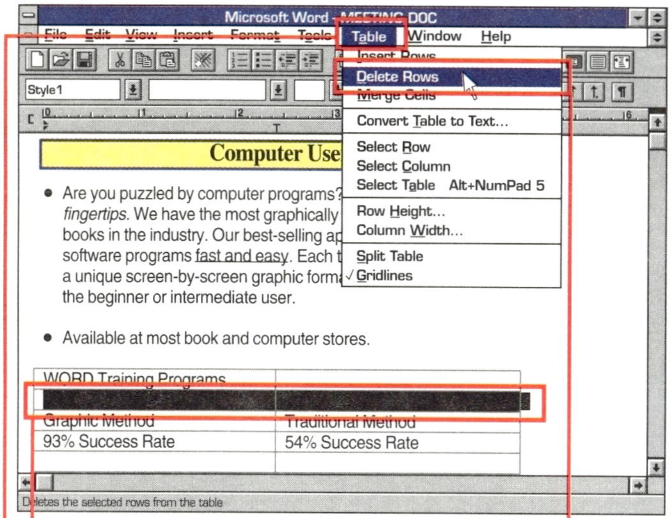

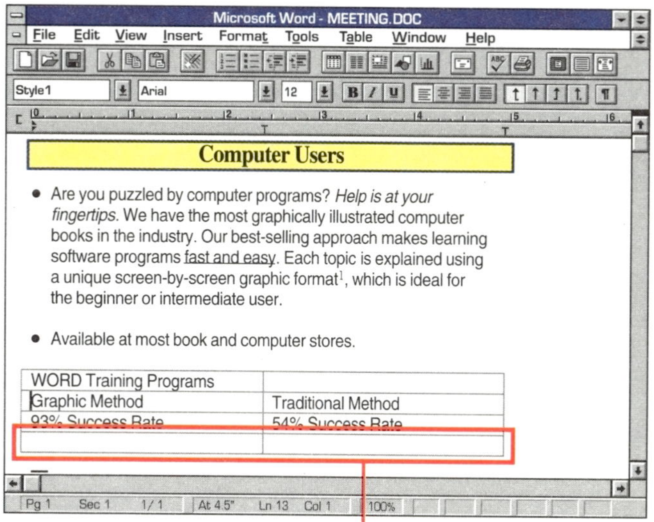

1 Select the row you want to delete.

2 Click **Table** to open its menu.

3 Click **Delete Rows**.

■ The row is deleted.

4 To delete another row, repeat steps 1 to 3.

INSERT OR DELETE A COLUMN

RESIZE COLUMNS

Insert a Column

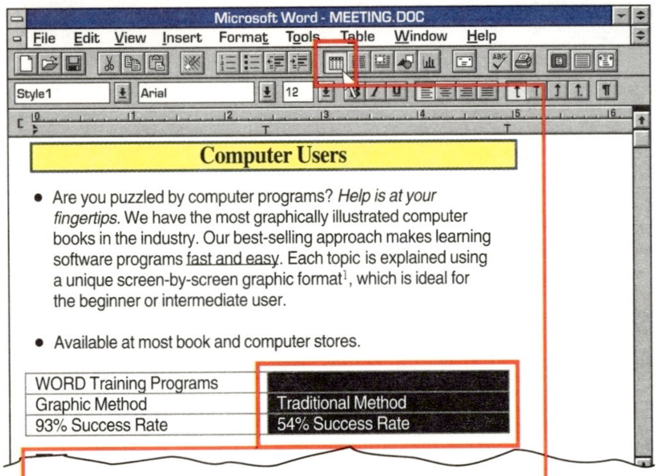

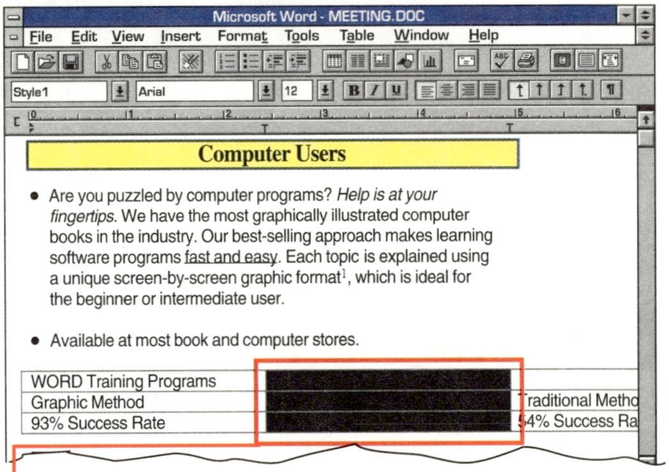

1 Select the column you want to move to the right to make room for a new column.

2 Click the **Table** button.

■ A new column is inserted.

Resize Columns

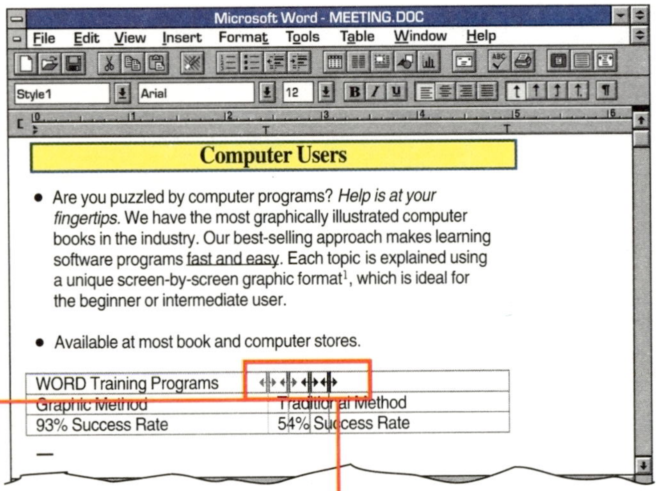

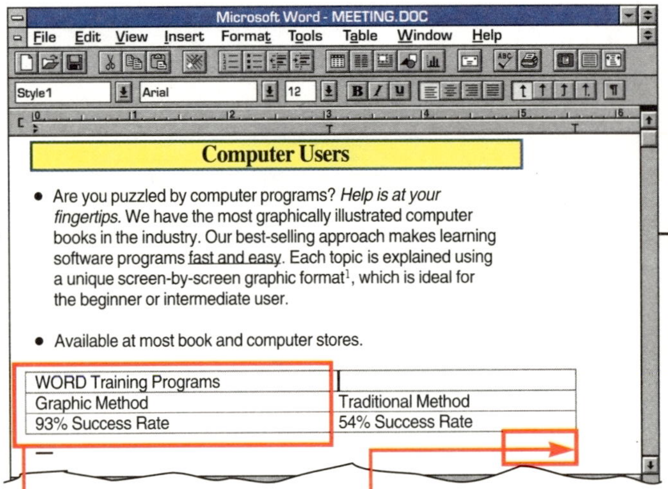

When you resize a column, the right edge of the table will move to accommodate the change.

1 Position the mouse pointer over the cell border you want to move and it changes to ◆||◆.

Note: If you only want to change the column width for a few rows, select the row(s) before step **1**.

2 Click and hold down the left mouse button as you drag the border to a new location.

3 Release the mouse button and the column width is changed.

■ The right edge of the table moved to accommodate the change.

Delete a Column

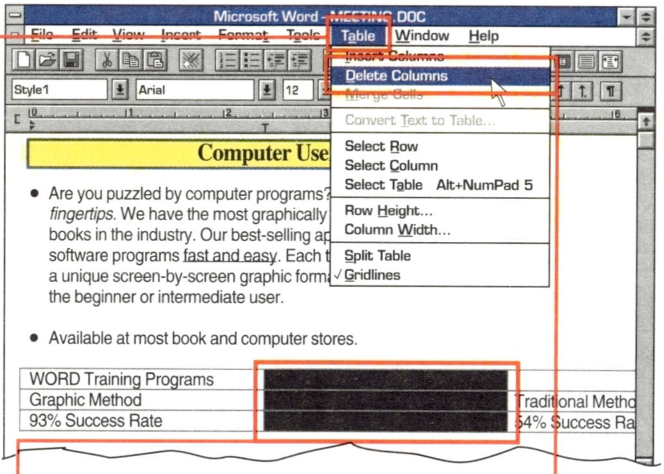

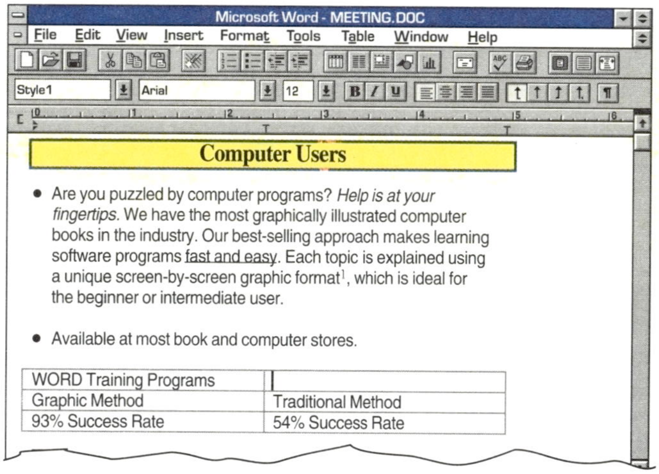

1 Select the column you want to delete.

2 Click **Table** to open its menu.

3 Click **Delete Columns**.

■ The column is deleted.

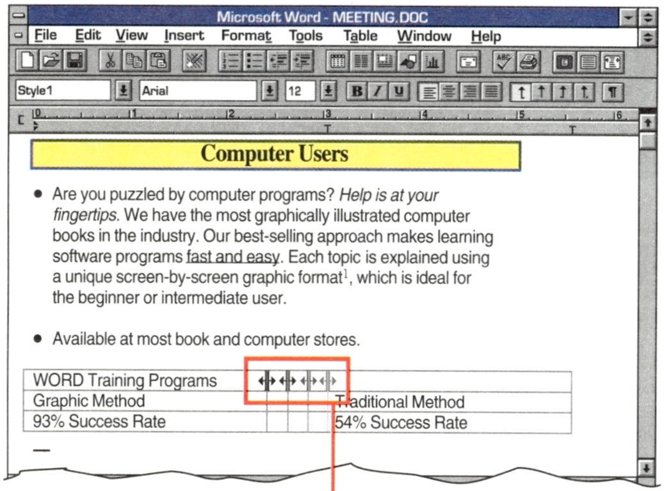

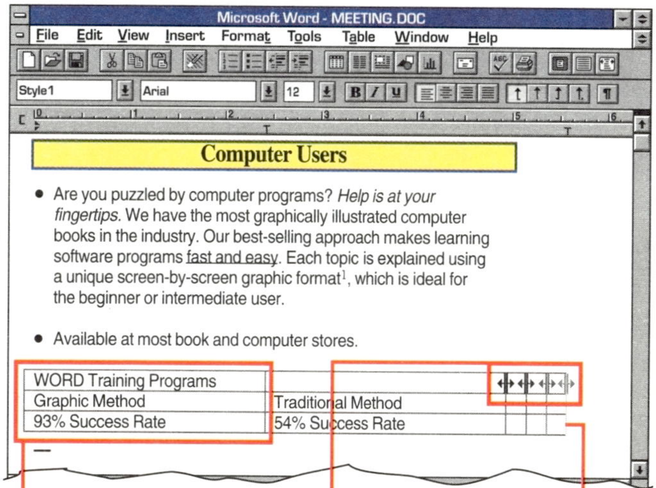

You can resize a column without changing the overall table width.

1 Press and hold down the **Shift** key.

Note: If you only want to change the column width for a few rows, select the row(s) before step 1.

2 Position the mouse pointer over the cell border you want to move and it changes to ⟺.

3 Click and hold down the left mouse button as you drag the border to a new location.

4 Release the mouse button, then the **Shift** key, and the column width is changed.

■ The right edge of the table did not move.

5 To resize another column using this method, repeat steps 1 to 4.

MERGE CELLS

FORMAT TEXT IN A TABLE

ADD BORDERS TO A TABLE

Merge Cells

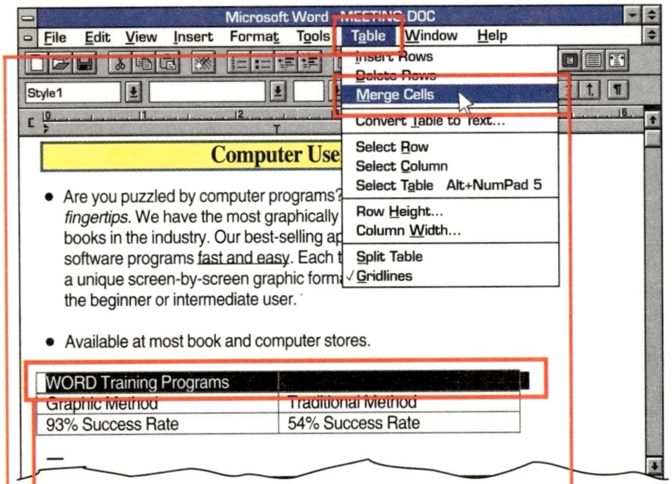

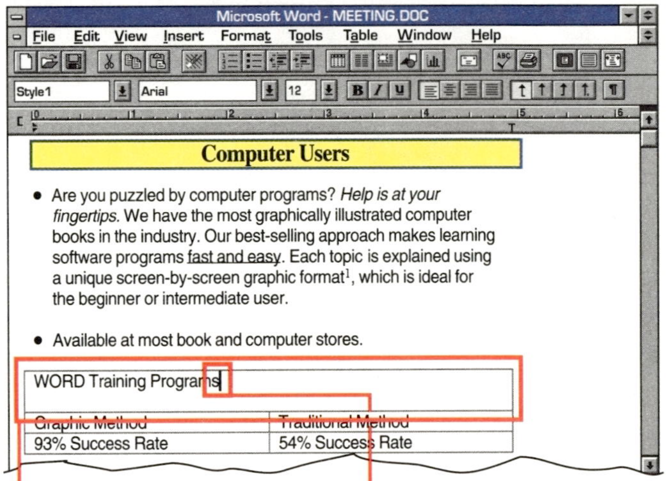

1 Select the cells you want to join together.

2 Click **Table** to open its menu.

3 Click **Merge Cells**.

■ The cells are merged.

Note: To split a merged cell, select the cell. Click ***Table****, then click* ***Split Cells****.*

4 To remove the extra line that was created, position the insertion point at the end of the text. Then press the **Delete** key.

Add Borders to a Table

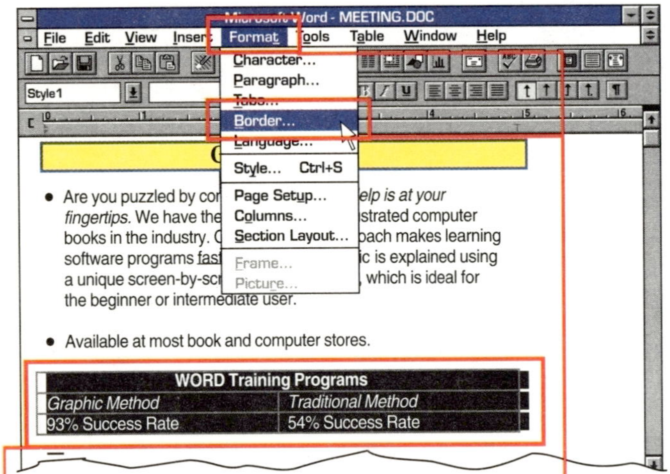

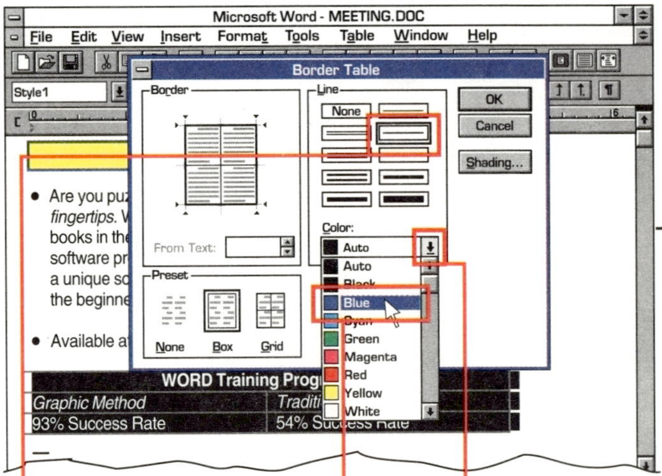

The dotted lines around the table cells do not appear when you print the document.

1 Select the table you want to add borders to.

2 Click **Format** to open its menu.

3 Click **Border** and the **Border Table** dialog box appears.

4 Click the desired line style.

5 To color the line, click the arrow ⬇ beside **Color:**.

6 Click the desired color (example: **Blue**).

Format Text in a Table

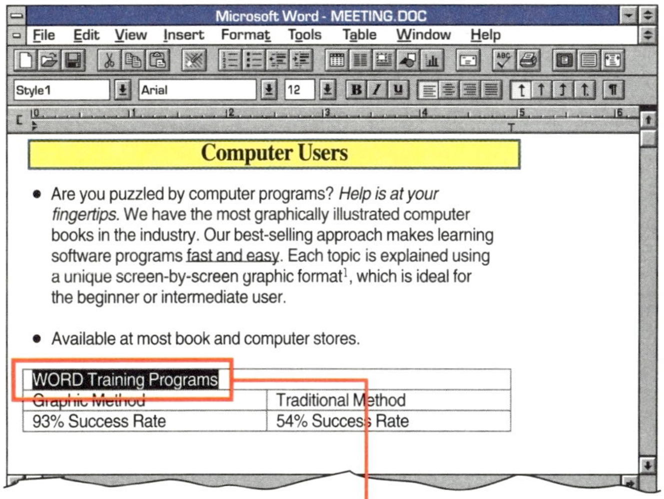

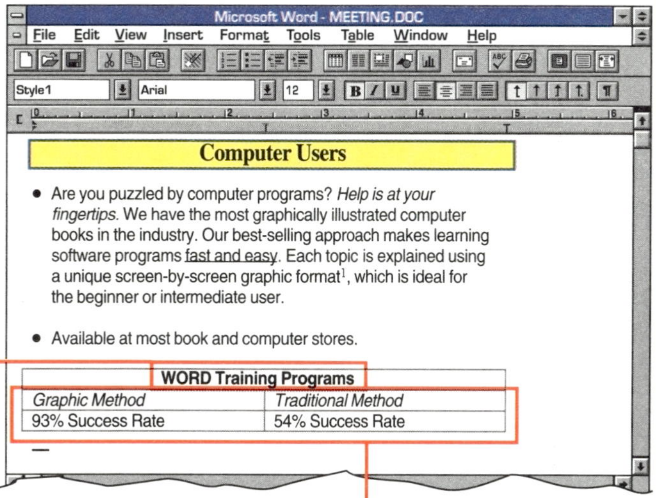

When formatting text in a table, use the same methods you learned when formatting text in a document.

1 Select the text you want to format.

2 Format the text (example: bold, center).

3 Format the rest of the text in the table.

Note: For more information on formatting text, refer to pages 40-43.

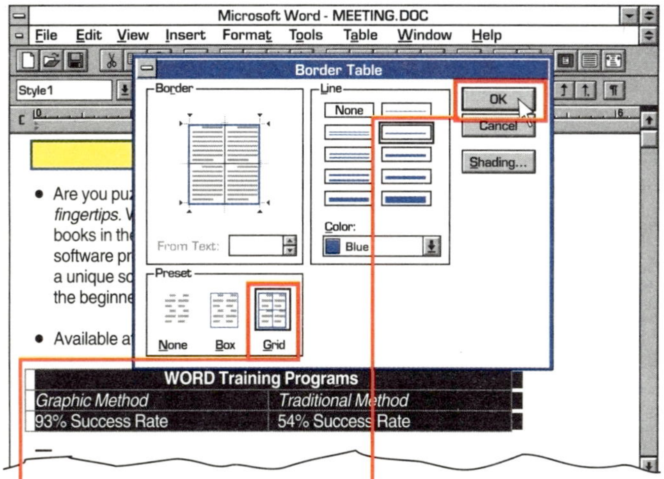

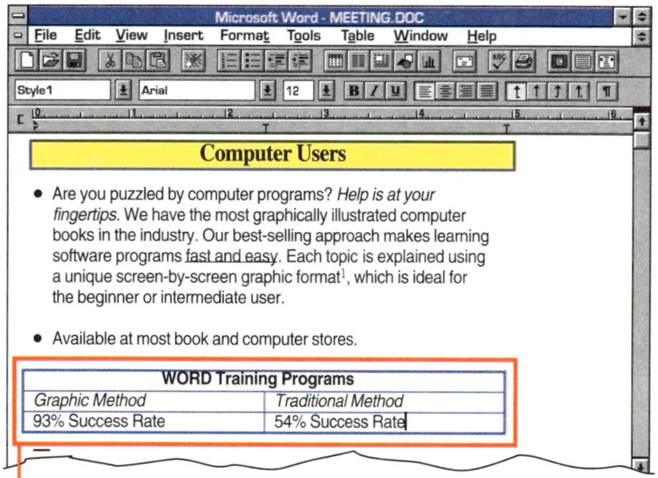

7 Click the desired border type (example: **Grid**).

*Note: To remove borders, click **None**.*

8 Click the **OK** button.

The borders are displayed.

Note: To deselect text, click anywhere on the screen.

INSERT A FRAME

INSERT A GRAPHIC

Insert a Frame

A Word frame is similar to a regular picture frame. Both give shape and support to a picture (graphic) or a group of words. If you move the frame, the contents inside move with it.

A Word frame can also be resized, causing the contents inside to become either smaller or larger.

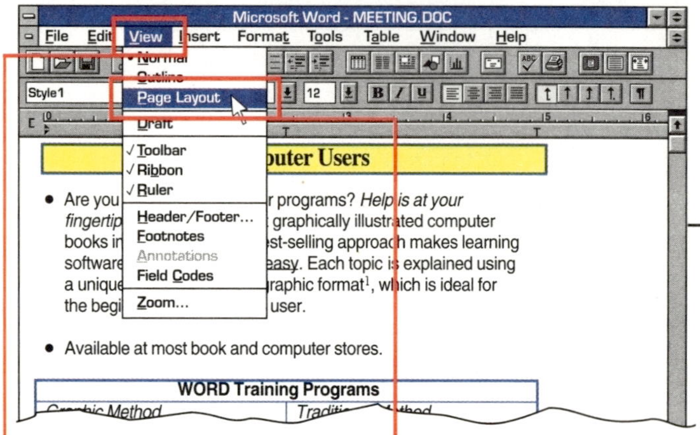

Before inserting a frame, you must switch to the Page Layout view.

1 Click **View** to open its menu.

2 Click **Page Layout**.

Note: For more information on the Page Layout view, refer to page 62.

Insert a Graphic

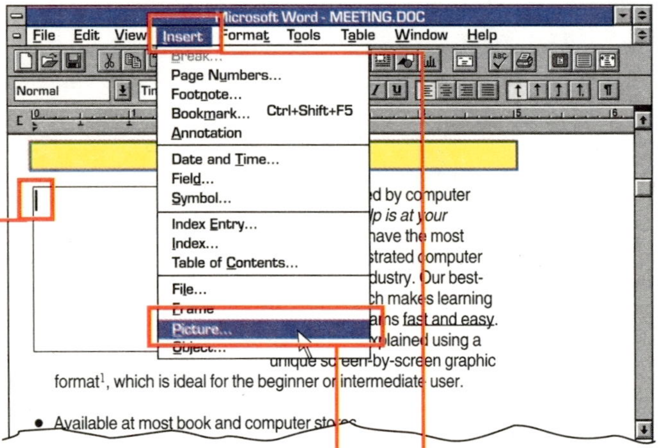

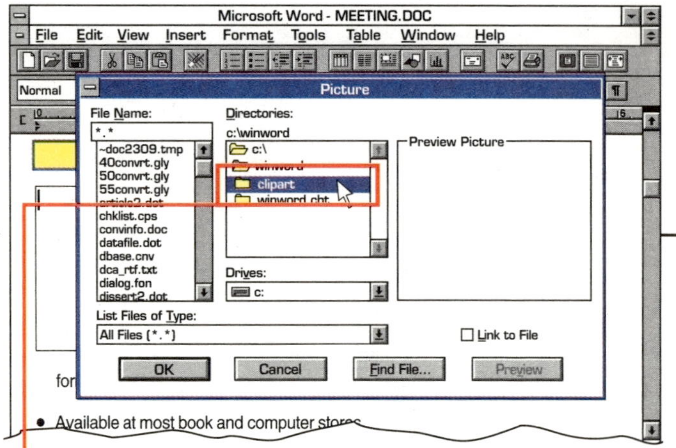

Word supplies you with many different graphics that can easily be inserted into your document.

1 Position the insertion point inside the frame you want to add the graphic to.

2 Click **Insert** to open its menu.

3 Click **Picture** and its dialog box appears.

4 To view the graphic files supplied by Word, double click **clipart**.

Note: To view the contents of another directory, double click that directory's name.

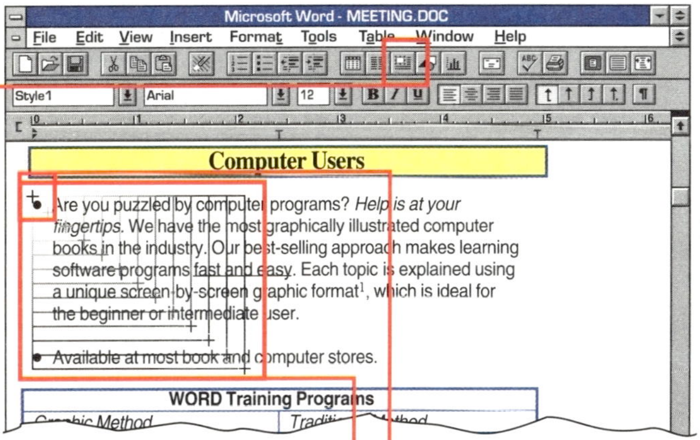

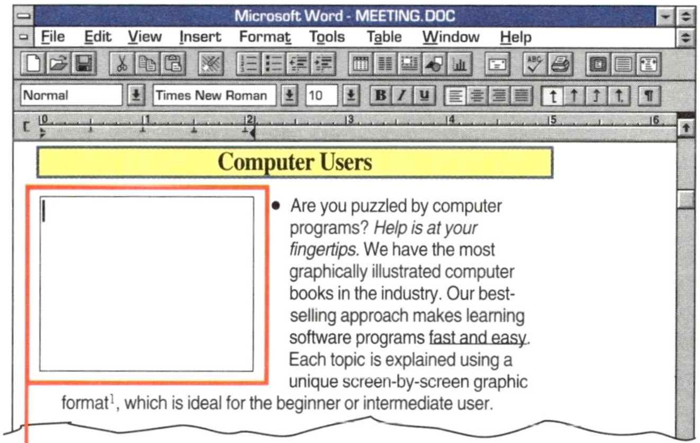

3 Click the down ⬇ or up ⬆ scroll arrow to view the area where you want to place the frame.

4 Click the **Frame** button and the mouse pointer ↖ changes to +.

5 Position the mouse pointer + where you want to locate the top left corner of the frame.

6 Click and hold down the left mouse button as you drag the frame to the desired size.

7 Release the mouse button and the frame is displayed.

■ You can insert a graphic, or type text into the frame. The frame can then be sized, and/or moved to any location in the document.

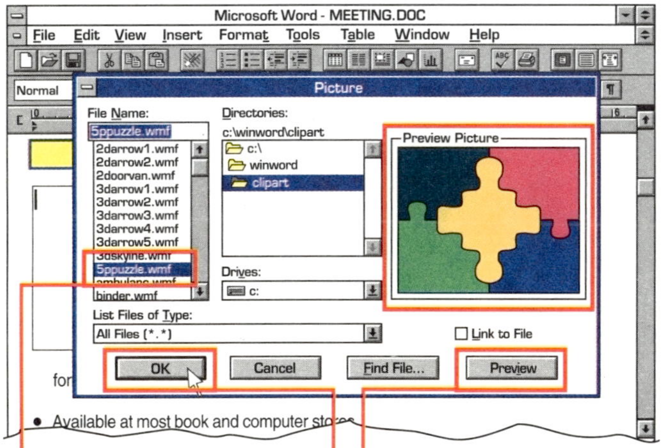

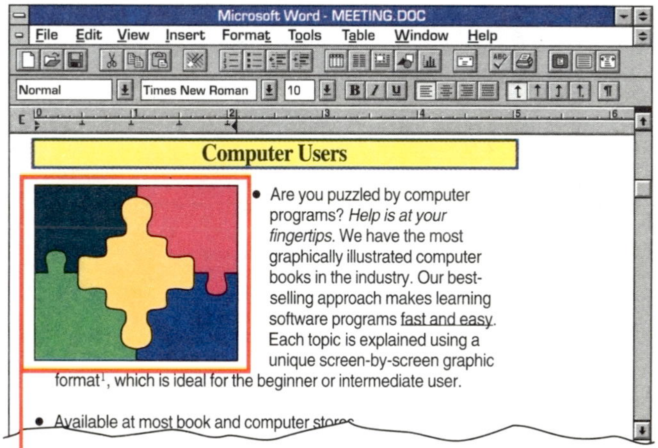

5 Click the name of the graphic you want to insert into the document (example: **5ppuzzle.wmf**).

Note: To view more graphic file names, click the down ⬇ scroll arrow.

6 Click the **Preview** button to view the graphic before inserting it into the document.

7 Click the **OK** button.

■ The graphic is inserted into the document.

Size a Graphic

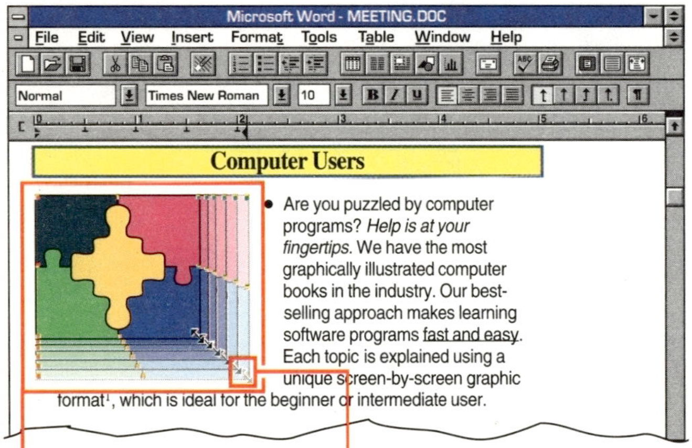

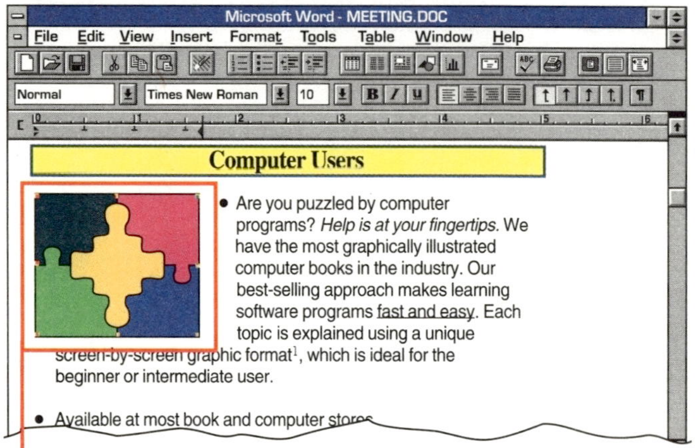

1 To select a graphic to be sized, click anywhere on the graphic and squares ■ appear around its edges.

2 Position the mouse pointer over any sizing handle ■ and it changes shape (example: ⤡).

3 Click and hold down the left mouse button as you drag the edges of the graphic to the desired size.

4 Release the mouse button and the graphic is sized.

Move a Graphic

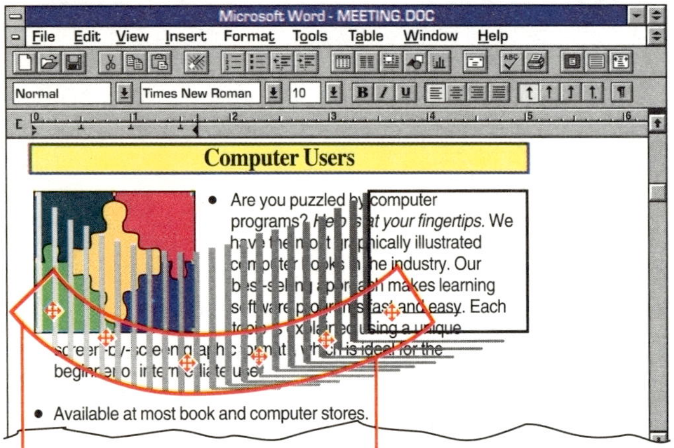

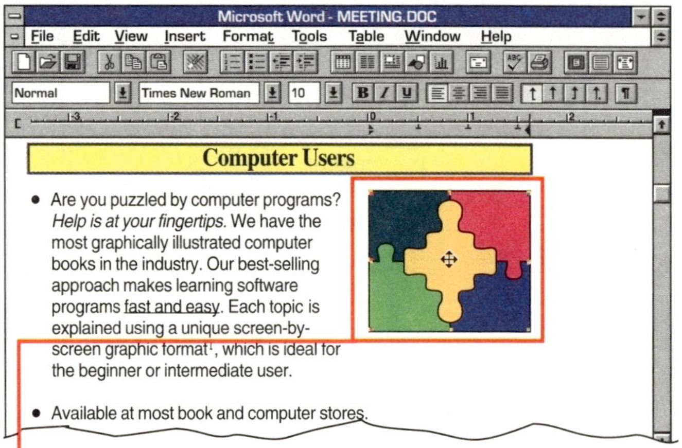

1 Position the mouse pointer over the graphic and it changes to ✥.

2 Click and hold down the left mouse button as you drag the graphic to a new location.

3 Release the mouse button and the graphic is moved.

Note: To deselect a graphic, click outside the graphic area.

DELETE A GRAPHIC

Delete

1 Click anywhere on the graphic to select it.

2 Press the **Delete** key.

Return to the Normal View

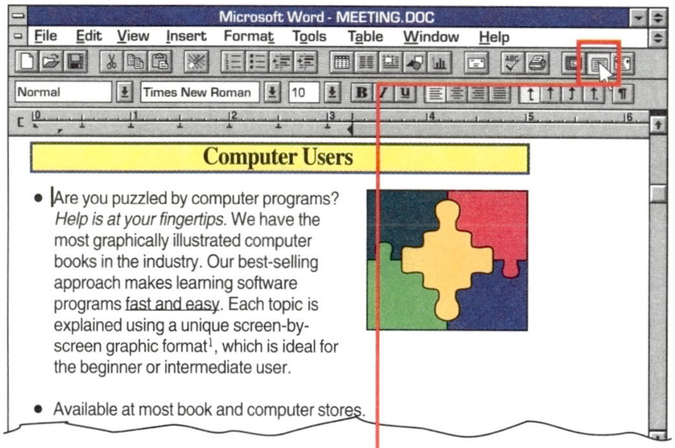

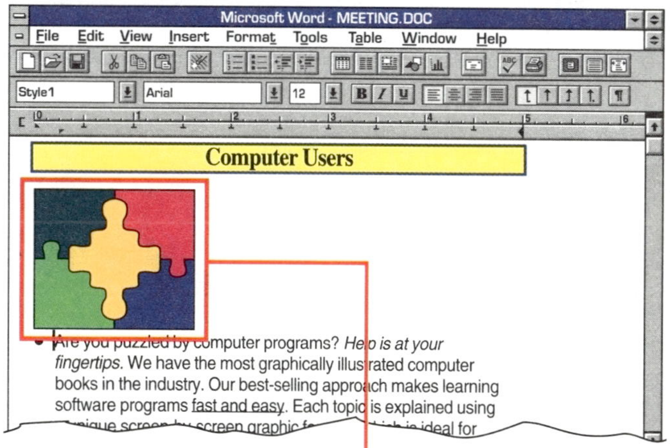

Since the Page Layout view displays the graphic in its actual position, the computer is slower when changes are made. To make text changes, switch back to the Normal view.

1 To return to the Normal view, click this button.

Note: For more information on changing views, refer to page 62.

■ The document is displayed at full size in the Normal view.

■ The Normal view does not display the graphic in its actual position.

*Note: To return to the Page Layout view, click **View**. Then click **Page Layout**.*

CHANGE PAGE SIZE AND ORIENTATION

PREVIEW A DOCUMENT

Change Page Size and Orientation

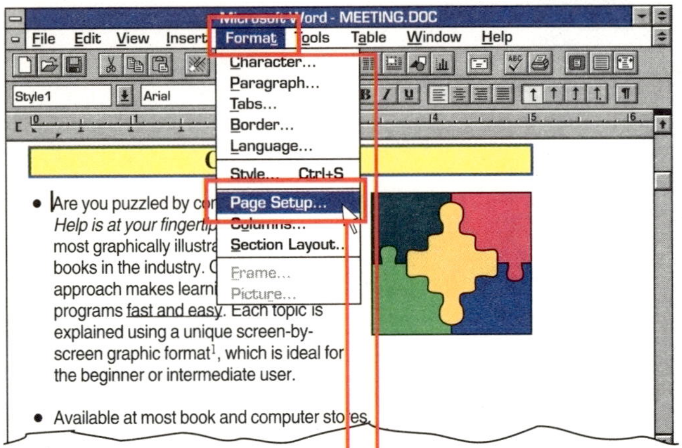

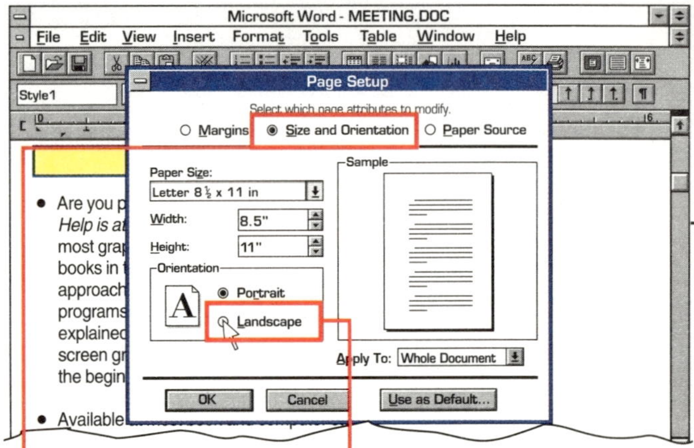

Word has the page size set at 8 1/2 by 11 inches, with a portrait orientation. You can change these settings.

*Note: The **Portrait** (vertical) orientation prints the document down the length of the paper.*

1 Click **Format** to open its menu.

2 Click **Page Setup** and its dialog box appears.

3 Click the circle beside **Size & Orientation**.

4 To change the orientation to **Landscape**, click the circle beside **Landscape** and ○ becomes ◉.

*Note: The **Landscape** (horizontal) orientation prints the document across the width of the paper.*

Preview a Document Before Printing

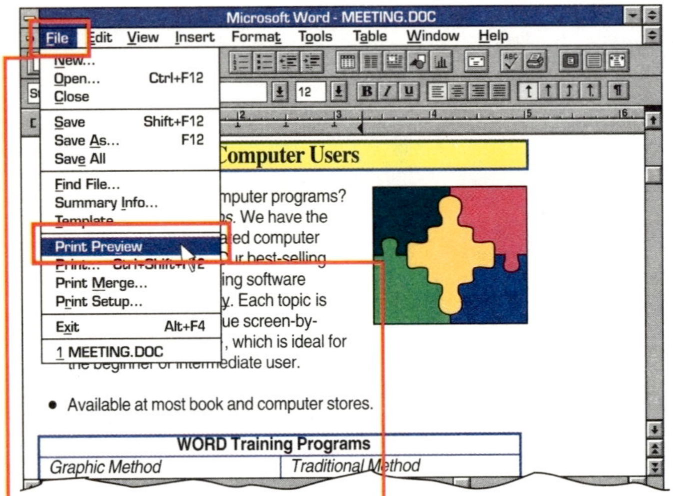

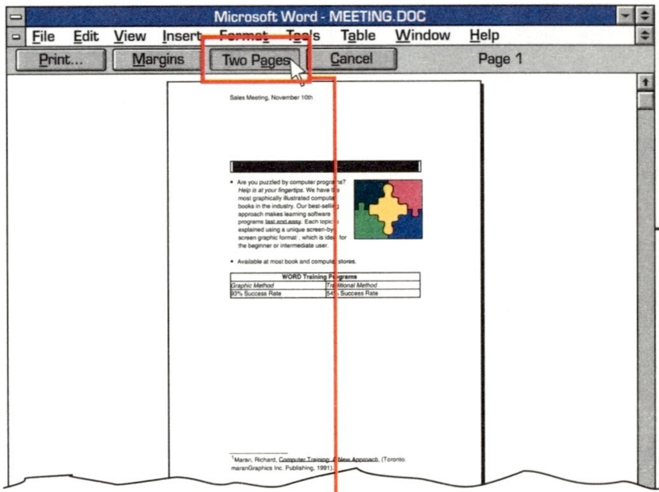

You can see how the document will look on a printed page before you actually print it.

1 Click **File** to open its menu.

2 Click **Print Preview**.

■ The Print Preview window displays the current page as it will look when printed.

Note: You cannot edit text in the Print Preview window.

3 If the document contains more than one page, press the **Page Down** key to view the next page.

4 To view two pages side-by-side, click the **Two Pages** button.

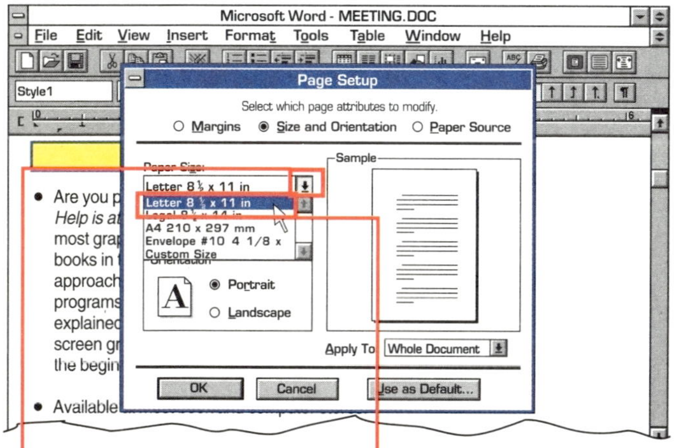

5 To change the paper size, click the arrow under **Paper Size:** and a list of the available paper sizes for your printer appears.

6 Click the desired paper size.

*Note: If the size you want is not listed, click **Custom Size**.*

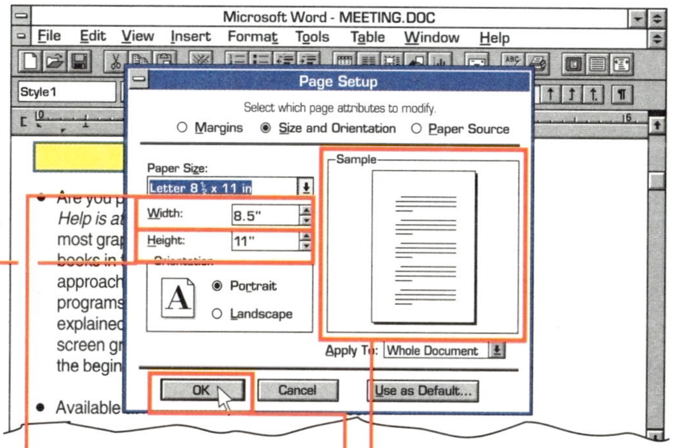

7 If you selected **Custom Size** in step 6, double click in the **Width:** box, and type the desired width of the page.

8 Double click in the **Height:** box, and type the desired height of the page.

■ A sample of the selected page size and orientation is displayed in the **Sample** box.

9 Click the **OK** button to close the **Page Setup** dialog box.

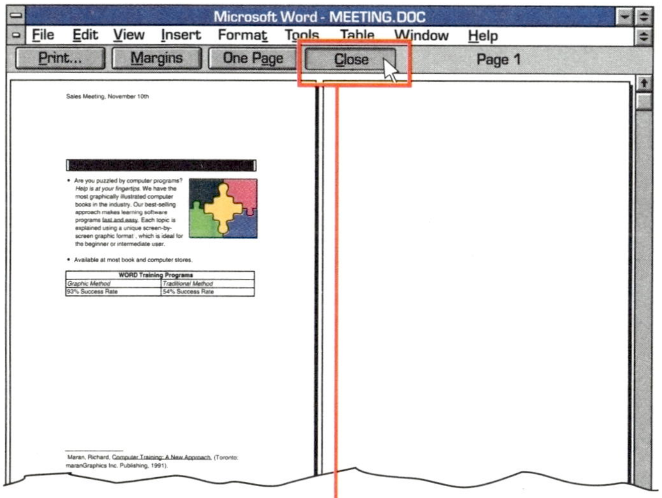

■ The two pages are viewed side-by-side.

*Note: To view only one page, click the **One Page** button.*

5 Click the **Close** button to return to the document.

PRINT A DOCUMENT

Print a Document

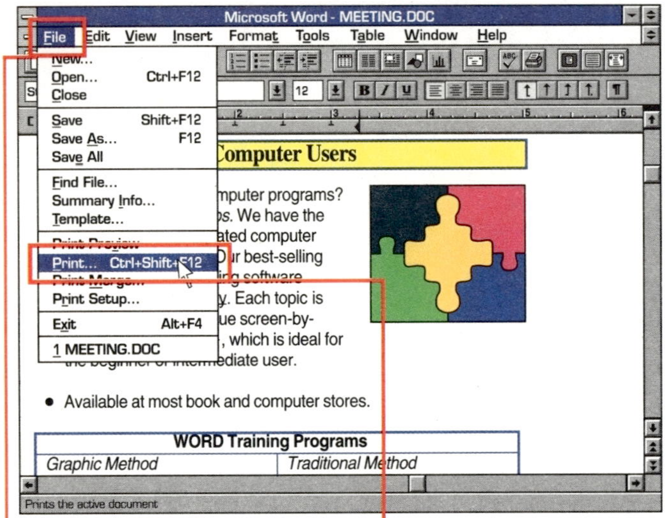

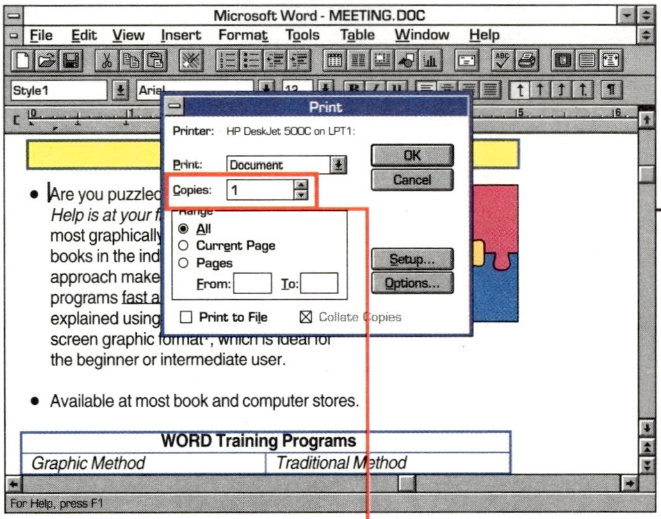

1 Click **File** to open its menu.

Note: To print only the current page, make sure there is no text or graphic selected before performing step **1**.

2 Click **Print** and the **Print** dialog box appears.

Number of copies

■ The default setting is **1** copy.

3 To print multiple copies, double click in the **Copies:** box. Then type the number of copies you want to print.

PRINT SELECTED PART OF DOCUMENT

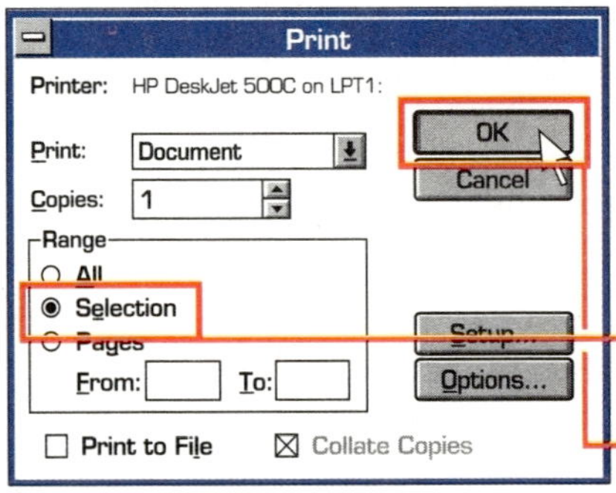

1 Select the graphic or text area you want to print.

2 Click **File** to open its menu.

3 Click **Print** and the **Print** dialog box appears.

4 Click the circle beside **Selection**.

5 Click the **OK** button.

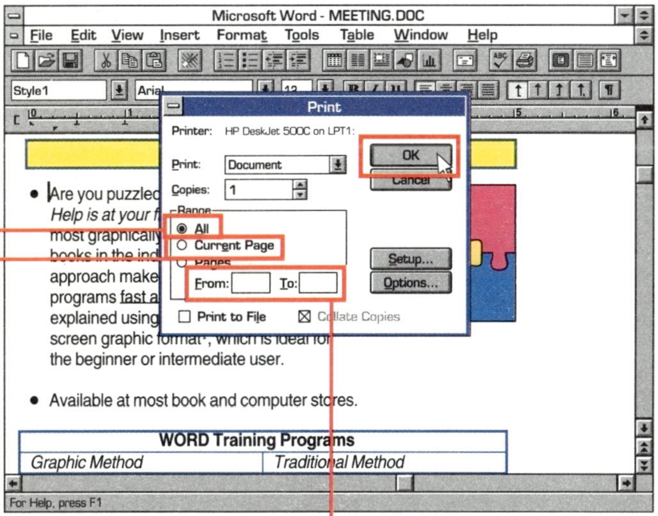

Print range

■ **All** is the default setting. All pages in the document will be printed.

4 To only print the page the insertion point is currently in, click the circle beside **Current Page** and ○ becomes ◉.

5 To print specific pages instead of all pages, click in the **From:** box. Then type the starting page number.

6 Click in the **To:** box and type the last page number.

7 Click the **OK** button, or press **Enter**.

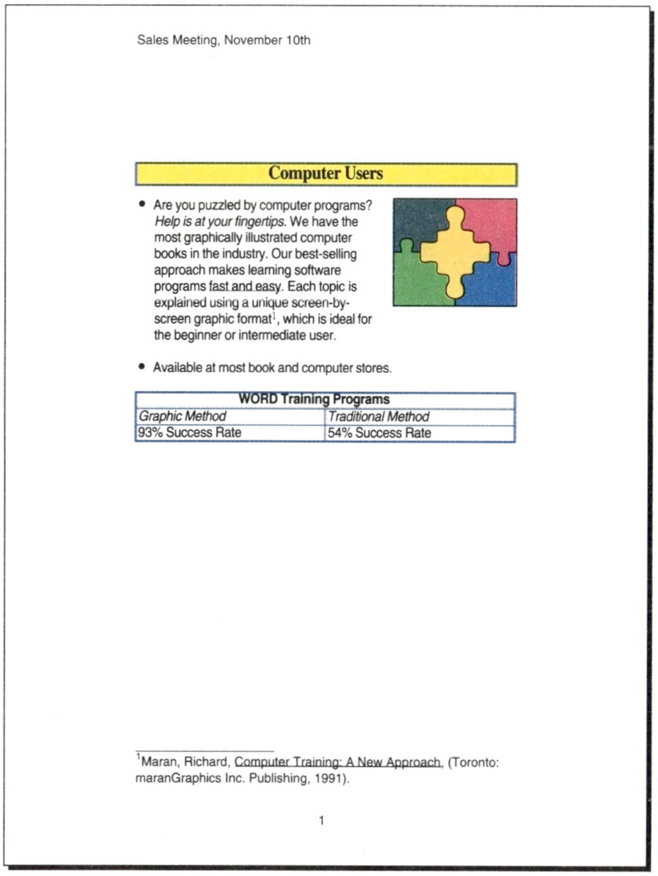
Sales Meeting, November 10th

Computer Users

- Are you puzzled by computer programs? *Help is at your fingertips.* We have the most graphically illustrated computer books in the industry. Our best-selling approach makes learning software programs fast and easy. Each topic is explained using a unique screen-by-screen graphic format[1], which is ideal for the beginner or intermediate user.
- Available at most book and computer stores.

WORD Training Programs	
Graphic Method	*Traditional Method*
93% Success Rate	54% Success Rate

[1]Maran, Richard, Computer Training: A New Approach, (Toronto: maranGraphics Inc. Publishing, 1991).

1

■ The page(s) is printed.

Note: The number of colors, and the quality of the printed document depends on the type and model of printer attached to your computer system. For more information, refer to your printer's manual.

QUICKLY PRINT A DOCUMENT

Click the **Print** tool to quickly print the document using the current settings.

PRINT OPTIONS

CREATE AN ENVELOPE

Print Options

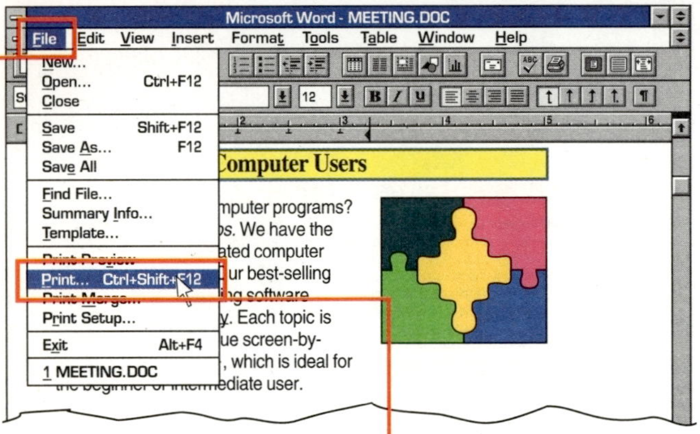

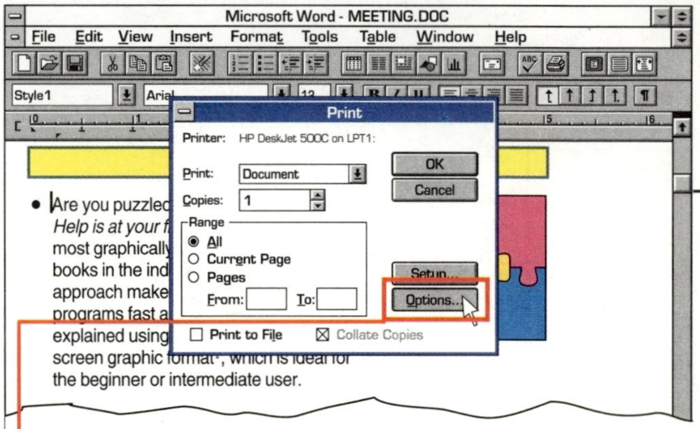

1 Click **File** to open its menu.

2 Click **Print** and the **Print** dialog box appears.

3 Click the **Options** button and the **Options** dialog box appears.

Create an Envelope

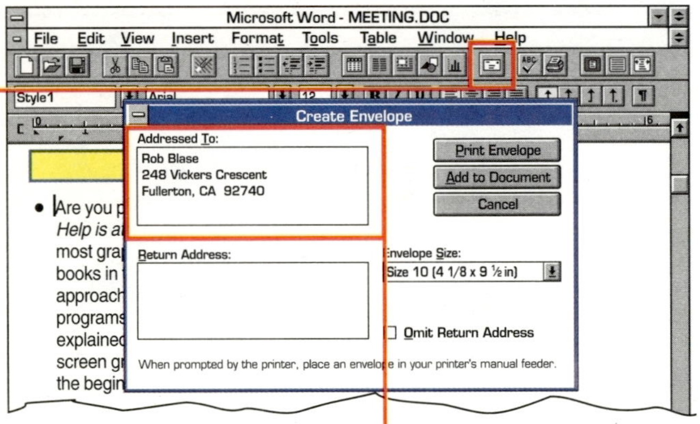

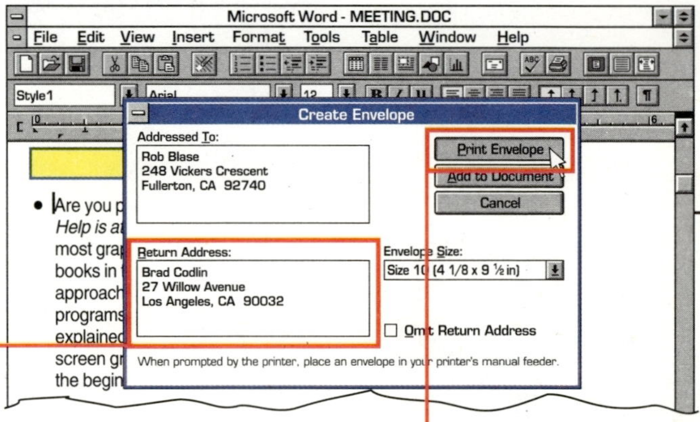

1 Click the **Envelope** button and the **Create Envelope** dialog box appears.

2 Type the address, pressing **Enter** after you type each line of text.

*Note: To specify a different sized envelope, click the arrow under **Envelope Size:**. Then click the desired size.*

3 To print a return address, click anywhere in the **Return Address:** box.

4 Type the return address, pressing **Enter** after you type each line of text.

*Note: If you do not want to print a return address, click the box beside **Omit Return Address**.*

5 Click the **Print Envelope** button to print the envelope.

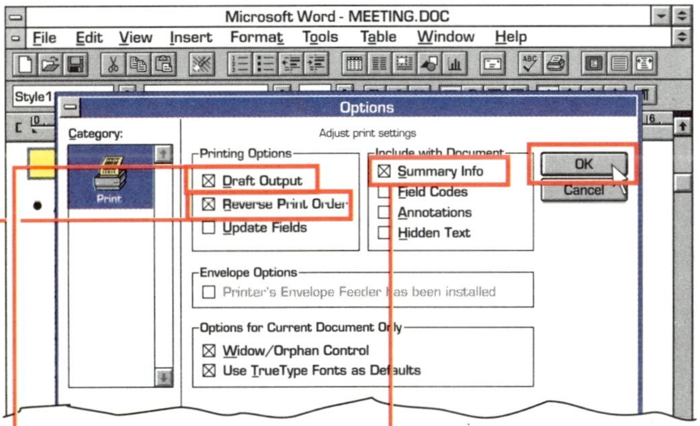

4 To produce a faster, lower quality printout, click the box beside **Draft Output**.

5 To print the pages in your document from last to first, click the box beside **Reverse Print Order**.

6 To print the file's summary information, click the box beside **Summary Info**.

Note: ☒ indicates an option is on. ☐ indicates an option is off.

7 Click the **OK** button to close the **Options** dialog box.

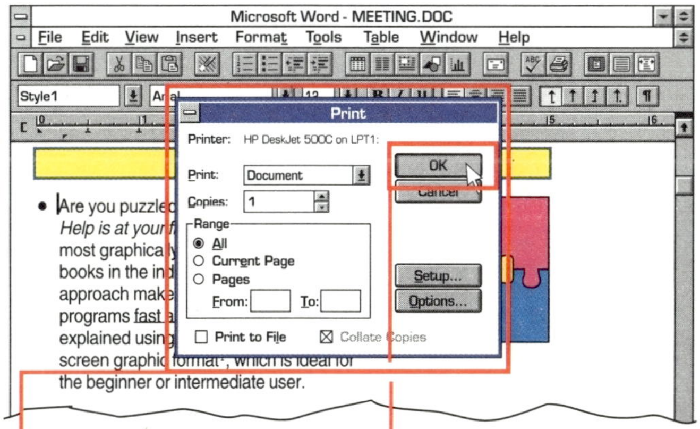

■ The **Print** dialog box reappears.

8 To print the document, click the **OK** button.

*Note: For more information on the **Print** dialog box, refer to page 78.*

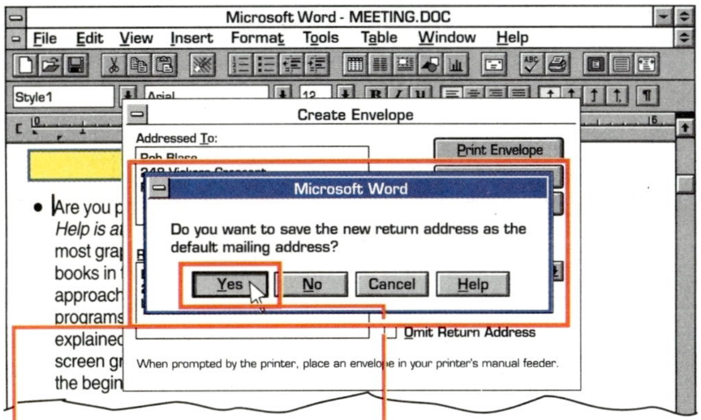

■ Word asks if you want to save the new return address as the default mailing address.

6 Click the **Yes** button to save the address.

*Note: Click the **No** button if you do not want to save the address.*

■ The envelope is printed.

GETTING STARTED • MANAGING YOUR FILES • EDIT A DOCUMENT • FORMAT TEXT • FORMAT A DOCUMENT • TABLES • GRAPHICS • PRINT • MERGE • OUTLINING

MERGE DOCUMENTS INTRODUCTION

CREATE THE MAIN DOCUMENT

Merge Documents Introduction

MAIN DOCUMENT

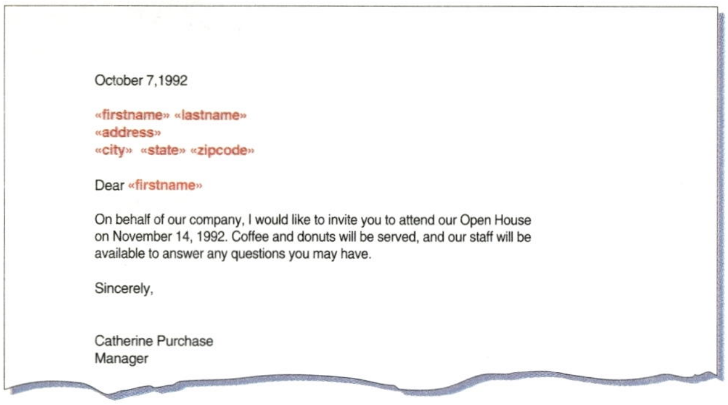
October 7,1992

«firstname» «lastname»
«address»
«city» «state» «zipcode»

Dear «firstname»

On behalf of our company, I would like to invite you to attend our Open House on November 14, 1992. Coffee and donuts will be served, and our staff will be available to answer any questions you may have.

Sincerely,

Catherine Purchase
Manager

The main document contains the text you want to appear in each letter. It also contains codes that tell Word where you want to insert the information from the data file.

DATA FILE

firstname	lastname	address	city	state	zipcode
David	Ross	12 Willow Avenue	Los Angeles	CA	90032
Jim	Devries	11 Linton Street	Atlanta	GA	30367
Heather	Matwey	56 Devon Road	San Diego	CA	92121
Carol	Smith	34 Ford Drive	Denver	CO	80207

The data file contains the information for each person to whom you want to send the letter. When you merge the documents, Word inserts this data into the main document.

Create the Main Document

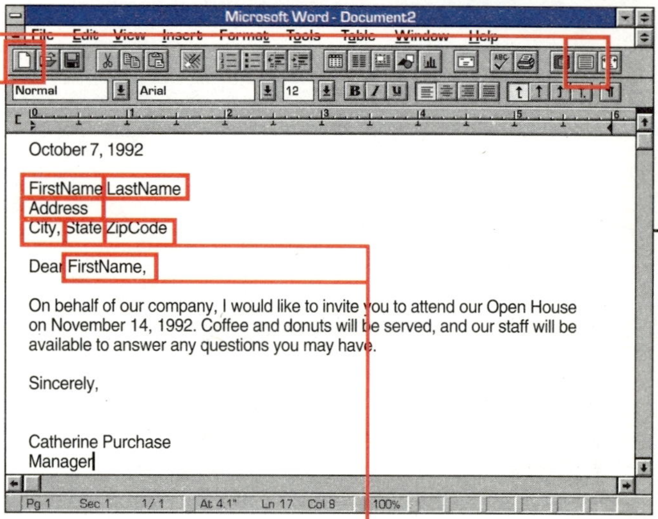

1 To open a new document, click the **New** button.

2 To return to the Normal view, click this button.

3 Begin typing the letter just as you would any other document in Word.

4 When you are at a position where you want to insert information from the data file, type a generic name for the text (example: **FirstName**). Later on you will replace this text with codes that Word can recognize.

MERGED FILE

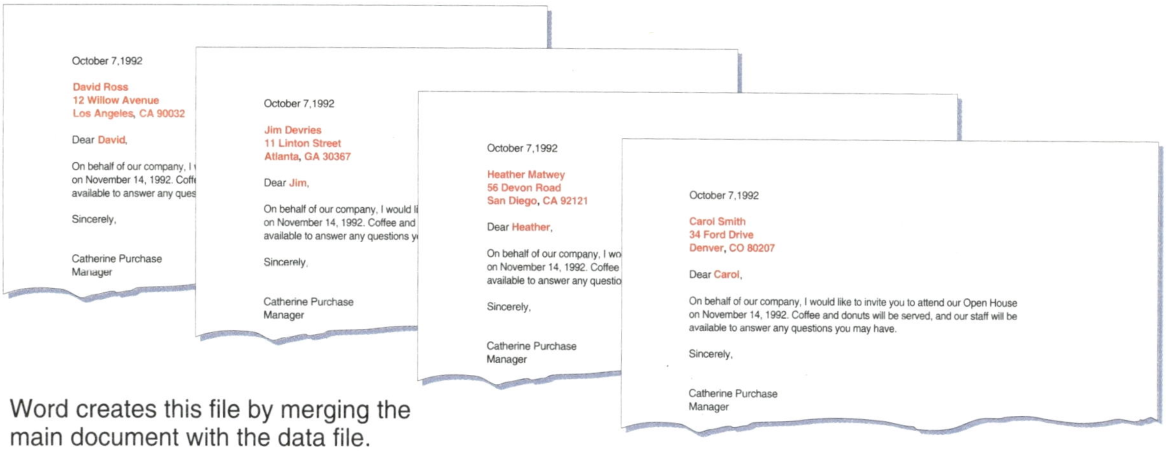

Word creates this file by merging the main document with the data file.

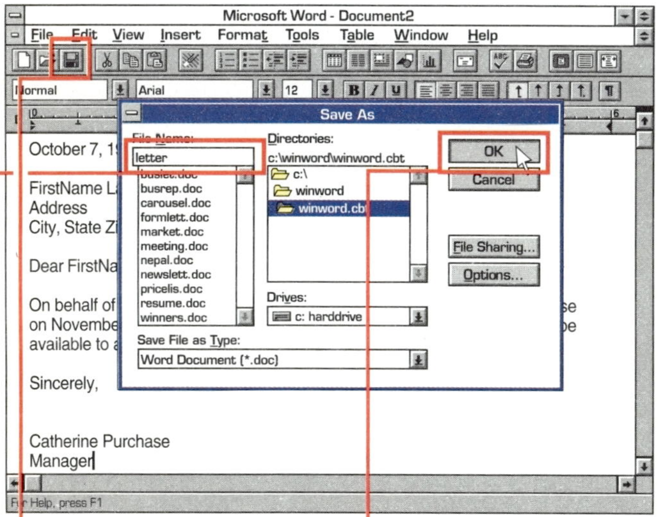

5 To save the document, click the **Save** button and the **Save As** dialog box appears.

6 Type a name for the main document (example: **letter**).

Note: To change directories, double click the name of the directory you want to change to.

7 Click the **OK** button.

*Note: The **Summary Info** dialog box appears. If you do not want to enter summary information, press **Enter**. For more information, refer to page 16.*

CREATE THE DATA FILE

Create the Data File

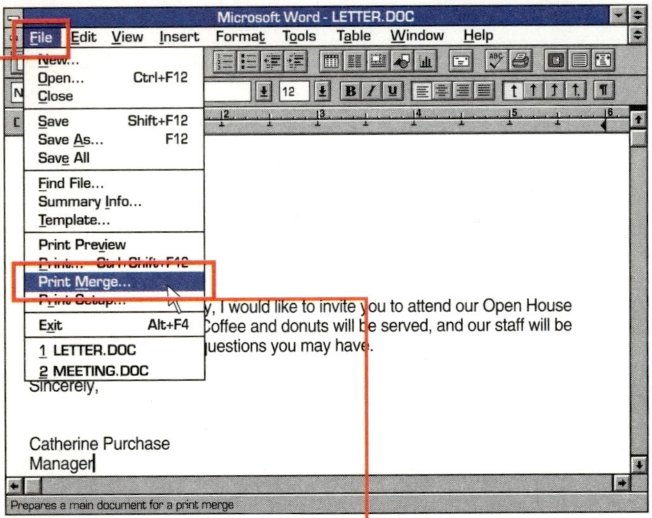

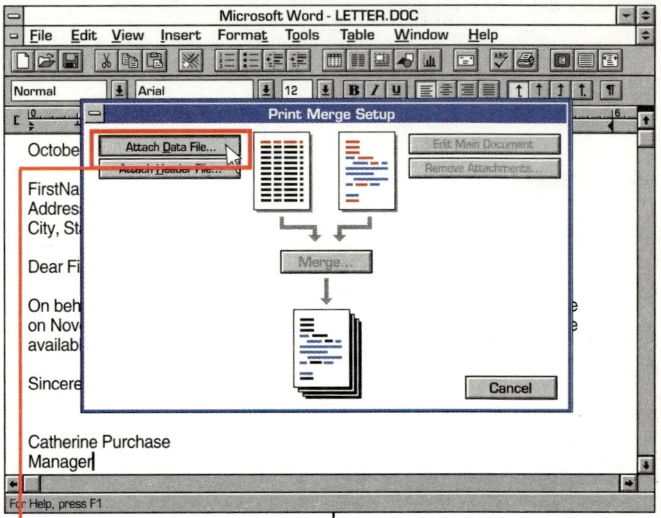

The data file contains the text that varies from letter to letter (example: names, addresses).

1 Click **File** to open its menu.

2 Click **Print Merge** and the **Print Merge Setup** dialog box appears.

3 Click the **Attach Data File** button and its dialog box appears.

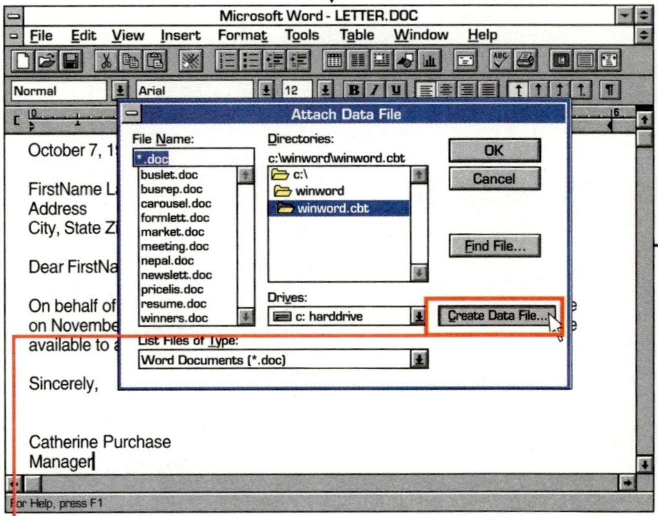

4 Click the **Create Data File** button and its dialog box appears.

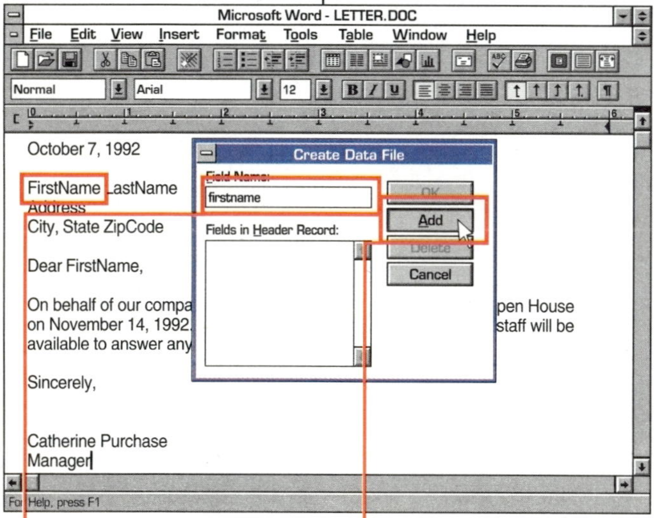

5 Type a name for the first field (example: **firstname**).

Note: Spaces between characters are not allowed.

6 Click the **Add** button, or press **Enter**.

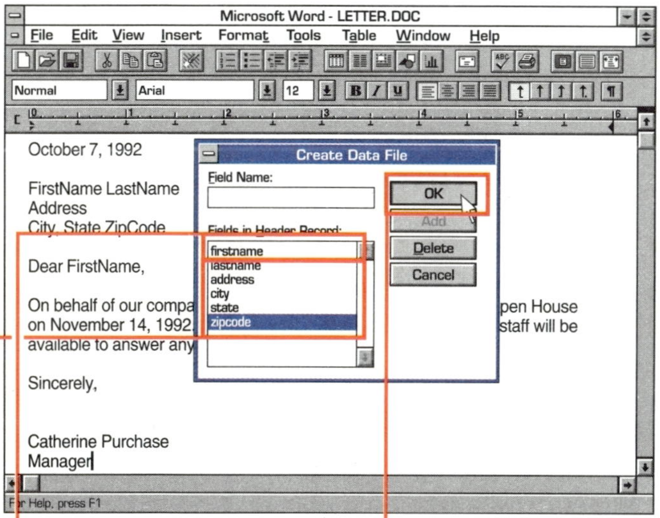

■ The field is added.

7 Repeat steps **5** and **6** for each field you want to add.

8 Click the **OK** button and the **Save As** dialog box appears.

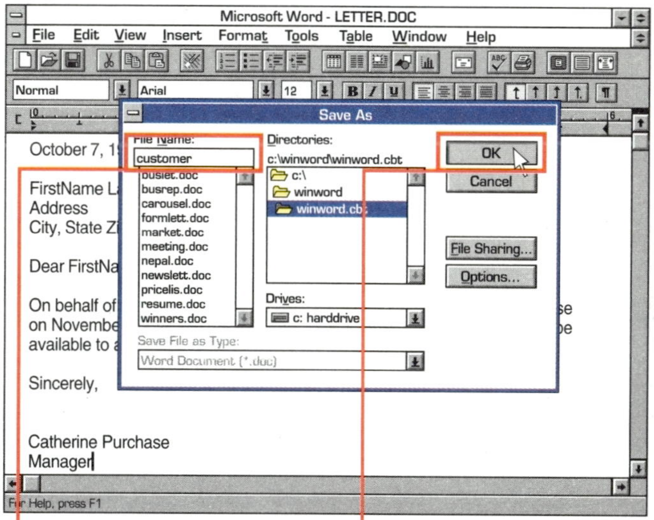

9 Type a name for the data file (example: **customer**).

Note: To change directories, double click the name of the directory you want to change to.

10 Click the **OK** button and Word opens a new document.

Note: Refer to page 86 to enter data into the data file.

ENTER DATA IN THE DATA FILE

ADD FIELDS TO MAIN DOCUMENT

PRINT

Enter Data in the Data File

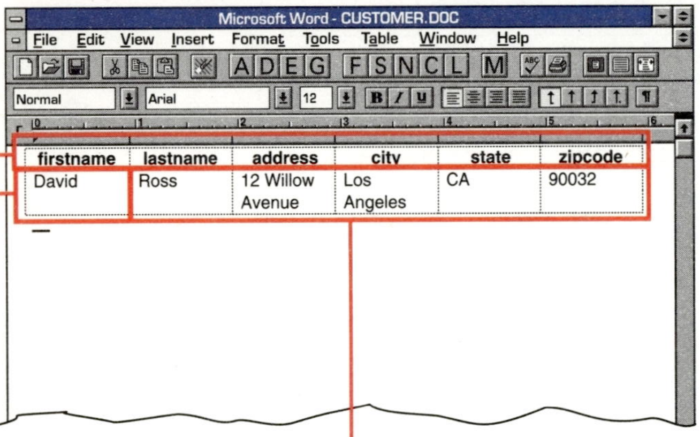

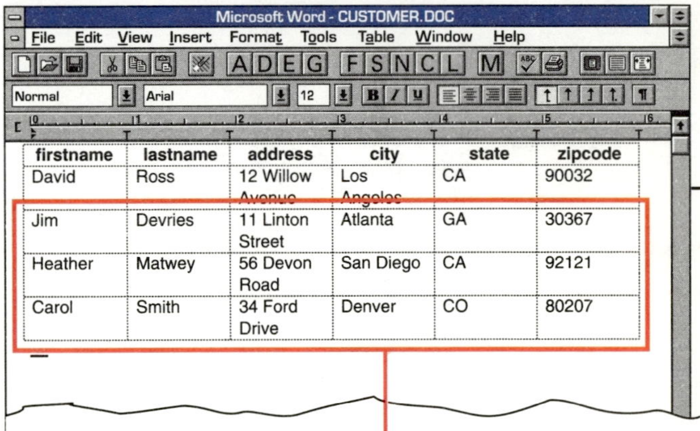

■ The fields you specified earlier appear in the first row of the table.

1 Type the data that corresponds to the first column heading (example: **David**).

Note: For visual clarity, the font was changed to Arial, 12 point.

2 Press the **Tab** key to move to the next cell.

3 Type the remaining data for that customer.

4 Press the **Tab** key to insert a new row.

Note: Although some text you type may not fit on one line in the table, it will print on one line when Word inserts the text into the main document.

5 Repeat steps **1** to **3** for each record.

Add Fields to the Main Document

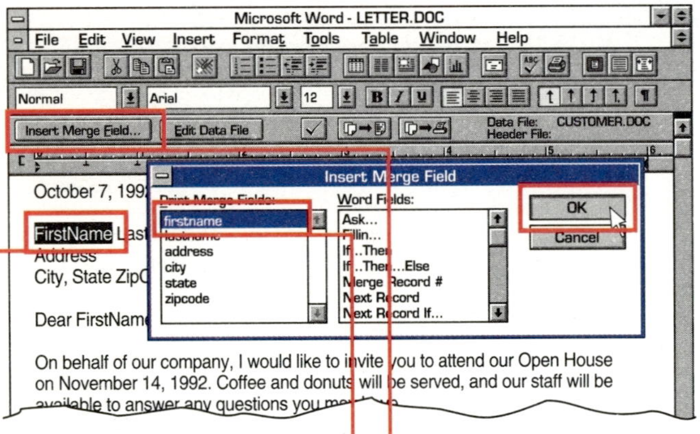

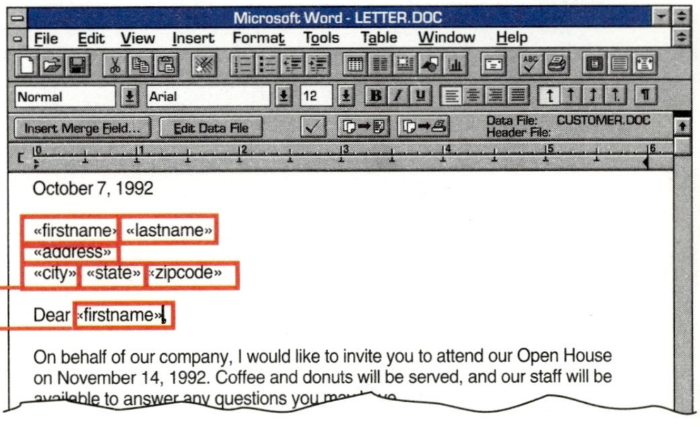

1 Select the text you want to replace with a merge field.

Note: Make sure you do not select the space before or after the text, since this can effect the spacing of the merged document.

2 Click the **Insert Merge Field** button and its dialog box appears.

3 Click the desired field name (example: **firstname**).

4 Click the **OK** button, or press **Enter**.

5 Repeat steps **1** to **4** for each merge field you want to insert into the document.

■ When you merge the main document and data file, Word replaces the merge fields with information from the data file to create a letter for each person.

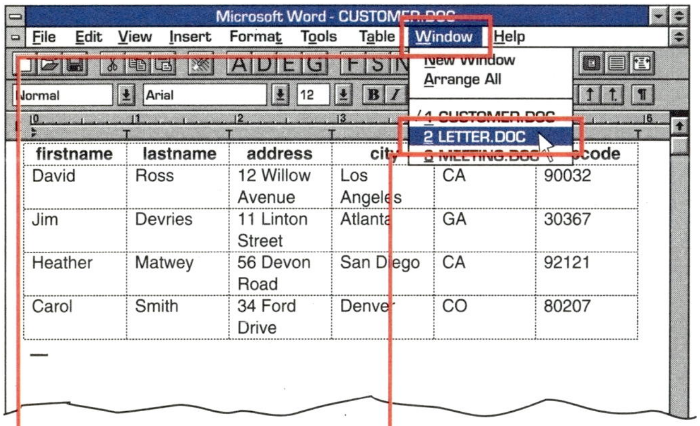

6 To switch to the main document, click **Window** to open its menu.

7 Click the name of the document (example: **LETTER.DOC**).

Print a Merged Document

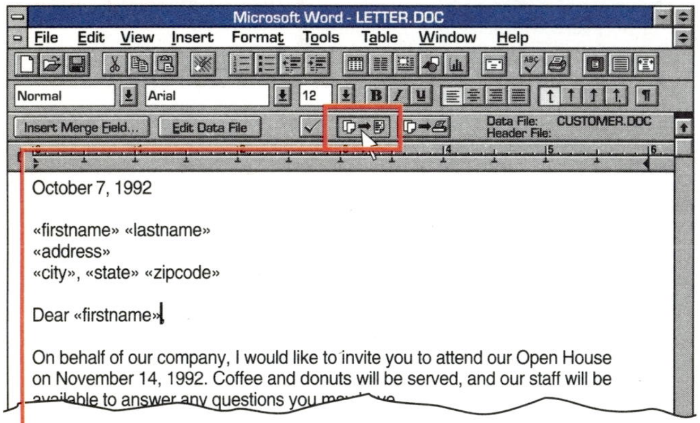

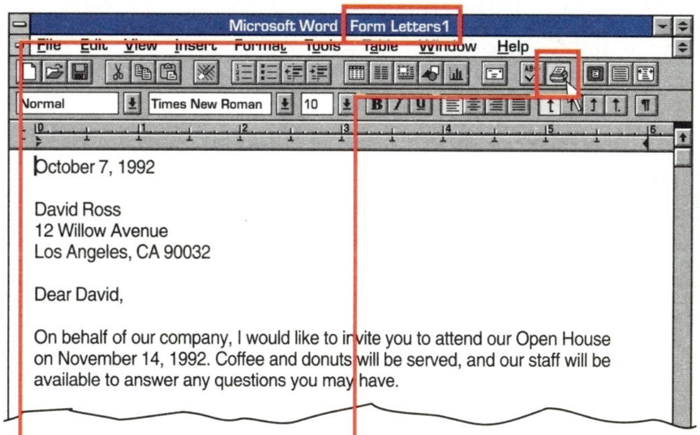

1 Click the **Merge to New Document** button.

Note: To print the merged documents without creating a new document, click the ***Merge to Printer*** *button* .

■ A new document called **Form Letters1** appears.

2 To quickly scroll through the document, press the **Page Down** key.

3 If desired, edit the letters.

4 Click the **Print** button to print the document.

Note: For more information on printing, refer to page 78.

CREATE AN OUTLINE

SWITCH TO OUTLINE VIEW

SELECT TEXT

Create an Outline

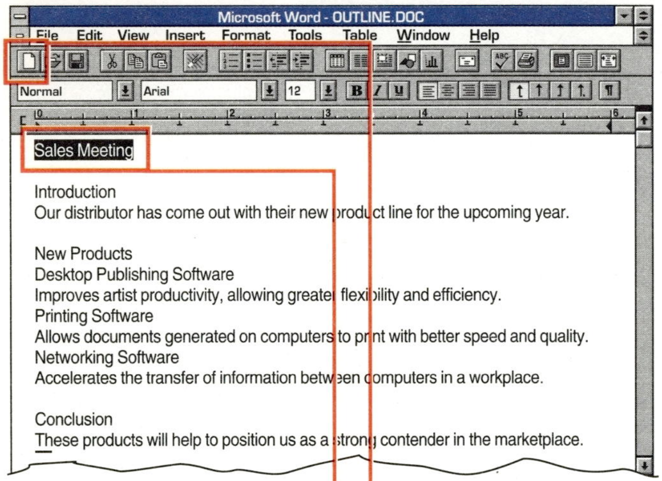

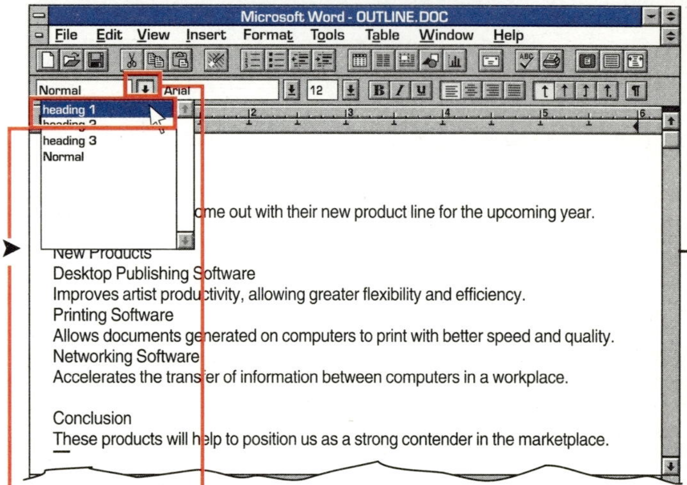

Viewing a document in outline form gives you a unique perspective for restructuring your document.

Outlining emphasizes your main/key ideas so you can easily access and reposition portions of the document. You can then switch back to the Normal view for detail work.

To create an outline, classify each heading in your document as a level one, two or three heading.

1 To open a new document, click the **New** button.

2 Type the text for your document.

3 Select the text you want to classify as a heading.

4 Click the arrow beside the **Style** box.

5 Click the desired heading style (example: **Heading1**).

Note: To classify text as a level two heading, click ***Heading2****.*

To classify text as a level three heading, click ***Heading3****.*

Switch to the Outline View

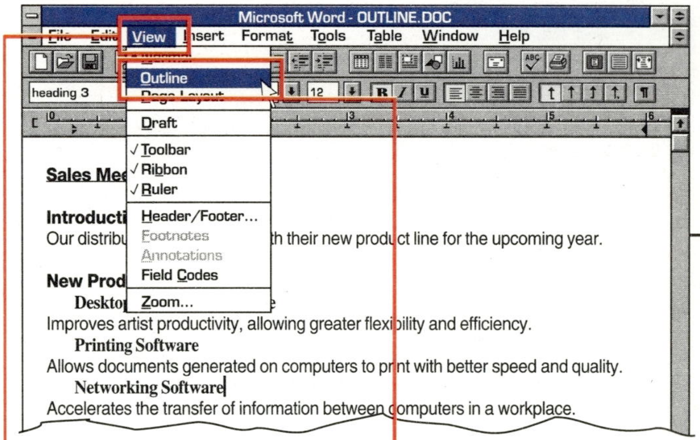

1 Click **View** to open its menu.

2 Click **Outline**.

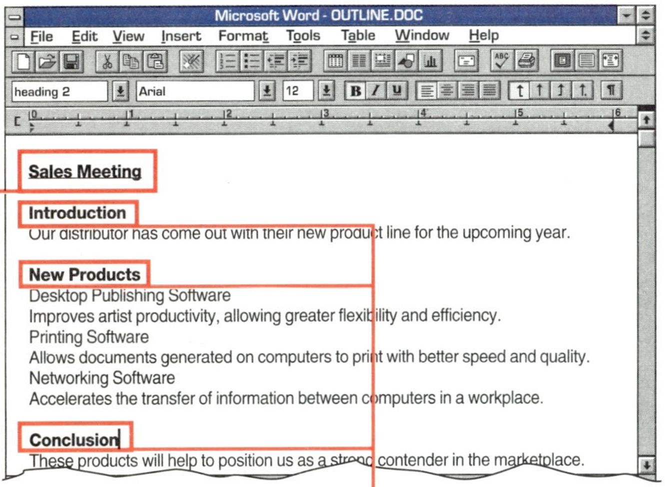

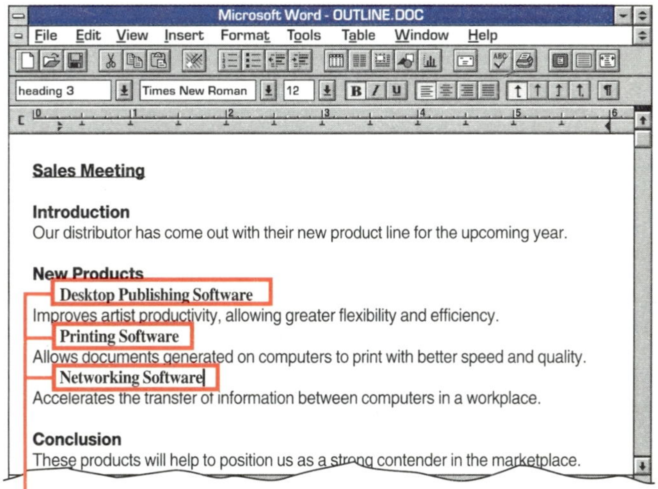

■ The text is displayed in the selected style.

Note: To deselect text, click anywhere on the screen.

6 Repeat steps **3** to **5** for the text you want to classify as a level two heading.

7 Repeat steps **3** to **5** for the text you want to classify as a level three heading.

Select Text in the Outline View

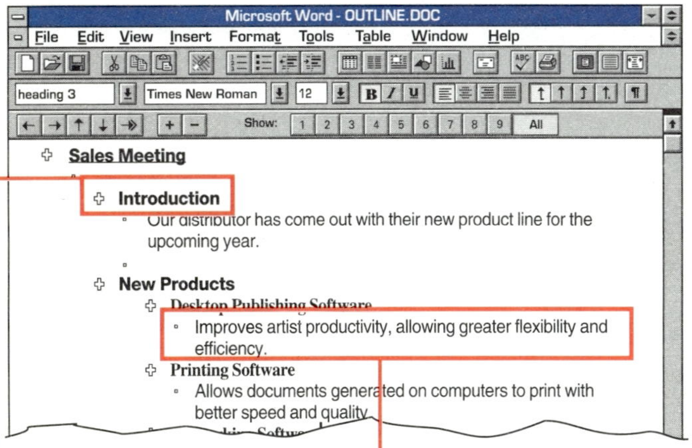

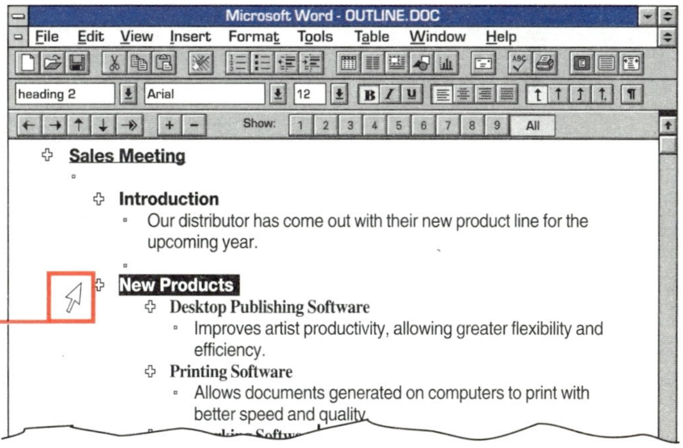

■ The ✥ symbol tells you the text is a heading with text below it.

■ The ▭ symbol tells you the text is a heading with no text below it.

Note: In the above example, all headings have text below them, therefore no headings display the ▭ symbol.

■ The ▫ symbol tells you the text is body text. Body text is not a heading.

You can select text using the same methods as in the Normal view.

1 Position the mouse pointer to the left of the paragraph you want to select.

2 Click the left mouse button.

SHORTCUT

To quickly select a heading and its subtext, position the insertion point over the symbol beside the heading and it changes to ✥. Click the left mouse button.

PROMOTE OR DEMOTE TEXT

MOVE TEXT

HIDE OR DISPLAY SUBTEXT

Promote or Demote Text

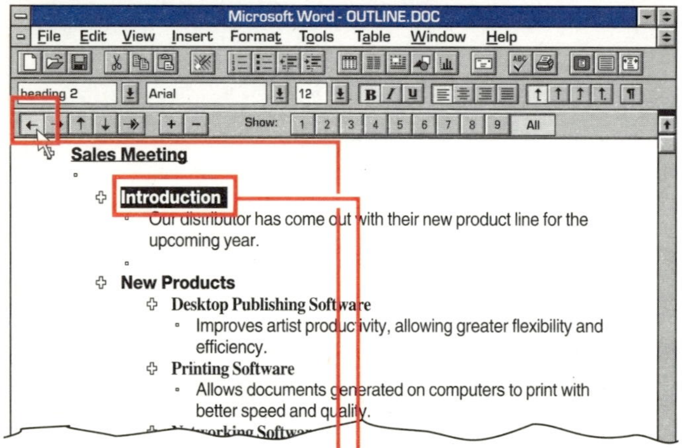

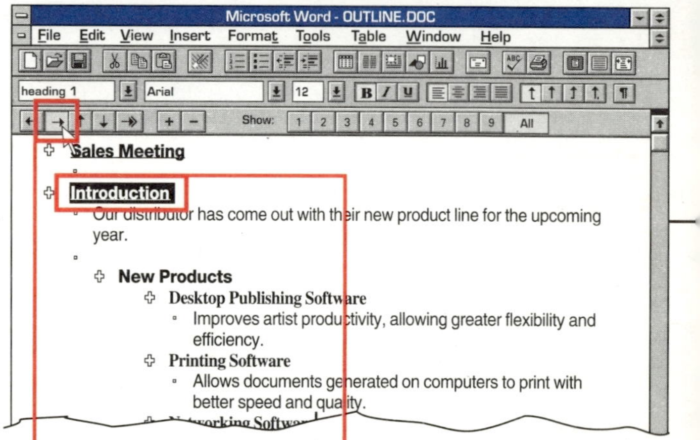

You can move a heading to a higher or lower heading level.

Promote text

1 Select the heading or body text you want to promote.

2 Click the **Promote Heading Level** button.

■ The text is promoted.

Demote text

1 Select the heading you want to demote.

2 Click the **Demote Heading Level** button.

Move Text

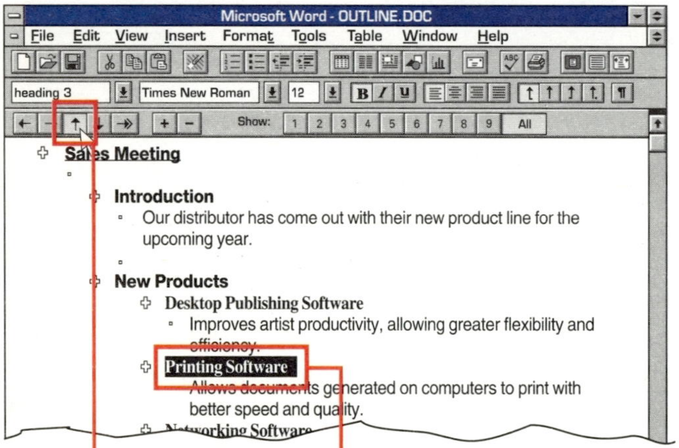

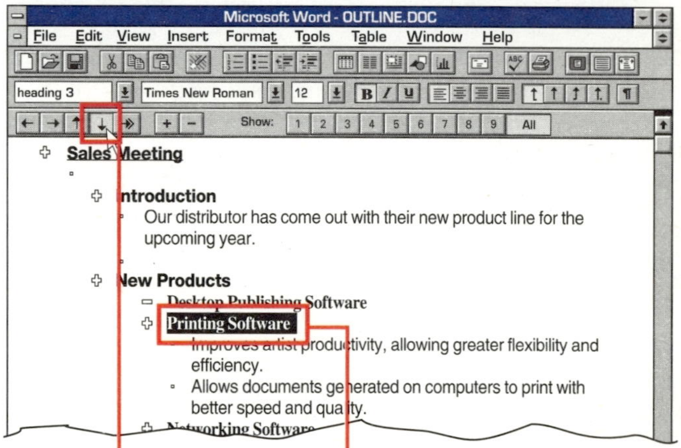

You can relocate portions of text within the document.

Move one paragraph up

1 Select the text you want to move one paragraph up.

2 Click the **Move Paragraph Up** button.

■ The text is moved one paragraph up.

Move one paragraph down

1 Select the text you want to move one paragraph down.

2 Click the **Move Paragraph Down** button.

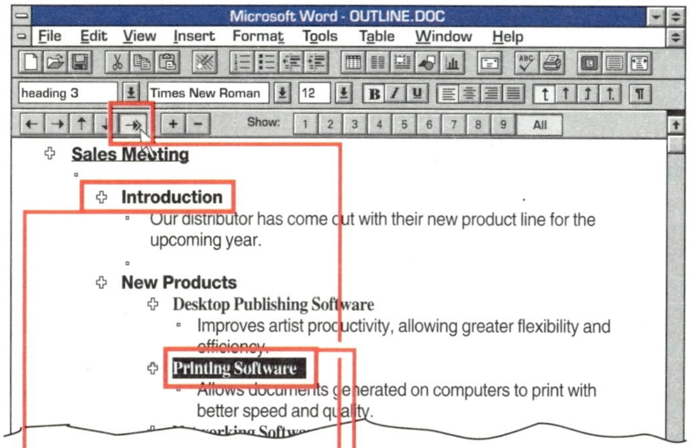

The text is demoted.

Demote heading to body text

1 Select the heading you want to demote to body text.

2 Click the **Demote Heading to Body Text** button.

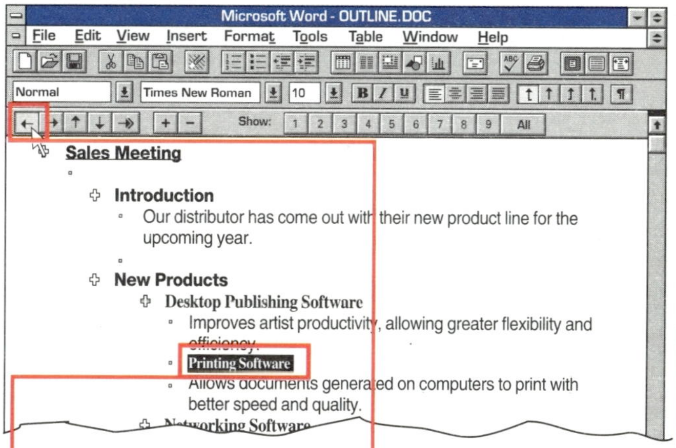

The heading is demoted to body text.

3 To promote body text back to a heading, click the **Promote Heading Level** button.

Hide or Display Subtext

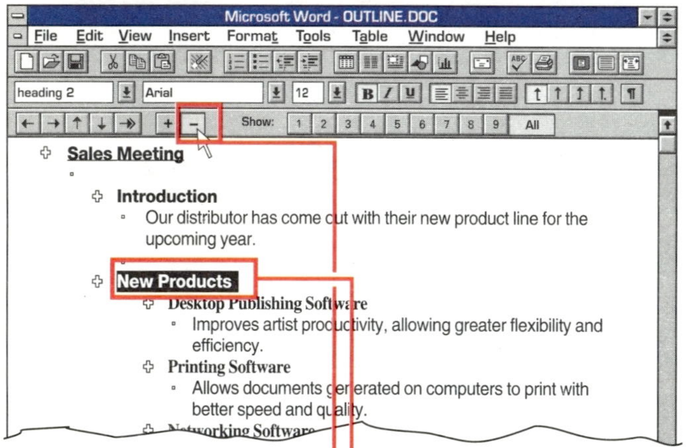

You can hide text to focus on the main ideas/ headings in the document, or display text to view the document in more detail.

Hide subtext

1 Select the heading that has the subtext you want to hide.

2 Click the **Hide Subtext** button.

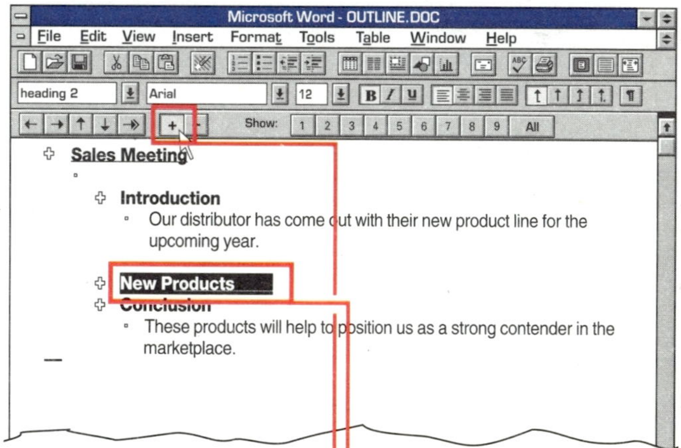

The subtext is hidden.

Display subtext

1 Select the heading that has the subtext you want to display.

2 Click the **Show Subtext** button.

CHANGE LEVEL DISPLAYED

NUMBER AN OUTLINE

Change Level Displayed

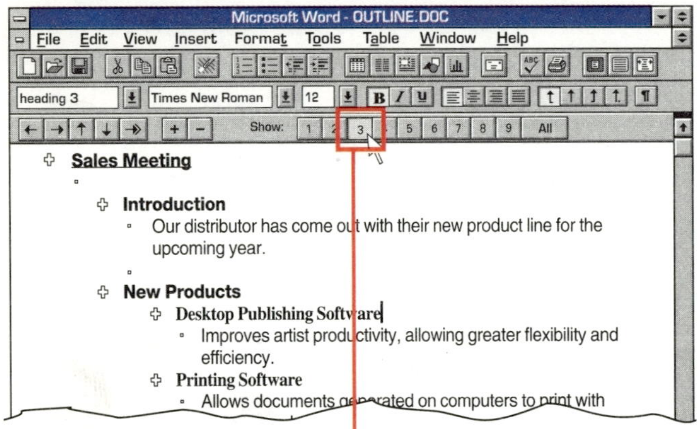

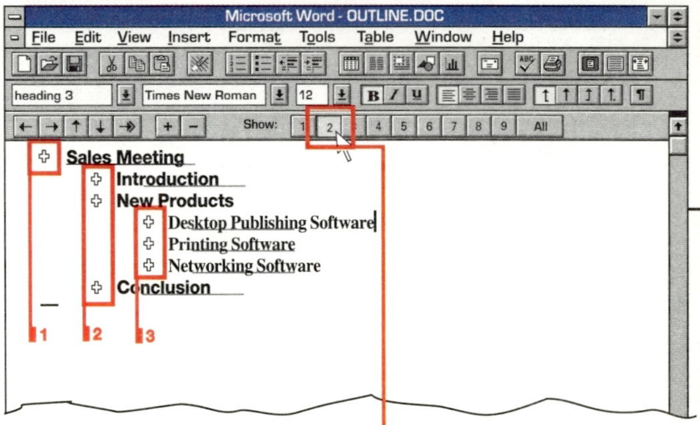

Changing the level of displayed information allows you to focus on a specific portion of your document or see the whole document condensed to main ideas/headings. This is valuable when editing and assessing the document.

■ When you first switch to the Outline view, all levels are displayed.

1 Click a button beside **Show:** to display a different level of information (example: **3**).

■ Three levels of information are displayed.

2 Click a button beside **Show:** to display another level of information (example: **2**).

Number an Outline

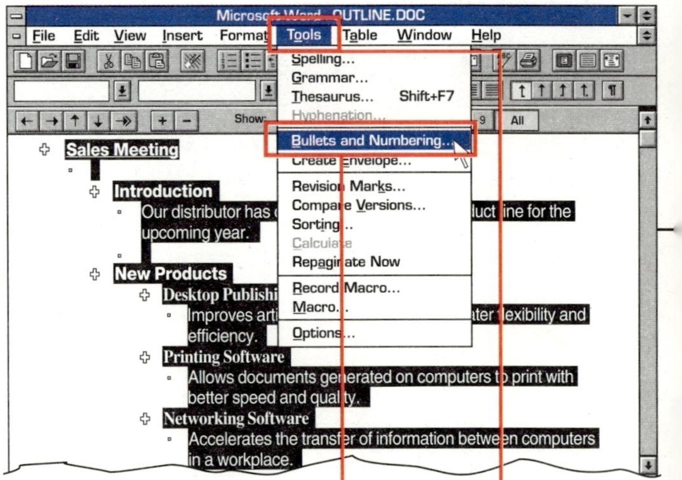

Word can number an outline to create a numbered list.

1 Select the part of the outline you want to number.

Note: To select the entire document, refer to page 10.

2 Click **Tools** to open its menu.

3 Click **Bullets and Numbering** to open its dialog box.

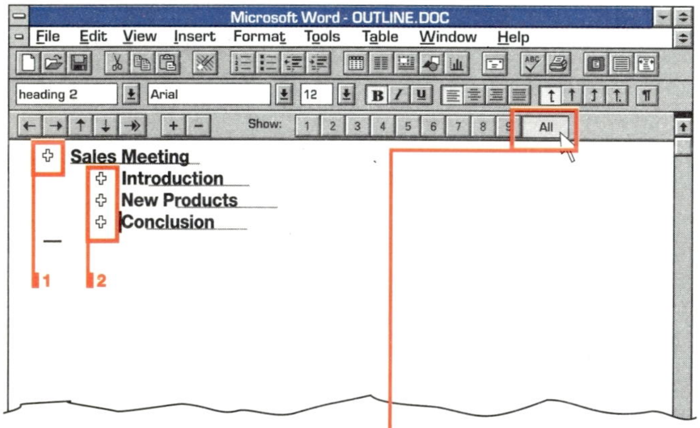

■ Two levels of information are displayed.

3 Click this button to again display all levels of information.

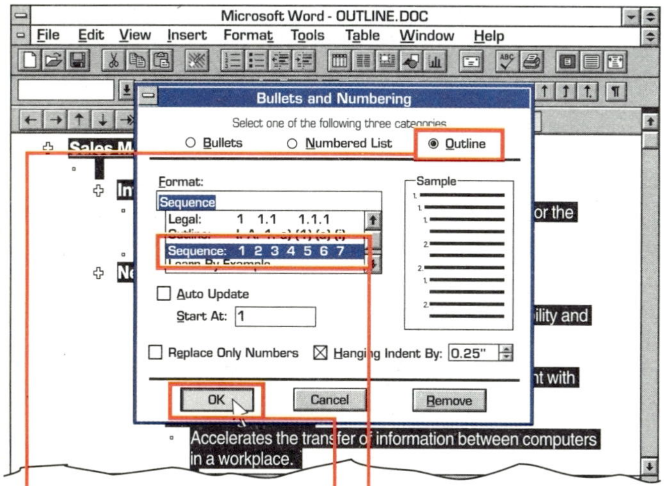

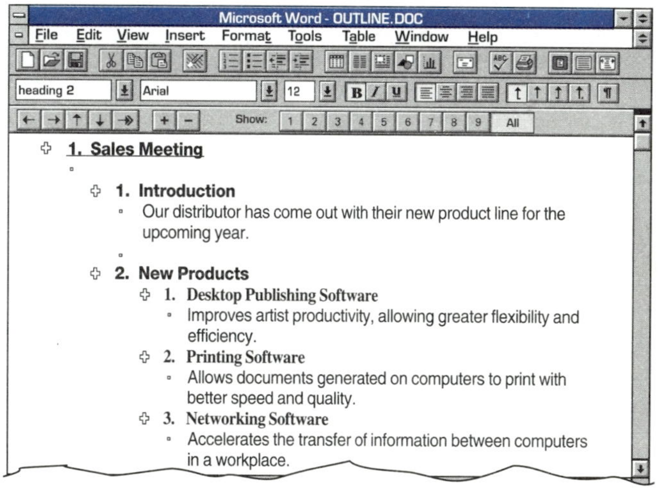

4 Click the circle beside **Outline**.

5 Click the desired number format.

Note: Click the ***Remove*** *button to remove a numbered list from an outline.*

6 Click the **OK** button.

■ The outline is numbered.

Note: To deselect text, click anywhere on the screen.

Rs. 150/—

Index